Erratum

Encyclopedia of Language and Education

isbn 0-7923-4936-9 (set)

On page iv should appear:

Acknowledgement

Cover picture:*The Tower of Babylon,* Pieter Bruegel the Elder
Museum Boymans-van Beuningen, Rotterdam

ENCYCLOPEDIA OF LANGUAGE AND EDUCATION

Encyclopedia of Language and Education

VOLUME 1: LANGUAGE POLICY AND POLITICAL ISSUES IN EDUCATION

The volume titles of this encyclopedia are listed at the end of this volume.

Encyclopedia of Language and Education

Volume 1

LANGUAGE POLICY AND POLITICAL ISSUES IN EDUCATION

Edited by

RUTH WODAK

Department of Linguistics
University of Vienna
Austria

and

DAVID CORSON

The Ontario Institute for Studies in Education
University of Toronto
Canada

KLUWER ACADEMIC PUBLISHERS

DORDRECHT / BOSTON / LONDON

Library of Congress Cataloging-in-Publication Data

Language policy and political issues in education / edited by Ruth
  Wodak and David Corson.
      p.   cm. -- (Encyclopedia of language and education ; v. 1)
    Includes bibliographical references and index.
    ISBN 0-7923-4713-7 (alk. paper). -- ISBN 0-7923-4596-7 (set : alk.
  paper)
    1. Language and education. 2. Language policy.   I. Wodak, Ruth,
  1950-   . II. Corson, David. III. Series.
  P40.8.L37 1997
  418'.007--dc21   97-30201

ISBN 0-7923-4928-8 (PB)   ISBN 0-7923-4713-7 (HB)
ISBN 0-7923-4936-9 (PB-SET)   ISBN 0-7923-4596-7 (HB-SET)

Published by Kluwer Academic Publishers,
P.O. Box 17, 3300 AA Dordrecht, The Netherlands

Sold and distributed in the U.S.A. and Canada
by Kluwer Academic Publishers,
101 Philip Drive, Norwell, MA 02061, U.S.A.

In all other countries, sold and distributed
by Kluwer Academic Publishers Group,
P.O. Box 322, 3300 AH Dordrecht, The Netherlands

Printed in the Netherlands (on acid-free paper)

TABLE OF CONTENTS

VOLUME 1: LANGUAGE POLICY AND POLITICAL ISSUES IN EDUCATION

GENERAL EDITOR'S INTRODUCTION

ENCYCLOPEDIA OF LANGUAGE AND EDUCATION

This is one of eight volumes of the Encyclopedia of Language and Education published by Kluwer Academic. The publication of this work signals the maturity of the field of 'language and education' as an international and interdisciplinary field of significance and cohesion. These volumes confirm that 'language and education' is much more than the preserve of any single discipline. In designing these volumes, we have tried to recognise the diversity of the field in our selection of contributors and in our choice of topics. The contributors come from every continent and from more than 40 countries. Their reviews discuss language and education issues affecting every country in the world.

We have also tried to recognise the diverse interdisciplinary nature of 'language and education' in the selection of the editorial personnel themselves. The major academic interests of the volume editors confirm this. As principal volume editor for Volume 1, Ruth Wodak has interests in critical linguistics, sociology of language, and language policy. For Volume 2, Viv Edwards has interests in policy and practice in multilingual classrooms and the sociology of language. For Volume 3, Bronwyn Davies has interests in the social psychology of language, the sociology of language, and interdisciplinary studies. For Volume 4, Richard Tucker has interests in language theory, applied linguistics, and the implementation and evaluation of innovative language education programs. For Volume 5, Jim Cummins has interests in the psychology of language and in critical linguistics. For Volume 6, Leo van Lier has interests in applied linguistics and in language theory. For Volume 7, Caroline Clapham has interests in research into second language acquisition and language measurement. And for Volume 8, Nancy Hornberger has interests in anthropological linguistics and in language policy. Finally, as general editor, I have interests in the philosophy and sociology of language, language policy, critical linguistics, and interdisciplinary studies. But the thing that unites us all, including all the contributors to this work, is an interest in the practice and theory of education itself.

People working in the applied and theoretical areas of education and language are often asked questions like the following: 'what is the latest research on such and such a problem?' or 'what do we know about such

R. Wodak and D. Corson (eds), Encyclopedia of Language and Education,
Volume 1: Language Policy and Political Issues in Education, vii–ix.
© *1997 Kluwer Academic Publishers. Printed in the Netherlands.*

and such an issue?' Questions like these are asked by many people: by policy makers and practitioners in education; by novice researchers; by publishers trying to relate to an issue; and above all by undergraduate and postgraduate students in the language disciplines. Each of the reviews that appears in this volume tries to anticipate and answer some of the more commonly asked questions about language and education. Taken together, the eight volumes of this Encyclopedia provide answers to more than 200 major questions of this type, and hundreds of subsidiary questions as well.

Each volume of the Encyclopedia of Language and Education deals with a single, substantial subject in the language and education field. The volume titles and their contents appear elsewhere in the pages of this work. Each book-length volume provides more than 20 state-of-the-art topical reviews of the literature. Taken together, these reviews attempt a complete coverage of the subject of the volume. Each review is written by one or more experts in the topic, or in a few cases by teams assembled by experts. As a collection, the Encyclopedia spans the range of subjects and topics normally falling within the scope of 'language and education'. Each volume, edited by an international expert in the subject of the volume, was designed and developed in close collaboration with the general editor of the Encyclopedia, who is a co-editor of each volume as well as general editor of the whole work.

The Encyclopedia has been planned as a necessary reference set for any university or college library that serves a faculty or school of education. Libraries serving academic departments in any of the language disciplines, especially applied linguistics, would also find this a valuable resource. It also seems very relevant to the needs of educational bureaucracies, policy agencies, and public libraries, particularly those serving multicultural or multilingual communities.

The Encyclopedia aims to speak to a prospective readership that is multinational, and to do so as unambiguously as possible. Because each book-size volume deals with a discrete and important subject in language and education, these state-of-the-art volumes also offer authoritative course textbooks in the areas suggested by their titles. This means that libraries will also catalogue these book-size individual volumes in relevant sections of their general collections. To meet this range of uses, the Encyclopedia is published in a hardback edition offering the durability needed for reference collections, and in a future student edition. The hardback edition is also available for single-volume purchase.

Each state-of-the-art review has about 3000 words of text and most follow a similar structure. A list of references to key works cited in each review supplements the information and authoritative opinion that the review contains. Many contributors survey early developments in their topic, major contributions, work in progress, problems and difficulties, and future directions for research and practice. The aim of the reviews, and of the Encyclopedia as a whole, is to give readers access to the international literature and research on each topic.

David Corson
General Editor Encyclopedia of Language and Education
Ontario Institute for Studies in Education of the University of Toronto
Canada

INTRODUCTION

> Most people take for granted the language into which they are born, the one spoken in
> their home and by their playmates. They learn it as a matter of course, and it appears
> to be of no more consequence to them than the air they breathe. Yet without either
> one they could not grow up to be human beings: lack of air would kill their bodies,
> but lack of language would kill their minds (Haugen 1985: p. 4).

In his famous article "Linguistic Pluralism as a Goal of National Policy"
(1985) Einar Haugen states some of the basic principles of language policy
and describes the development of language policies in several countries.
The problems which he discusses are critical ones: How did language
diversity within nations come about? What policies have major powers
adopted to meet this problem? And finally, can a policy of linguistic pluralism be implemented as a satisfactory solution to the problem? (1985: p. 5)
These problems have not been solved up to now, but there have been
many recent theoretical and empirical attempts which differ from country
to country which are very dependent on the socio-historical context of
the specific country and also on legal provisions and decisions taken on a
global level (see Skutnabb-Kangas, and Hastings in this volume).

In the *Handbook of Sociolinguistics* (1996) Denise Daoust (1996:
p. 448ff) reviews and summarizes the most important trends in language
policy and language planning and emphasizes the corpus/status dichotomy
introduced by Kloss (1969: p. 81). Thus corpus planning refers to all actions aiming at modifying the language itself, whereas status planning
concerns the level of societal strategies in raising or lowering the status
of a language. Overall, Daoust points to the relevance of education and
educational systems in establishing diversity, but without elaborating the
details of the possibilities of language education and language curricula in
the midst of this process.

This is why we dedicate this first volume of the Encyclopedia to questions of language policy and education – because we think that the core
of the problems mentioned already by Haugen and the possible solutions
to language conflicts, language maintenance and multiculturalism manifest themselves in the educational system and can also be partially solved
through education. Thus, education is embedded in the power systems of
society; the knowledge of languages and specifically of high status languages allows access to many important institutions; the acquisition of
languages, the choice of the specific languages taught and the methods of
teaching them are all dependent on the policies of social elites (see Corson

1995; Wodak 1996 and contributions by David Corson, Hilary Janks and John Baugh in this volume).

Sociolinguistics from the outset has provided us with theoretical approaches to explain and interpret inequality in education. I would just like to mention Basil Bernstein's so-called "Deficit Theory", William Labov's "Difference Theory" and Pierre Bourdieu's theory of the "linguistic market" (see Leodolter 1975; Coulmas 1992, and John Baugh and David Corson in this volume). More recently, scholars in Critical Applied Linguistics (Alastair Pennycook in this volume) and Critical Language Awareness (see the review by Clark and Ivanic in volume 6) have developed more differentiated proposals in describing and solving the domination and oppression of minorities through language.

Sociolinguistic research emphasises three domains where language is central in the socialisation process and in schools:

- as L1 which determines the identity and the intellectual and cognitive development of individuals;
- as mode for transfer of knowledge and for interaction between teacher and student;
- as object of knowledge and critical reflection in both L1 and L2 education.

This volume covers many aspects of these three domains and reviews the most recent research and findings relating to these basic dimensions, on a more general level (Section One, Theoretical Issues, Section Two, Minorities and Education), for many countries (Section Three, Specific Areas) and also for educational practice (Section Four, Practical and Empirical Issues).

The theoretical issues in Section One cover very important general aspects of language policy: on the one hand, the impact of power on educational issues is discussed, as well as the influence of language attitudes on teaching and language acquisition (Herbert Christ). Already this first part of the volume manifests the interdisciplinary and critical approach taken by most of the authors. The complex area of language policy and education cannot be analyzed and observed from the point of view of Linguistics and language by themselves. Many thoughts, findings and concepts from other neighbouring disciplines are seen to be relevant. We have to include historical, sociological, sociopsychological and pedagogical frameworks in our discussions (Fairclough/Wodak 1997). The contributions of John Baugh, Duncan Waite, Mark Fettes and Alastair Pennycook emphasize this point.

Section Two discusses the situation of minorities and minority languages from a general perspective: the legal solutions and restrictions are presented, both on national and on global levels (Tove Skutnabb-Kangas, W.K. Hastings); clearly, the globalisation of our world leads to new problems in dealing with language minorities. Specifically, this is the case for the European Union where the tensions between national languages and minority languages on the one hand, and dominant languages like English and French become manifest on many levels, and the social practice and realities prove that legal measures by themselves cannot cope with nationalistic and power issues as well as with existing racism and ethnicism (Wodak/DeCillia 1995; Robert Phillipson and Jan Branson and Don Miller in this volume). Section Three offers insight into the language situation of different countries: it becomes very clear that it is not possible to generalize about language policies, that the historical and social development in each country leads to different policies, curricula and solutions. Thus, – to mention a few –, the attempts of Australia (Michael Clyne) to become a multicultural country are relatively successful, the developments in South Africa after apartheid are still unfolding (Ute Smit), the situation in India is very complex due to the period of colonization and the many languages (Khubchandani) and the situation in Great Britain nowadays with its minorities is again very different (Naz Rassool).

In Section Four, practical issues of implementation are discussed. The impact of modern media and the attempts to integrate media into curricula and into a critical educational perspective are outlined by Theo van Leeuwen. New critical materials which could be used in schools are introduced by Hilary Janks, a field where the findings of Applied Linguistics and Sociolinguistics should be used on a much wider scale. Stephen May illustrates practical language policies mainly in Great Britain, an example which could be carefully generalized to other countries; and finally, Robert Phillipson is concerned with the role of the English language nowadays, as the dominant language of the elites and politics. We hope that this volume will enhance the debate on these very important issues and will at least lead to critical reflection. But more optimistically, we hope it will lead to creative and new solutions in the development and implementation of language policies.

REFERENCES

Corson, D. (ed.): 1995, *Discourse and Power in Educational Organizations*, Hampton Press, Cresskill, NJ.

Coulmas, F.: 1992, *Language and Economy*, Blackwell, Cambridge.

Coulmas, F. (ed.): 1996, *The Handbook of Sociolinguistics*, Blackwell, Cambridge.

Daoust, D.: 1996, 'Language planning and language reform', in Coulmas (ed.), 436–520.

Fairclough, N. & Wodak, R.: 1997, 'Critical discourse analysis', in T. Van Dijk (ed.), *Discourse in Social Interaction*, Sage, London, 258–284.

Haugen, E.: 1985 'The language of imperialism: Unity or pluralism', in N. Wolfson & J. Manes (eds.), *Language of Inequality*, Mouton, Amsterdam, 3–20 [first appeared under the title "Linguistic Pluralism as a Goal of National Policy", Language and Society 1969, 65–82].

Kloss, H.: 1969, *Research possibilities on Group Bilingualism; A Report*, Université Laval,
    C.I.R.B., Quebec.
Leodolter, R. [=Wodak]: 1975, *Das Sprachverhalten von Angeklagten bei Gericht.* Kron-
    berg/Ts: Scriptor.
Wodak, R.: 1996, *Disorders of Discourse*, Longman, London.
Wodak, R. & DeCillia, R. (eds.): 1995, *Sprachenpolitik in Europa,* Passagen, Vienna.

Ruth Wodak

Section 1

Theoretical Issues

HERBERT CHRIST

LANGUAGE ATTITUDES AND EDUCATIONAL POLICY

Educational policy is deeply influenced by language attitudes, for language is a central mediating factor in education (Kelly 1969). Schools, universities and institutions of further education are thus determined by language(s) and attitudes towards language. This occurs in several ways:

- through the language(s) of instruction chosen or prescribed;
- through contact with other languages in use within the broader environment of a given educational institution (e.g., the mother tongue of pupils and students where these differ from the local language);
- through the range of curricular options offered under the rubric of "foreign languages";
- through instruction on the topic of language (reflection on language[s], comparison and evaluation of languages, grammar lessons);
- through the contribution made by educational institutions to the standardization and "purification" of language.

Decisions concerning educational policy on these various levels are based on traditional and current attitudes on the part of political groupings and the public towards language, languages, and language usage, along with laws, regulations and even specific clauses in national constitutions. All this points to the existence of attitudes towards language ratified by collective consensus or majority acceptance.

EARLY DEVELOPMENTS

The present historical retrospective is limited to the post-Renaissance period. There is, of course, earlier evidence indicating a connection between educational policy and attitudes towards language and/or language(s). In the late fifteenth century, however, two revolutionary developments began which were to be of universal significance and whose influence has persisted until the present day: the formation of national vernaculars and the gradual democratization of education ("education for all").

The year 1492 is important in marking a shift in attitudes towards language. It was in this year that Antonio Nebrija presented the King of Spain with his *Gramática castellana,* in the foreword of which it was stated that language (the Spanish tongue – not Latin) was the constant companion of royal governance ("*la compañera del imperio*"; Eberenz

R. Wodak and D. Corson (eds), *Encyclopedia of Language and Education,*
Volume 1: Language Policy and Political Issues in Education, 1–11.
© *1997 Kluwer Academic Publishers. Printed in the Netherlands.*

1992; Sanchez Pérez 1992). This is the birth certificate of a European national vernacular, which, that same year, embarked upon a worldwide career.

Almost at the same time, in another European country – Germany – a widespread movement was under way advocating general and universal education. The reformer Martin Luther demanded of the municipalities and princes of the land that they found schools so that the population might learn to read. Luther, who had himself been responsible for the translation of the Bible into the vernacular, argued that the people should be enabled to read the Bible in their mother tongue. There were thus political, theological and religious reasons for a change in attitude towards language and for the concomitant gradual implementation of universal education, the latter, in its turn, bringing about a further radical shift in attitudes towards language.

Only the barest outline can be provided here of the various stages in the development of vernacular languages towards the universal significance they enjoy today, particularly in respect of language attitudes and the growing influence of educational institutions on this development. When, for instance, the oft-cited Abbé Grégoire, as a member of the French Constituent Assembly, attacked the use of *patois* (dialect) and argued that all French citizens should learn (standard) French as the language of the nation, then this was not motivated originally by considerations of language policy but by broader political considerations: the French should learn French in order to understand the laws of the new Republic and obey them. For this purpose, every village was to have its school. Grégoire's demand, however, also had enormous consequences in terms of language policy. Opposition to *patois* had a profound influence on French attitudes towards language, particularly the French language (Caput 1972/1975; Settekorn 1988); it altered the linguistic map of France, making the country today a practically monolingual territory. The best proof of this is the fact that the struggle for the right to regional dialects is conducted almost exclusively in standard French (see the review by Corson in this volume: 99–109).

But it was not only in France that aspirations towards national unity received support through language policy in particular. Analogous tendencies can be found in other European nation-states, and these frequently led to conflict. Language was and remains for many people one of the basic elements in the movement towards political unity (Italy being a case in point: see Salvi 1975).

Of problematical consequence was the "export" of languages to other countries, as occurred in the wake of European overseas colonization, as well as during the continental expansion of such colonial powers as Russia and China. Nebrija's dictum concerning language as the constant companion of governance was readily construed as encouraging the export of language: i.e., the use of the language of the conquerors and colonizers in occupied territories. It cannot be said that the attitudes of conquerors and colonizers towards their own language and the languages of the conquered were unanimous – but they did tend to assert the primacy of the colonizers' tongue, be this for practical reasons (to facilitate communication between conqueror and conquered, from periphery to metropole) or on explicitly civilizing grounds (the language of the colonizers providing the colonized with a conduit to the blessings of European civilization). In both cases, the consequences for the colonized were the same: subordination, both physically (by military, political, and economic power) and culturolinguistically (see Calvet 1974; Phillipson 1992).

MAJOR PROBLEMS TODAY

Educational policy is confronted with particular problems in the following areas: governmental or social enforcement of the use of particular languages; tendencies towards linguistic standardization; the consequences of colonization, migration, economic globalization, and developments in communication technology; and, finally, the political interrelationships between states.

It has already been indicated that the establishment and maintenance of national vernaculars is a problem area of universal relevance. Educational policy is ineluctably drawn into these conflicts, and cannot escape them. In extreme cases, this means open conflict; in more favourable instances, compromise may be sought. Well-known examples of conflict involving language include the problematical status of Kurdish in the Republic of Turkey, Basque in Spain, and Berber in North Africa. Attempts at consensual regulation include Switzerland (with four languages), Paraguay (bilingual), and South Africa (multilingual).

Educational policy and attitudes towards language can also be influenced by attempts at standardization; recent examples include Dutch ("*Allgemeen beschaaft Nederlands*"), Basque, Quechua (Peru), Bahasa Indonesia, and Bahasa Malaysia. Standardization becomes obvious whenever languages assume written form, and whenever unified orthographic and grammatical norms are applied. But even long-standardized written languages experience problems of normative usage that need to be solved from time to time (Haarmann 1988).

Languages can be standardized on levels other than their external linguistic form. For example, many states have stipulations regarding the use of technical terminology and place restrictions on the assigning of personal names. In practically all countries there are prescriptions concerning the use of languages in public institutions, government offices, parliamentary assemblies and courts of law. In a number of countries, the influence of foreign or minority languages on the majority tongue is closely monitored. Regulations are occasionally passed to protect certain speech communities: for example, the language of the workplace or of advertising (for Quebec as a classic case, see Laurin 1977 and see the review by Burnaby).

Colonization and decolonization have also had long-lasting consequences in terms of educational policy. Doubtless noteworthy is the fact that the great majority of colonized peoples, long after their liberation, have continued to employ the language of the colonial powers or the local languages favoured by the latter. This is hardly surprising in the case of the first wave of decolonization in the Americas. In North America and in the Spanish and Portuguese colonies of South and Central America, those who sought independence were primarily discontented inhabitants of European origin – that is to say, themselves part of the mass of colonizers – who were obviously competent in the language of the colonial power.

A quite different aspect, however, is presented by African and Asian states which gained their independence in the twentieth century. The formerly colonized peoples discovered in the languages of the colonizers a bonding agent with which to unify infant nations. By retaining colonial languages, these countries avoided or postponed controversy about linguistic alternatives. Official, political reasons were given for retaining these languages, but there were also other, tacit grounds, including the fact that classes and social groups that had successfully acquired the language of the former colonial masters were thereby ensuring themselves the privileges which such acquisition brought with it (see the reviews by Egbo in Volume 2 and by Obondo in Volume 5).

The consequences of these developments for educational policy are clear: colonial languages (not only English, French, Portuguese and Spanish, but also such languages as Chinese and Russian) have become languages of instruction far beyond the bounds of those employing them as their mother tongue, and exert great influence on attitudes towards language and cultural traditions.

The worldwide process of diaspora in the postwar period, which is in part a result of colonization, has also had consequences for educational policy. On the one hand, migrants must acquire the language of their host country as a second language. On the other, migrants not only use the language of their former homeland in private life, but also demand the right to employ it in public and seek its use in school instruction and in the media. The language of migrant origin may be not only the official language of the former homeland (i.e. not infrequently the language of the colonizer) but also an African or Asian language – and it is particularly the right to speak and to learn in one of these latter languages that is being argued for. How host countries react to such demands on the part of immigrants is an interesting and as yet little-researched question. In this area, educational policy should not be considered in isolation, but attention needs to be given to the activities of immigrant minorities themselves in political parties, social organizations, the press, and the electronic media. One is prompted to observe that migration can create more favourable conditions for particular groups to use and receive instruction in their own language than was the case in their homeland, where they were disadvantaged through the rigorous promotion of an official tongue.

At first glance, it would seem that economic globalization and advances in communication technology have resulted in one language – English – gaining primacy over all others (see the review by Phillipson. Closer inspection, however, reveals something different. Globalization, in compelling reconsideration of such questions as production location and international cooperation, has granted communication a far higher value than ever before. If global communication is to function optimally, then much greater linguistic effort is required in the domain of international exchange. How far can one go strategically with a particular language, and how far with others? It would be a mistake to regard languages merely as *means* of communication; languages are also forms of personal and emotional expression, as well as being bearers of cultural traditions. To try and replace the manifold richness of languages with a single language is not only illusory but also counter-productive. Wherever cooperation, mutual agreement, trust, team spirit, creativity and the willingness to learn are criteria for success, faith needs to be placed in the multiplicity of tongues. It is for this reason that the current economic globalization and improvements in communication *technology* are demanding increased efforts in the teaching and learning of languages – especially, of course, those languages that have greatest currency. And such developments have their effect on educational policy.

It goes without saying that increasing international integration on the political level also influences the educational sphere; one need only recall the current restructuring of defence alliances, or supranational political associations such as the European Union. The latter, in particular, is an interesting example not only of a tactful handling of the question of language but also of a prudent approach to educational policy (European Commission 1995).

WORK IN PROGRESS

Research into attitudes towards language should be distinguished from research into its consequences in terms of educational policy. Language attitudes are of interest to researchers both as an individual and as a collective phenomenon. Most studies at the individual level have been dedicated to the phenomenon of bilingualism in early childhood, with a focus on *language acquisition*. Ranging from early empirical-descriptive studies (e.g., Ronjat 1913) to useful surveys of the state of research (e.g., Baker 1987; Hagège 1996), much effort has been expended in treating this phenomenon under the heading: "How does one become a bilingual (or multilingual) individual?" A further question – for a long time the subject of heated controversy – concerns the relative merits of bilingualism. It is commonly accepted today that the advantages of bilingualism outweigh any disadvantages (see Volume 5).

Another perspective is that of *language possession*. The linguist Wandruszka (1979) has described this phenomenon, proceeding from the linguistic capacity of the human individual. By virtue of his or her language and its unique, individual stratification, every human being is multilingual. Not only does every language contain elements from many other languages, but every speaker moves among various levels of his or her language, e.g., in dialects and regiolects, sociolects and language for specific purposes, the language of intimacy and the language of distance. To this extent, every human being is in effect multilingual. Wandruszka concludes that it should not be a difficult task, under such circumstances, to train large numbers of people to become truly multilingual.

Attitudes of monolingual individuals to their language, by contrast, has hitherto been the subject of little research. One exception is a study by Ingrid Gogolin (1994), who observed and questioned teachers from various countries in respect to their attitude towards the language of instruction employed. Gogolin characterized the attitude revealed in this occupational context as a *monolingual mindset* ("*monolingualer Habitus*"), i.e. as a self-explanatory, undiscussed and unproblematized attitude towards the language in which children are taught. The absence of problematization has much less to do with questions of teaching methodology than with the underlying disposition of the teacher: the language of instruction is regarded as a value in itself.

Attitudes of language learners to foreign languages, however, have been more frequently investigated. A good example of a comparative (German/French) study is Candelier and Hermann-Brennecke (1993), which reveal the great significance of attitudes in determining the choice of a particular foreign language in school, how much these attitudes influence learning success, and, finally, how far attitudes are responsible for learners continuing with a language or dropping it (on this group of topics, see also Hermann 1980).

Individual attitudes towards language can be distinguished from collective attitudes – such as the attitude of the inhabitants of a country to the official language, to territorial multilingualism, and to minority languages. The collective attitude towards languages is a social phenomenon which is determined by a great number of different forces. Official language policy has an important function in this context (for an example, see Coulmas 1991), in that it serves within the social process to express the will and guiding principles of the political class and of prevailing political opinion. However, political discourse alone cannot suffice to describe the phenomenon. All social forces need to be considered: social classes, levels of education, age groups, gender, occupational groups, residential areas, places of work, organizations and associations. These all play their part in constituting and developing collective attitudes towards language.

Nevertheless, official language policy is a variable which deserves special attention. Three examples may serve to direct attention to international aspects of language policy. Robert Phillipson has published a critical study entitled *Linguistic Imperialism* (1992 see his review) which considers the relationship of English to other languages. "Linguistic imperialism" constitutes a special instance of the category of *linguicism*, which can be defined as follows: "Ideologies, structures, and practices which are used to legitimate, effectuate, and reproduce an unequal division of power and resources (both material and immaterial) between groups which are defined on the basis of language" (Phillipson 1992: p. 47). Phillipson shows how, since the beginnings of British colonial history, structures based on this ideology have been created which have made English into the internationally dominant language par excellence, maintaining it in this role far beyond the period of classical colonialism as such. British English provides Phillipson with his prime example, though the role of American English is also examined. In the case of a polycentric language such as English, the reader must, of course, also consider centres of English language policy beyond Great Britain and the USA. Areas where direct and indirect measures are taken on the basis of this language policy range from foreign affairs, international alliances, and defence to the promotion of scientific research and the establishment of the profitable macro-industry called "ELT" (English Language Teaching).

Phillipson's critical reflections concern less the fate of English than the fate of the languages that have undergone domination – a topic that is also dealt with by Louis-Jean Calvet (1974, 1987). Calvet employs the concept of colonialism and the metaphors of "*glottophagie*" (linguistic cannibalism) and of "*the war of tongues*" in order to show the effects which such dominance (in Calvet's studies, that of French) has within and beyond the borders of the territory of linguistic origin. Calvet's study recounts the resistance within France to regional language variants (see the example of l'Abbé Grégoire, above) as well as the methods used in disseminating the French language throughout the colonies and the present-day promotion of French worldwide. It is neither the spread of a language in itself that constitutes a problem, nor the extent to which it is taught. What is potentially pernicious is the resulting attitudes towards other languages; these are made to compare unfavourably with the glottophagic language that is being promoted, and are thereby condemned as inferior, unworthy of support, and incapable of development.

The third study to be cited here concerns the German language. In contrast to Phillipson's language-political and Calvet's ideology-critical approaches, Ulrich Ammon's methodology (1991) is sociolinguistic and empirical, restricting itself essentially to the immediate present (insofar as this is possible in the case of a sociolinguistic topic). What interests Ammon is the use of the German language both within and beyond the discrete ethnocultural radius of the language, in all relevant domains – politics, administration, culture, science, the media, tourism. Ammon also examines the teaching of German as a foreign language and the official promotion of this polycentric language by both state and publicly financed private institutions. The author is at the same time aware of the fact that there are autochthonous language minorities existing within areas dominated by German, as well as numerous new minorities formed since the Second World War, for which the language policies pursued in German-speaking countries present a new challenge. The overall phenomenon dealt with by Ammon is thus the same as that examined by Calvet and Phillipson: the question of the politics and ecology of language.

PROBLEMS AND DIFFICULTIES

The consequences for educational policy arising out of language attitudes have as yet not been analysed systematically. However, as there obviously are consequences, these urgently require consideration.

Research on teaching principles and practice has treated some problems of more immediate relevance to the area, but without establishing an explicit connection to the question of language attitudes. To this category belong problems of *literacy acquisition* among children and adults, as well as the mediation of universal literacy, particularly in respect of the special conditions of our audiovisual age. In what language or languages is literacy to be effected, and with what purpose? How can reading competence be ensured, writing competence exercised and improved? How best should the *evaluation* of language performance among pupils and students take place? What weight should be placed here on orthographical and grammatical correctness, "refined" pronunciation, and stylistic facility, and what significance do such factors have in one's further schooling and career? Research findings on the nature of success and failure at school, it is clear, have always revealed the presence of language attitudes.

The language attitudes of teachers and school administrators are of decisive importance, particularly for the school career of children from linguistic minorities (see Gogolin 1994, discussed above). How do these attitudes influence a pupil's success at school? Further problems include the range of options for second-language instruction offered to adult migrants, and the attitudes of migrants themselves, and of others in the broader community, towards language acquisition as a means of social integration.

Foreign language instruction as a whole (as a service accessible to all citizens) and foreign language instruction for specific purposes (e.g., professional or technical) belong increasingly among the areas of investigation that are of central relevance to research into language attitudes. The attitudes of language learners and the public at large play an essential role in any decision to learn a language and to do so successfully (see Candelier & Hermann-Brennecke 1993; Hermann 1980). Attitudes are closely linked to motivation and the willingness to learn.

In recent decades, forms of foreign language acquisition have been practised which have revolutionized foreign language teaching, such as total immersion programmes and "bilingual instruction". In the case of immersion programmes, learners are submerged in a total language-bath by instructing them exclusively *in a foreign language*. What they experience, then, is similar to what is generally expected of children from a language minority who are obliged to learn in a language of instruction that is quite new to them. Bilingual instruction, on the other hand, mediates content *in two languages of instruction*: the usual medium of instruction and a foreign language. Common to both approaches is the fact that the foreign language is not treated as the object of instruction but as the linguistic medium itself. The attention of the learner is thus not primarily directed at the linguistic form but at the material that is being mediated. These practical approaches have only recently become the object of research interest. A useful survey of the present state of development in selected European countries can be found in Fruhauf, Coyle and Christ (1996); an annotated bibliography on the state of research has been published (Landesinstitut 1996; also see Volume 5).

Much more clearly than is the case with immersion programmes and bilingual instruction, the area of *early foreign language teaching* has revealed just how massively attitudes towards the teaching and learning of foreign languages have changed in recent times. Soon after World War One, a worldwide FLES movement (Foreign Languages in Elementary Schools) got under way, with support from numerous interdisciplinary research projects. This constituted a breaking of the taboo which stated that only people who had largely completed the acquisition of their mother tongue were capable of learning foreign languages. The 1980s saw a renaissance of interest in early foreign language instruction. Still controversial, however, is the question of what form of "encounter" with foreign languages is most appropriate for young children. The extreme positions currently being contested are those of *language awareness* (e.g., Hawkins 1987) and "enseignement précoce" or *early foreign language teaching* (e.g., Garabédian &Weiss 1991). Gompf and Karbe (1995) provide a competent survey of the present state of discussion.

FUTURE DIRECTIONS

In the future, attitudes towards language and languages will doubtless receive more attention than before in terms of educational policy. Both individual and collective language attitudes clearly influence teaching and learning, and must therefore be granted due consideration in research and in policy applications. A prime research objective will be the tracing of changes and developments in individual and collective attitudes. How, if at all, can the latter be influenced and channelled? On the assumption that attitudes are shaped over time and constitute psychological dimensions that are resistant to change, it must be determined whether and to what extent education can affect these processes of formation. It is undeniable that educational policy and practice will have to reckon with their presence and incorporate such attitudes into their considerations.

Conversely, attention must be paid to the question of whether and to what extent educational policy measures – their objectives; teaching practice; the behaviour patterns of teachers and learners – serve to strengthen or even create attitudes towards language. Do such measures stimulate discussion and problematization of these attitudes, incorporating them in a broader frame of linguistic policy which is suited to given social conditions and which encourages peaceful and fruitful coexistence among speakers of different languages? Language attitudes possess their very own political dimension – a fact of which educational policy needs to take productive cognizance.

REFERENCES

Ammon, U.: 1991, *Die Internationale Stellung der deutschen Sprache*, de Gruyter, Berlin & New York.
Baker, C.: 1987, *Key Issues in Bilingualism and Bilingual Education*, Multilingual Matters, Clevedon.
Calvet, L.-J.: 1974, *Linguistique et colonialisme: Petit traité de glottophagie*, Payot, Paris.
Calvet, L.-J.: 1987, *La Guerre des langues et les politiques linguistiques,* Payot, Paris.
Candelier, M. & Hermann-Brennecke, G.: 1993, *Entre le choix et l' abandon: Les langues étrangères à l'école, vues d'Allemagne et de France*, Didier, Paris.
Caput, J.P.: 1972/1975, *La Langue française: Histoire d'une institution*, 2 vols., Larousse, Paris.
Chervel, A.: 1977, *Et il fallut apprendre à écrire à tous les petits Français: Histoire de la grammaire scolaire*, Payot, Paris.
Coulmas, F.: 1991, *A Language Policy for the European Community: Prospects and Quandaries,* Berlin & New York.
Eberenz, R.: 1992, 'Spanisch: Sprache und Gesetzgebung/Lengua y legislación', *Lexikon der Romanistischen Linguistik* 6.1. Niemeyer, Tübingen, 368–78.
European Commission: 1996, *Teach and Learn: Towards the Cognitive Society*, First Report on the Consideration of Cultural Aspects in Education. Office for Official Publications of the European Union, Luxemburg.
Fruhauf, G., Coyle, D. & Christ, I.: 1996, *Teaching Content in a Foreign Language: Practice and Perspectives in European Bilingual Education*, Stichting Europees Platform voor het Nederlandse Onderwijs, Alkmaar.
Garabédian, M. & Weiss, F. (coordonné par): 1991, *Enseignements/apprentissages précoces des langues: Le Français dans le monde; Recherches et Applications*, Edicef, Paris.

Gogolin, I.: 1994, Der monolinguale Habitus der multilingualen Schule, Waxmann, Münster & New York.

Gompf, G. & Karbe, U.: 1995, 'Erwerb von Fremdsprachen im Vorschul- und Primarschulalter', in K.R. Bausch et al. (eds.), Handbuch Premdsprachenunterricht, Francke, Tübingen, 436–42.

Haarmann, H.: 1988, 'Allgemeine Strukturen europäischer Standardsprachenentwicklung', Sociolinguistica: International Yearbook of European Sociolinguistics 2. Niemeyer, Tübingen, 10–51.

Hagège, C.: 1996, L'Enfant aux deux langues, Editions Odile Jacob, Paris.

Hawkins, E.: 1987, Awareness of Language: An Introduction, Cambridge University Press, Cambridge.

Hermann, G.: 1980, 'Attitudes and success in children's learning of English as a second language: The motivational vs. the resultative hypothesis', English Language Teaching Journal 34, 247–54.

Howatt, A.P.R.: 1984, A History of English Language Teaching, Oxford University Press, Oxford.

Kelly, L.G.: 1969, Twenty-Five Centuries of Language Teaching, Newbury House, Rowley, Mass.

Landesinstitut für Schule und Weiterbildung (ed.): 1996, Fremdsprachen als Arbeitssprachen im Unterricht: Eine Bibliographie zum bilingualen Lernen und Lehren, Verlag für Schule und Weiterbildung, Soest.

Laurin, C.: 1977, Le Français, langue du Québec, Editions du jour, Québec.

Pennycook, A.: 1994, The Cultural Politics of English as an International Language, Longman, London & New York.

Phillipson, R.: 1992, Linguistic Imperialism, Oxford University Press, Oxford.

Ronjat, J.: 1913, Le développement du langage observé chez un enfant bilingue, Paris.

Salvi, S.: 1975, Le lingue tagliate: Storie delle minoranze linguistiche in Italia, Rizzoli Editore, Milano.

Sanchez Pérez, A.: 1992, Historia de la enseñanza del español como lengua extranjera, Sociedad General Española de Librería, Alcobendas (Madrid).

Settekorn, W.: 1988, Sprachnorm und Sprachnormierung in Frankreich: Einführung in die begrifflichen, historischen und materiellen Grundlagen, Niemeyer, Tübingen.

Wandruszka, M.: 1979, Die Mehrsprachigkeit des Menschen, Piper, München & Zürich.

MARK FETTES

LANGUAGE PLANNING AND EDUCATION

The choice of the language or languages of instruction in schools presupposes the *existence* of language varieties suitable for the task. In the
most widespread model of schooling, such a language of instruction is
expected to be highly standardized (so that many different schools can
use the same curricular and human resources) and both prestigious and
widely used (so that education promotes economic mobility and inter-
group communication). These are not "natural" characteristics for any
language: they are the result of the more-or-less conscious influence of
various powerful groups and institutions on sociolinguistic norms. In its
most conscious, explicit and rationalized form, such influence is known as
language planning.

DEVELOPMENT OF THE TRADITION

The term 'language planning' was coined nearly forty years ago by Einar
Haugen (1959, 1966) to describe the process of developing of a new standard national language in Norway following independence from Denmark.
In the course of the next few years, dozens of European colonies and overseas territories raised their own national flags, and the Norwegian case
suddenly appeared to be of worldwide relevance. From within the broader
study of the 'language problems of developing nations' (Fishman et al.
1968; Rubin & Jernudd 1971), language planning soon grew to be recognized as a discipline in its own right (Fishman 1974; Rubin et al. 1977;
Cobarrubias & Fishman 1983).

This mainstream tradition of language planning took the model of standard national European languages as its point of departure. Such a language
was seen as an instrument that could be shaped and wielded by the state
to promote national unity and efficient communication within its borders.
It was soon realized that such goals require at least two different types of
intervention: *corpus* planning, aimed at defining and developing a national
standard, and *status* planning, aimed at encouraging its use in preference
to other language varieties (Kloss 1969). Much of the language planning
literature, including the references cited above, is concerned with applying
these concepts to specific national situations, for instance the development
of Hebrew as the national language of Israel or the attempts to develop a
national language for the Philippines on the basis of Tagalog. There has

R. Wodak and D. Corson (eds), Encyclopedia of Language and Education,
Volume 1: Language Policy and Political Issues in Education, 13–22.
© *1997 Kluwer Academic Publishers. Printed in the Netherlands.*

also been considerable interest in the ongoing reform and modernization of the national European languages.

While influential, the 'modernist paradigm' just described has never held a monopoly in the field of language planning. Another long-established formula holds that any 'systematic, theory-based, rational, and organized societal attention to language problems' may be termed language planning (Cooper 1989: p. 31). Understood this way, language planning comprises all systematic language policy development and implementation, including 'foreign language planning' (Lambert 1994) and 'language-in-education planning' (Ingram 1990; Paulston & McLaughlin 1994). The principal difficulty with this interpretation is that a great deal of language policy-making goes on in a haphazard or uncoordinated way, far removed from the language planning ideal. Therefore language planning in this wider sense must be linked to the critical evaluation of language policy: the former providing standards of rationality and effectiveness, the latter testing these ideas against actual practice in order to promote the development of better (more sophisticated, more useful) language planning models. Such a field of study would be better described as 'language policy and planning', LPP (Grabe 1994).

As will become clear, this broader definition seems far more relevant to important contemporary issues than the restrictive modernist paradigm. The latter, however, has gone furthest in developing a standard set of analytical tools, for example the three-fold typology proposed by Cooper (1989) and used to organize the following section. Here the corpus-status distinction is augmented by *acquisition* planning. As used here, the term refers to all planning activities that focus on language teaching and learning, rather than on more general aspects of language development and status. It would be a mistake, however, to equate acquisition planning with 'language-in-education planning'; rather, as Paulston and McLaughlin (1994) recognize, all aspects of language planning are potentially relevant to education, and vice versa (for illustrations from the early planning literature, see Kennedy 1984). The links should become clearer as we proceed.

MAJOR CONTRIBUTIONS

The classical theory of language planning was developed around the model of a single standard national language. However, any language variety used in education, whether large or small, is likely to be the product of a certain degree of planning, in the sense that it will have been chosen according to certain criteria, it will probably have a writing system of some kind, and its acquisition is expected to promote certain social and cognitive goals. The major contribution of the modernist paradigm has been to make explicit some of the assumptions involved in developing a language in this way, to test these against the effects of various language policies in different social settings, and thus to provide a framework for further policy development on the basis of *future-oriented, realistic problem-solving* (Rubin 1984).

This having been said, three important caveats must be added. In general, language planning research has been more successful in highlighting problems and analyzing policies than in reproducing successes. This is because language change is intimately linked to social change, and involves all the uncertainties of any social enterprise. Political and social forces constrain the application of theory, and language planning has developed along rather narrow analytical lines which have not encouraged a broad social analysis or links with other applied social science disciplines (Fishman 1984). Furthermore, language planning does not take place in a neutral context, but is used by particular groups to advance their own goals at the expense of others; and the gradual broadening of the field's concerns has called into question some of the central assumptions behind the classical theory. These themes will be taken up again below.

Corpus Planning

The challenges of corpus planning were the original inspiration for conceiving of language planning as an independent discipline. Its aims are readily understandable for educators: the development of writing systems for different language varieties ('graphization'), the definition of 'correct' language ('standardization'), and the introduction of new terms for new concepts ('modernization'). Modern school systems are, of course, one of the chief means by which such standards are propagated and reinforced. Interestingly, teachers appear in general to exert a highly conservative influence on language use, which reinforces the importance of acquisition planning for the diffusion of linguistic innovations (Cooper 1989).

Corpus planning is important for nearly all standard languages; indeed, English may be the only such language without a clear planning tradition. In the national languages of the industrialized countries, the chief concern is modernization – assuring intertranslatability with other modern languages, and in particular with English, as the language with the highest production rate of scientific and technological terms. Occasionally such terminological work is accompanied by orthographical or other types of language reform. Graphization and standardization are processes more characteristic of non-national languages, for example the indigenous languages of the Americas and Asia and most of the languages of Africa and the Pacific. However, it should be noted that some Central Asian national languages, for example, are still undergoing this type of development, adopting new writing systems in a break with the Soviet past and modifying their lexicon to bring it closer to the models employed in other Turkic or Iranian languages (Coulmas 1994; Fierman 1991). Obviously such reforms place huge demands on the education systems of these countries.

Language planning research has been successful in identifying a number of factors which may affect the success of corpus planning. In the area of graphization, a common discovery is that the highly precise transcriptions favoured by linguists are felt by the language community to be too unwieldy for everyday use. Another major hurdle to establishing a written standard is the problem of dialectal variation, which generally means that a given writing system will provide a more phonetic representation of some varieties than others. (The grapholects of most existing standard languages are based on the variety of the national capital, or of a historically dominant region of the country.) These points, and their implications for education, are well illustrated by current developments in North American Aboriginal languages (Burnaby 1985; St. Clair & Leap 1982).

Modernization is also a controversial activity, in which the homogenizing pressure exerted by languages of regional or global power, leading towards 'internationalization' of the lexicon, is commonly opposed by the countervailing force of linguistic purism (Thomas 1991). Such conflicts often divide along class lines, for instance in India, where a 'purist', elite-driven approach to the modernization of Hindi has failed to take root in popular linguistic practice (Khubchandani 1983; see his review). Some knowledge of the diversity of strategies for language reform (Fodor & Hagège 1983), i.e. the ways in which languages around the world are being developed and modified to meet social goals, could help prepare teachers for the open and critical discussion of linguistic norms in the classroom (Fairclough 1990). A more fundamental concern at the global level, however, is whether corpus planning, through the pursuit of intertranslatability, is accelerating the loss of non-European means of knowledge and expression (Mühlhäusler 1996; and below).

Status Planning

The paradigmatic act of status planning is the adoption by a state of one or more official languages. The apparent simplicity of such a move is belied by the difficulty of assessing its consequences. It was soon discovered, for instance in the African context (Bamgbose 1991), that official declarations in themselves had little effect on language behaviour. 'Status', operationalized as the 'functional allocation of language varieties' (Cooper 1989), turned out to be intimately bound up with questions of identity, prestige, perceived benefit and other attitudinal factors that are difficult to influence in a predetermined way (McGroarty 1996). As a result, the 'national' languages adopted by many post-colonial states have often remained mired in political controversy or social indifference, and even the more successful examples, such as Tanzanian Swahili or Indonesian, have had to contend with the stubborn prestige of former colonial languages and the continuing risk of igniting local nationalist passions (see many articles in the edited collections cited above). The implications for the educational systems of developing countries have been enormous, including the entrenchment of small elites with command of the former colonial languages (estimated at 4% of the population in such countries as Kenya and India; see the review by Obondo in Volume 5), the continued dominance of a Western-oriented curriculum, and the inability to sustain high levels of popular literacy (Phillipson 1992).

The problem of status is also salient in relation to non-dominant ('non-official', 'minority') languages. The early planning literature was largely silent about the fate of these other varieties, reflecting dominant Western practices at the time. In the early 1980s, a review of OECD policies (Churchill 1986) established a six-stage typology for what might be called 'status planning for minority languages', and demonstrated that most government policies were located at the lowest stages: that is, the treatment of minority languages as a problem rather than a resource. In fact, such practices are the corollary of the 'standard national language' planning framework developed in Western Europe and exported throughout the world (Luke et al. 1990; Tollefson 1991; Phillipson 1992; Mühlhäusler 1996). As in the case of developing countries, this had disastrous consequences for the educational status of linguistic minorities (Skutnabb-Kangas & Cummins 1988).

The 1990s, however, have brought political, economic, technological and cultural changes with far-reaching effects on linguistic attitudes and policies (Coulmas 1994). The value of multilingualism is now being reassessed by Western scholars (Ouane 1995; Skutnabb-Kangas 1995) and linguistic human rights are evolving into a distinct field of inquiry (Skutnabb-Kangas & Phillipson 1994; see the review by Skutnabb-Kangas in this volume). Educational issues are of central importance to this evolving pluralist paradigm, which promises to transform both the theory and practice of language planning (Grabe 1994 and below).

Acquisition Planning

Within the modernist paradigm, language acquisition was seen as an aspect of status planning: that is, if a language standard could be established in terms of societal norms, its teaching and learning would follow as a matter of course. As Cooper (1989) pointed out, however, many countries, including those with highly standardized national languages, still face considerable challenges in cultivating an adequate knowledge of the standard among new immigrants and various non-dominant groups that use a different language variety among themselves. In this light, the exclusion of education research from the field of language planning, and the use the separate term 'applied linguistics' to refer to the study and improvement of language teaching and learning, appears decidedly unhelpful. Recent reviews of 'language-in-education planning' (an applied linguistics term) in fact demonstrate close affinities with classical work in language planning (Ingram 1990, 1994; compare Rubin 1984). Conversely, one current use of the term 'language planning' refers to the development of national foreign language curricula (Lambert 1994). Cooper's three-fold typology does away with such unhelpful distinctions, and focuses attention on what language policies and planning are supposed to achieve.

Scarcely any literature exists on 'acquisition planning' under that name, but a great deal of work is relevant to it, ranging from efforts to teach a national standard variety to speakers of regional or ethnic varieties, through the teaching of 'standard-as-a-second-language' to immigrants and involuntary minorities and 'standard-as-a-foreign-language' to those of other backgrounds, to language maintenance and revitalization programs for non-dominant languages. It should be clear at once that no 'systematic, theory-based, rational, and organized societal attention to language problems' (to return to our earlier definition of language planning) can afford to neglect such issues, which together cover most of the traditional domain of applied linguistics (or 'language in education') and merit detailed treatment on their own grounds.

Of principal interest in the present context is how this research is, or could be, used to guide the development and implementation of language policy. Here a distinction can be drawn between national policies, which set overall language goals for the education system, and lower-level policies within schools, literacy organizations, and so on. An influential example of the former was Australia's ground-breaking National Policy on Languages (Lo Bianco 1987 and see Clyne's review), which was exceptional in its attempt to integrate policy in all of the areas mentioned above. However, the policy has also been criticized for not paying sufficient attention to issues of implementation and evaluation, allowing it to be politically sidelined (Ingram 1994). Another much-cited example of comprehensive acquisition planning in a more limited area is the Dutch National Action Program on Foreign Languages (Van Els 1994). Unfortunately such examples are rare, and most acquisition planning throughout the world appears to take place on a fragmented and ad hoc basis (e.g. Bergentoft 1994). Even where overwhelming empirical evidence on some aspect of language acquisition is available, for instance regarding the inefficacy of 'submersion' or 'early-exit' bilingual programs in promoting competence in the dominant language, educational policies are rarely refashioned accordingly (Cummins 1993).

Given the incoherence of most acquisition planning at the national level, there is an important potential role for schools and school districts in formulating 'language policy [across the curriculum]' (Corson 1990; 1998). This approach constitutes, in effect, a language planning paradigm for educational institutions, including status, corpus and acquisition issues. It may well be that most acquisition planning takes place, and will continue to take place, at this level (see the review by May in this volume), in which case the importance of educational research for the field of language planning as a whole can scarcely be overstated. In the following section, it is suggested that this is but one of the factors involved in the emergence of a new conception of the field.

FUTURE DIRECTIONS

Mühlhäusler (1996) aptly characterizes the classical tradition in language planning as the 'streamlining approach': one language variety for as many functions as possible, and others relegated to inconspicuous niches in the social order. However, as the above review makes clear, this description no longer fits much of what goes on under the label of language planning. As the field's scope has broadened to include the full range of language varieties and language-related institutions in society, so the modernist paradigm has gradually ceded ground to a postmodernist acceptance and revalorization of diversity. Central figures of the field have recently posited language planning as a means to broker compromise solutions rather than to favour one language over another (Jernudd 1993), or turned their attention to strategies for strengthening small languages in the face of linguistic homogenization (Fishman 1991). While not yet fully visible, a new paradigm is clearly struggling to be born.

One noteworthy and perhaps unexpected contribution to this process has come from interlinguistics, the 'science of planned languages' (Schubert 1989). Long marginalized in academic discourse, the planned language tradition has developed an extensive critique of the modern language order as a means of producing and reproducing inequalities and barriers to communication (Tonkin 1979; Dasgupta 1987; Piron 1994), paralleling the postmodern shift in the language planning paradigm. Unlike most critiques, however, this one is coupled with a positive proposal stressing the viability of a planned neutral 'lingua franca' as a means of achieving a balance of power between different language groups, based largely on a century-long experiment involving Esperanto (Tonkin 1987; Janton 1994). A serious dialogue with this related tradition has begun and promises to be highly enriching (Dasgupta 1987).

A revised conception of language planning, capable of incorporating the full range of approaches and insights described above, might view it as a set of theories and practices for managing linguistic ecosystems as called for by Mühlhäusler (1996). A useful analogy can be drawn with agricultural science, which in the Western tradition was long synonymous with crop monoculture, but which has more recently been developed in the direction of 'permaculture', the design of self-sustaining crop-yielding ecosystems (Bell 1992). The fundamental notion is that societies need not be, and indeed should not be, constructed on an ideal of monolingualism. Rather, it is possible (and beneficial) for many languages to coexist in a complex web of relationships where many or most people are bilingual or multilingual and experience this as a resource worth preserving. Convincing arguments have been made that this is or was the case in the Pacific (Mühlhäusler 1996), Southern Asia (see the review by Khubchandani in this volume), and Africa (Akinasso 1994); Skutnabb-Kangas and her colleagues (1995) are convinced that it could be equally true of Europe and the world of the future.

Such an 'ecological approach' to language planning would have far-reaching implications for education, including the proliferation of bilingual classrooms and, possibly, the widespread teaching of Esperanto in an intercultural framework. There is, admittedly, a wide gap between such a vision and the present realities of language policy-making. Today the 'streamlining approach' continues to be applied by many governments in disregard for linguistic human rights and cultural sustainability. Yet a rising tide of resistance, and the changing tone of political discourse, suggest that the era of its unquestioned dominance is past.

University of Toronto
Canada

REFERENCES

Akinasso, F.N.: 1994, 'Linguistic unification and language rights', *Applied Linguistics* 15(2), 139–168.
Baldauf, Jr., R. & Luke, A. (eds.): 1990, *Language Planning and Education in Australasia and the South Pacific*, Multilingual Matters, Clevedon.
Bamgbose, A.: 1991, *Language and the Nation: The Language Question in Sub-Saharan Africa*, Edinburgh University Press, Edinburgh.
Bell, G.: 1992, *The Permaculture Way: Practical Steps to Create a Self-Sustaining World*, Thorsons, London.
Bergentoft, R.: 1994, 'Foreign language instruction: A comparative perspective', in R.D. Lambert (ed.), *Language Planning Around the World: Contexts and Systemic Change*, National Foreign Language Center, Washington, 17–46.
Burnaby, B. (ed.): 1985, *Promoting Native Writing Systems in Canada*, OISE Press, Toronto.
Churchill, S.: 1986, *The Education of Linguistic and Cultural Minorities in OECD Countries*, Multilingual Matters, Clevedon.
Cobarrubias, J. & Fishman, J. (eds.): 1983, *Progress in Language Planning: International Perspectives*, Mouton, Berlin.
Cooper, R.L.: 1989, *Language Planning and Social Change*, Cambridge University Press, Cambridge.
Corson, D.: 1990, *Language Policy Across the Curriculum*, Multilingual Matters, Clevedon.
Corson, D.: 1998, *Language Policy in Schools*, Erlbaum, New York.
Coulmas, F.: 1994, 'Language policy and planning: Political perspectives', *Annual Review of Applied Linguistics* 14, 34–52.

Cummins, J.: 1993, 'Bilingualism and second language learning', *Annual Review of Applied Linguistics* 13, 51–70.

Dasgupta, P.: 1987, 'Towards a dialogue between the sociolinguistic sciences and Esperanto culture', *Language Problems and Language Planning* 11, 305–334.

Fairclough, N. (ed.): 1990, *Critical Language Awareness*, Longman, London.

Fierman, W.: 1991, *Language Planning and National Development: The Uzbek Experience*, Mouton de Gruyter, Berlin.

Fishman, J.A.: 1984, 'Language modernisation and planning in comparison with other types of national modernisation and planning', in C. Kennedy (ed.), *Language Planning and Language Education*, Allen and Unwin, London, 37–54.

Fishman, J.A.: 1991, *Reversing Language Shift: Theoretical and Empirical Foundations of Assistance to Threatened Languages*, Multilingual Matters, Clevedon.

Fishman, J. (ed.): 1974, *Advances in Language Planning*, Mouton, The Hague.

Fishman, J.A., Ferguson, C.A. & Das Gupta, J. (eds.): 1968, *Language Problems of Developing Nations*, John Wiley and Sons, New York.

Fodor, I. & Hagège, C. (eds.): 1983, *Language Reform: History and Future*, Buske Verlag, Hamburg.

Grabe, W.: 1994, 'Language policy and planning: foreword', *Annual Review of Applied Linguistics* 14(), vii–ix.

Haugen, E.: 1959, 'Planning for a standard language in Norway', *Anthropological Linguistics* 1(3), 8–21.

Haugen, E.: 1966, 'Linguistics and language planning', in W. Bright (ed.), *Sociolinguistics*, Mouton, The Hague, 50–71.

Ingram, D.E.: 1990, 'Language-in-education planning', *Annual Review of Applied Linguistics* 10, 53–78.

Ingram, D.: 1994, 'Language policy in Australia in the 1990s', in R.D. Lambert (ed.), *Language Planning Around the World: Contexts and Systemic Change*, National Foreign Language Center, Washington, 69–110.

Janton, P.: 1993, *Esperanto: Language, Literature, and Community*, translated and updated by H. Tonkin, J. Edwards & K. Johnson-Weiner, SUNY Press, Albany.

Jernudd, B.H.: 1993, 'Language planning from a management perspective: An interpretation of findings', in E. H. Jahr (ed.), *Language Conflict and Language Planning*, Mouton De Gruyter, Berlin.

Kennedy, C. (ed.): 1984, *Language Planning and Language Education*, Allen and Unwin, London.

Khubchandani, L.M.: 1983, *Plural Languages, Plural Cultures: Communication, Identity, and Sociopolitical Change in Contemporary India*, University of Hawaii Press, Honolulu.

Kloss, H.: 1969, *Research Possibilities on Group Bilingualism: A Report*, International Centre for Research on Bilingualism, Quebec.

Lambert, R.D. (ed.): 1994, *Language Planning Around the World: Contexts and Systemic Change*, National Foreign Language Center, Washington.

Lo Bianco, J.: 1987, *National Policy on Languages*, Australian Government Printer, Canberra.

Luke, A., McHoul, A.W. & Mey, J.L.: 1990, 'On the limits of language planning: Class, state and power', in R. Baldauf, Jr. & A. Luke (eds.), *Language Planning and Education in Australasia and the South Pacific*, Multilingual Matters, Clevedon, 25–44.

McGroarty, M.: 1996, 'Language attitudes, motivation, and standards', in S.L. McKay and N.H. Hornberger (eds.), *Sociolinguistics and Language Teaching*, Cambridge University Press, Cambridge, 3–46.

Mühlhäusler, P.: 1996, *Linguistic Ecology. Language Change and Linguistic Imperialism in the Pacific Region*, Routledge, New York.

Ouane, A. (ed.): 1995, *Vers une culture multilingue de l'éducation*, Institut de l'UNESCO pour l'Education, Hamburg.

Paulston, C.B. & McLaughlin, S.: 1994, 'Language-in-education policy and planning', *Annual Review of Applied Linguistics* 14, 53–81.

Phillipson, R.: 1992, *Linguistic Imperialism*, Oxford University Press, Oxford.

Piron, C.: 1994, *Le défi des langues: Du gâchis au bon sens*, L'Harmattan, Paris.

Rubin, J.: 1984, 'Bilingual education and language planning', in C. Kennedy (ed.), *Language Planning and Language Education*, Allen and Unwin, London, 4–16.

Rubin, J. & Jernudd, B. (eds.): 1971, *Can Language Be Planned? Sociolinguistic Theory and Practice for Developing Nations*, University Press of Hawaii, Honolulu.

Rubin, J., Jernudd, B.H., Das Gupta, J., Fishman, J.A. & Ferguson, C.A. (eds.): 1977, *Language Planning Processes*, Mouton, The Hague.

St. Clair, R. & Leap, W. (eds.): 1982, *Language Renewal Among American Indian Tribes: Issues, Problems and Prospects*, National Clearinghouse for Bilingual Education, Arlington.

Schubert, K. (ed.): 1989, *Interlinguistics: Aspects of the Science of Planned Languages*, Mouton de Gruyter, Berlin.

Skutnabb-Kangas, T. (ed.): 1995, *Multilingualism for All*, Swets & Zeitlinger, Lisse.

Skutnabb-Kangas, T. & Cummins, J. (eds.): 1988, *Minority Education: From Shame to Struggle*, Multilingual Matters, Clevedon.

Skutnabb-Kangas, T. & Phillipson, R. (eds.): 1994, *Linguistic Human Rights*, Mouton de Gruyter, Berlin.

Thomas, G.: 1991, *Linguistic Purism*, Longman, London.

Tollefson, J.W.: 1991, *Planning Language, Planning Inequality*, Longman, London.

Tonkin, H.: 1979, 'Equalizing language', *Journal of Communication*, Spring 1979, 124–133.

Tonkin, H.: 1987, 'One hundred years of Esperanto: A survey', *Language Problems and Language Planning* 11, 264–282.

Van Els, T.: 1994, 'Foreign language planning in The Netherlands', in R.D. Lambert (ed.) *Language Planning Around the World: Contexts and Systemic Change*, National Foreign Language Center, Washington, 47–68.

ALASTAIR PENNYCOOK

CRITICAL APPLIED LINGUISTICS AND EDUCATION

Critical Applied Linguistics (CALx) is not, as yet, a term that is widely used. Nevertheless, it appears to be a useful umbrella under which a number of emerging critical approaches to language and education can be described. Part of the difficulty in defining CALx lies in the difficulties in determining both what it is to be critical and what is meant by Applied Linguistics. The term critical has a number of senses, from the popular meaning of stating negative opinions (as in 'don't be so critical'), through the sense of the general practice of commentary (as in literary criticism), to a more psychological version of ways of thinking (as in critical thinking). The sense of critical being used here, however, derives from a line of cultural and political work ('Critical Theory'), which takes as its basic goal the need for critical analysis of the social, cultural, economic and political ways in which people are inequitably positioned.

Applied Linguistics is commonly defined as 'the study of second and foreign language learning and teaching' and 'the study of language and linguistics in relation to practical problems, such as lexicography, translation, speech pathology, etc' (Richards, Platt & Weber 1985: p. 15). As a broad interdisciplinary area which draws on (at the very least) linguistics, education, psychology, sociology, anthropology, and cultural studies, Applied Linguistics encompasses a wide variety of approaches to a wide variety of questions to do with language and education. It would be wrong, however, to consider CALx as nothing but a welding together of applied linguistic and political concerns. Rather, it is important to observe, first, that CALx often directs its critical focus on the positivistic and apolitical modes of analysis that predominate in a great deal of research on Applied Linguistics itself; thus, another aspect of CALx is its critique of normative applied linguistics. Second, by asking different questions in different ways, CALx does more than just add a political dimension to standard questions, but rather opens up a range of different issues for investigation. CALx, therefore, can be seen as addressing critical questions to do with gender, sexuality, ethnicity, cultural difference, ideology, inequality, identity, and subjectivity in the areas of language use, language learning and language teaching.

R. Wodak and D. Corson (eds), Encyclopedia of Language and Education,
Volume 1: Language Policy and Political Issues in Education, 23–31.
© *1997 Kluwer Academic Publishers. Printed in the Netherlands.*

BACKGROUND KNOWLEDGES

As a relatively new term within a relatively new domain, CALx does not have a long history. Nevertheless, as a pulling together of a number of different strands of critical work, the background to CALx can be conceptualised in terms of related critical approaches. As a developing focus within an interdisciplinary domain, therefore, its antecedents are best understood in terms of the critical domains on which it draws. These include, first, traditional areas of critical thought, such as Marxian structuralist analyses of society, studies in political economy, or theories of imperialism. From such areas have been gleaned macro-political understandings of the contexts in which language use and language education occur. Second, CALx has also started to reflect the changing nature of critical thought in general, thus looking increasingly to the work done in cultural studies, feminism, queer theory, or anti-racism, while drawing on postmodernist, poststructuralist and postcolonialist approaches to knowledge and the world. From these perspectives have emerged a far more complex understanding of the relationships between language, culture, discourse and subjectivity, and a belief that research needs to focus on an analysis of the micropolitics of the everyday. And third, CALx has drawn on more closely related domains of work such as Critical Pedagogy, Critical Literacy, Critical Linguistics, and Critical Discourse Analysis. From these allied foci have come ways of understanding both education and language as always political, as always concerned with issues of power and inequality.

MAJOR CONTRIBUTIONS AND CURRENT WORK

The term 'Critical Applied Linguistics' appears to have emerged in the late 1980s. In 1987, Chris Candlin (1990), in his plenary address to the 8th World Congress of Applied Linguistics (AILA) asked 'What happens when Applied Linguistics goes critical?' Candlin argued for a critical dimension to Applied Linguistics for two main reasons: First, because Applied linguistics had started to lose touch with the problems and issues around language faced by ordinary language users. Applied Linguistics, he argued, was becoming an arcane, sectarian and theory-oriented discipline that was increasingly distanced from the everyday concerns of language use. Second, he suggested, a critical dimension was needed to reveal 'hidden connections ... between language structure and social structure, between meaning-making and the economy of the social situation, but also connections between different branches of the study of language and their relationship to our central objective, the amelioration of individual and group existences through a focus on problems of human communication. A study of the socially-constituted nature of language practice' (1990: pp. 461–2). In this view, then, CALx can be seen as an attempt to make

Applied Linguistics matter, to remake the connections between discourse, language learning, language use and the social and political contexts in which these occur.

The first actual (written) use of the term may have come in an article in the first issue of a new student-run journal, *Issues in Applied Linguistics*, in which I made a strong plea for the development of CALx (Pennycook 1990). (Another aspect of CALx, as Canagarajah 1996, points out, must be not only to deal with critical concerns but also to attempt to write those concerns differently, and thus to question various academic norms and practices; hence my minor incursion here into encyclopedic style and the encyclopedic framing of knowledge by the use of 'I'.) Also taking issue with the sterile theorizing of Applied Linguistics, I argued that Applied Linguistics was problematically 'based on the tenets of modernism, especially its emphasis on universal, foundational, and totalizing theories as well as on teleological, progressivist and positivist understandings of the world' (p. 16). I went on to suggest that a CALx should be developed that draws on other critical work in related areas: critical linguistics, critical sociolinguistics, critical ethnography and critical pedagogy. Calling for major changes in how language was understood and research was conducted, I argued for a version of CALx that had explicit transformative goals, that sought not just to explore questions of language and inequality but sought also to change those conditions. These calls for a critical emphasis in Applied Linguistics above all signified a realization that, first, Applied Linguistics had become an approach to questions of language and education that was given more to sterile theorizing than to critical inquiry. This argument has been developed more recently by Rampton (1995), who suggests that Applied Linguistics may be starting to shift from an 'autonomous' to an 'ideological' model of language. Second, questions to do with language use in professional settings, language learning and language teaching were so inherently bound up with basic political issues that there was an urgent need for approaches to these domains that could draw connections between language and culture, society, ideology and politics.

One important area of work has been in the promotion of Language Rights. Taking issue with the conservative and often strangely apolitical domain of language planning (see Tollefson 1991), writers such as Phillipson and Skutnabb-Kangas (1995) have argued that language planning needs to start with a concept of the inalienable rights of minority groups to mother tongue education and other uses of their first language. This argument, furthermore, has not merely been conducted in the academic domain, but rather has been part of an active movement to have such rights endorsed in international human rights covenants. This work draws on two parallel sets of arguments, on the one hand the work done to promote minority language and bilingual education (Skutnabb-Kangas & Cummins 1988), and on the other the work that has focused critically on the implications of the global dominance of certain languages. In the latter context, Phillipson (1992: see his review) has coined the term 'English linguistic imperialism' to describe the ways in which 'the dominance of English is asserted and maintained by the establishment and continuous reconstitution of structural and cultural inequalities between English and other languages' (p. 47).

While Phillipson's (1992) analysis of linguistic imperialism has shed a great deal of light on the ways in which institutions such as the British Council have unceasingly promoted the global spread of English for economic and political purposes, the structuralist view of imperialism employed by Phillipson has also been criticised for not allowing sufficient space for the diverse ways in which English is used in the postcolonial world. Working from a more poststructuralist standpoint, I have suggested that we need to focus on the 'worldliness' of English in order to understand the many contradictory forces that surround English use globally and in order to develop a critical pedagogy of international English (Pennycook 1994a). Canagarajah (1993) has pursued these questions further by looking at how English and English teaching practices are resisted in Sri Lankan classrooms. Canagarajah also shows here the importance of investigating such questions through grounded critical ethnographies of actual language use.

This focus on the micropolitics of the classroom rather than the macro-politics of social organization has enabled a much more politicised understanding of language classrooms. While a lot of work in Applied Linguistics has tended to focus on classrooms as quasi-laboratories in which language acquisition occurs, CALx has sought to understand the relationships between classrooms and the broader institutional and social contexts in which they operate. This more critical view, therefore, starts with the understanding that language education is an inherently political process, that 'Pedagogical choices about curriculum development, content, materials, classroom processes, and language use, although appearing to be informed by apolitical professional considerations, are, in fact, inherently ideological in nature, with significant implications for learners' socioeconomic roles' (Auerbach 1995: p. 9, see her review in Volume 2). From this point of view, 'the classroom functions as a kind of microcosm of the broader social order' (ibid), that is to say the political relationships in the world outside the classroom are reproduced within the classroom. From this standpoint, Auerbach has advocated what she calls 'participatory action research', by which she means the development of research projects by the classroom participants themselves in order to focus on the issues of particular concern to them.

In addition to such explorations of the socioeconomic roles of language learners, gender has started to emerge (though remarkably slowly given the influence of work on gender and education elsewhere) as a key element in analysing language education. Sunderland's (1994) edited book draws together a number of issues to do with gender and English language teaching, including questions of language and gender, classroom interaction and gender, and women in the ESL workforce. Peirce's (1995) study of a group of non-English speaking immigrant women in Canada sheds light on the social relations that affect their participation in different discourses in English (see Norton's review in Volume 8). Sanguinetti's (1992/3) work with immigrant women ESL students in Australia leads her to argue for the importance of critical educational praxis within 'women-centred' learning environments. Also exploring how gender and ethnicity intersect in complex ways in ESL classes, Schenke (1991) points to the complexities and complicities engaged when students are called on to narrate autobiographical stories. By attending not so much to the stories themselves but rather to the voice through which they are narrated, she suggests, it is possible to 'touch upon the discursive formations of subjectivity and memory, and ... [to] work towards a more historicized and engaged practice of feminist/ESL teaching' (p. 48). Meanwhile, the interrelationships between gender, sexual orientation and language learning are only just starting to be explored (Nelson 1993).

These authors also draw on the area of critical and feminist pedagogy in their work, and indeed the influence of critical pedagogy can be found quite widely in CALx. In his work with immigrant farm workers in rural Colorado, for example, Graman (1988) draws explicitly on the pedagogy of Paulo Freire to develop an ESL 'education for humanization'. Graman argues that 'what is needed in the field of second language pedagogy is an approach that addresses the existential, political, and axiological questions touching the lives of both students and teachers. If the teachers and students want to encourage critically conscious second language learning, they should take action to put Freire's pedagogy into practice in the classroom' (p. 441). Drawing on similar critical pedagogical traditions, Walsh (1991) explores ways in which bilingual Puerto Rican students can develop a *voice,* through 'critical bilingualism – the ability to not just speak two languages, but to be conscious of the sociocultural, political, and ideological contexts in which the languages (and therefore the speakers) are positioned and function, and of the multiple meanings that are fostered in each' (pp. 126–7). The connections to Paulo Freire's work also open up a range of still relatively unexplored associations between CALx and work in critical literacy. Once we start to take seriously the idea that reading the word is also a practice in reading the world, profound questions start to emerge for how we understand reading and writing in both first and second languages.

A flourishing area of work in recent years has come under the broad umbrella of Critical Discourse Analysis (CDA: see the reviews by Norton and by Goldstein in Volume 8). While discourse analysis in Applied

Linguistics had previously concentrated on how stretches of language in use operate and achieve coherence, the more critical stance has sought to draw relationships between texts and broader social concerns. According to Kress (1990), critical discourse analysts share an interest in 'denaturalizing the discursive practices and the texts of a society' in order to 'show the imbrication of linguistic-discursive practices with the wider socio-political structures of power and domination' (p. 5). Wodak (1995) points to three concepts that 'figure indispensably in all CDA: the concept of *power*, the concept of *history*, and the concept of *ideology*'. The task for critical discourse analysts is to connect these concepts to discourse. Her own work (e.g. 1989), which has focused particularly on racism and anti-semitism, may be seen as a form of critical discourse sociolinguistics (Wodak 1995, 1996). van Dijk's (e.g. 1993) 'sociocognitive model' shares similar assumptions, the central concern being with 'the analysis of the complex relationships between dominance and discourse' (p. 252). The CDA approach to discourse, he argues, 'implies a political critique of those responsible for its perversion in the reproduction of dominance and inequality' (p. 253). Fairclough's work (1989, 1995) has probably received most attention. He argues that a social theory of discourse can start to account for the relationships between texts, discursive practices and wider social and cultural structures, and thus can show how the production and reception of texts is ideologically shaped by relations of power. His three-level analysis includes texts, discourse practices and social practices in an effort to explore not only the text itself but also its production and interpretation within a larger social context. This process of critical discourse analysis moves from detailed textual analysis, to explanation and interpretation. A key emerging area for this sort of analysis is on English Language Teaching textbooks, in an effort to display the interests and ideologies underlying their construction and interpretation (see Dendrinos 1992). Work in CDA has also been criticised for its sometimes deterministic account of the relationships between language, society and ideology, and its failure to account for interpretive possibilities. One controversial issue of debate has to do with the implications of poststructuralist approaches to language and discourse, a stance generally eschewed by these critical discourse analysts (see Pennycook 1994b).

This work in CDA has also been closely linked to the area of Critical Language Awareness. With the general move to reintroduce metalinguistic studies of language into school curricula ('language awareness'), writers such as Clark (1992) have argued that this awareness should be a critical awareness. Clark's work has aimed to 'empower students by providing them with the opportunities to discover and critically examine the conventions of the academic discourse community and to enable them to emancipate themselves by developing alternatives to the dominant conventions' (p. 137). This critical focus on teaching English for academic purposes

(EAP) has also been taken up by Benesch (1993), who argues that EAP has failed to question academic norms, presenting them instead as 'positive artifacts of a normative academic culture into which ESL students should be assimilated' (p. 710). The crucial issue here is how a critical approach to ESL writing can be developed which on the one hand provides students with the academic/writing tools to succeed academically, yet, on the other hand, nevertheless deals critically with the norms and expectations of academic writing, attempts to incorporate students' lives and cultures into the classroom, and sets a broader critical agenda that seeks to raise issues of social, economic and political concern.

PROBLEMS AND DIFFICULTIES

There are a number of concerns facing CALx. First, since CALx has to date only been loosely defined, it is important to consider whether it should seek firmer definition or continue in its disparate fashion. Since its strength has been in its resistance to definition and a politics that opposes exclusionary knowledge, it is to be hoped that a tendency to reify CALx in a body of canonical texts or authors will be resisted. A second problem is that there are a number of domains which are central to Applied Linguistics which seem hardly to have been touched by CALx. Language testing and second language acquisition suggest themselves here (though see Bourne 1988; Peirce 1995). It is to be hoped that these powerful domains of positivistic knowledge will be opened up to critical examination and developed from a critical perspective. Third, it is important that CALx develops a flexibility of research and knowledge frameworks. Some of the influential work in allied domains remains stuck within clumsy, neo-Marxian structuralism. If CALx is to progress, it must draw from more diverse ways of framing critical knowledge. Fourth, as with a number of critical domains of work, theory has tended to progress quickly in advance of grounded contexts of research. Critical studies of a diversity of contexts of language education are very much needed. And finally, much more work is needed to bridge the gap between the academic context of CALx theorizing, which currently tends to be White and Western, and the multiple contexts in which such ideas are already being practiced, which in many cases is by those silent Others of Applied Linguistics. As Oda (1995) has pointed out, this continuing imbalance has many effects, including the continued privileging of Native Speakers of English over Nonnative speakers, and the concomitant privileging of certain interests over others. It is important that CALx as discussed here is seen as relevant and is taken up by a far more extensive base of interested people around the world if it is to be able to claim any broad legitimacy.

FUTURE DIRECTIONS

First, as suggested above, there are a number of domains of Applied Linguistics that need opening up from a critical perspective. With the increasing interest being shown in CALx it is to be hoped that critical studies will emerge in second language acquisition, language testing, translation, speech therapy, and so on. Preferably, once these have gone beyond a period of critique, they will also develop critical and transformative perspectives of their own. Second, as modes of knowledge and research change elsewhere, CALx should start to draw on a range of new critical perspectives that are starting to emerge from studies in gender and sexuality, postcolonialism, cultural studies, postmodern ethnography, and so on. If a constant difficulty in Applied Linguistics has been the need to keep abreast of developments in psychology, education and so on, CALx presents an even greater challenge in the need to be aware of such broad and changing domains of work. If CALx can keep itself open to such influences, however, it may be able to bring to bear a range of challenging and diverse questions concerning, for example, sexuality and English language teaching, popular multiculturalism and language learning, language assessment for social equality, postcolonialism and English in the world, or the acquisition of discourses by second language learners.

University of Melbourne
Australia

REFERENCES

Auerbach, E.: 1995, 'The politics of the ESL classroom: Issues of power in pedagogical choices', In J. Tollefson (ed.), *Power and Inequality in Language Education*, Cambridge University Press, New York, 9–33.
Benesch, S.: 1993, 'ESL, ideology, and the politics of pragmatism, *TESOL Quarterly* 27, 705–717.
Bourne, J.: 1988, ' "Natural Acquisition" and a "Masked Pedagogy" ', *Applied Linguistics* 9, 83–99.
Canagarajah, A.S.: 1993, 'Critical ethnography of a Sri Lankan classroom: Ambiguities in student opposition to reproduction through ESOL', *TESOL Quarterly* 27, 601–626.
Canagarajah, A.S.: 1996, 'From critical research practice to critical research reporting', *TESOL Quarterly* 30, 321–331.
Candlin, C.: 1990, 'What happens when applied linguistics goes critical?', in M.A.K. Halliday, J. Gibbons & H. Nicholas (eds.), *Learning, Keeping and Using Language*, John Benjamins, Amsterdam.
Clark, R.: 1992, 'Principles and practice of CLA in the classroom', In N. Fairclough (ed.), *Critical Language Awareness*, Longman, London, 117–140.
Dendrinos, B.: 1992, *The EFL Textbook and Ideology*, N.C. Grivas, Athens.
Fairclough, N.: 1989, *Language and Power*, Longman, London.
Fairclough, N.: 1995, *Critical Discourse Analysis*, Longman, London.
Graman, T.: 1988, 'Education for humanization: Applying Paulo Freire's pedagogy to learning a second language', *Harvard Educational Review* 58, 433–448.

Kress, G.: 1990, 'Critical discourse analysis', in W. Grabe (ed.), *Annual Review of Applied Linguistics* 11, 84–99.

Nelson, C.: 1993, 'Heterosexism in ESL: Examining our attitudes',*TESOL Quarterly* 27, 143–150.

Oda, M.: 1995, 'Native and nonnative EFL teachers: Building the profession together', paper presented at The Twenty-Ninth Annual TESOL Convention, Long Beach, California, March 28–April 1, 1995.

Peirce, B.N.: 1995, 'Social identity, investment, and language learning', *TESOL Quarterly* 29, 9–31.

Pennycook, A.: 1990, 'Towards a critical applied linguistics for the 1990s', *Issues in Applied Linguistics* 1, 8–28.

Pennycook, A.: 1994a, *The Cultural Politics of English as an International Language,* Longman, London.

Pennycook, A.: 1994b, 'Incommensurable discourses?', *Applied Linguistics* 15, 115–138.

Phillipson, R.: 1992, *Linguistic Imperialism,* Oxford University Press, Oxford.

Phillipson, R. & Skutnabb-Kangas T.: 1995, 'Linguistic rights and wrongs', *Applied Linguistics* 16, 483–504.

Rampton, B.: 1995, 'Politics and change in research in applied linguistics', *Applied Linguistics* 16, 233–256.

Richards, J., Platt, J. & Weber, H.: 1985, *Longman Dictionary of Applied Linguistics,* Longman, London.

Sanguinetti, J.: 1992/3, 'Women, "empowerment" and ESL: An exploration of critical and feminist pedagogies', *Prospect* 8 (1&2), 9–37.

Schenke, A.: 1991, 'The "will to reciprocity" and the work of memory: Fictioning speaking out of silence in E.S.L. and feminist pedagogy', *Resources for Feminist Research* 20, 47–55.

Skutnabb-Kangas, T. & Cummins, J.: (eds.) 1988, *Minority Education: From Shame to Struggle,* Multilingual Matters, Clevedon.

Sunderland, J. (ed.): 1994, *Exploring Gender: Questions and Implications for English Language Education,* Prentice Hall, New York.

Tollefson, J.: 1991, *Planning Language, Planning Inequality,* Longman, London.

van Dijk, T.: 1993 'Principles of critical discourse analysis', *Discourse and Society* 4, 249–283.

Walsh, C.: 1991, *Pedagogy and the Struggle for Voice: Issues of Language, Power, and Schooling for Puerto Ricans,* OISE Press, Toronto.

Wodak, R. (ed.): 1989, *Language, Power, and Ideology: Studies in Political Discourse,* John Benjamins, Amsterdam.

Wodak, R.: 1995, 'Critical linguistics and critical discourse analysis', in J. Verschueren, J-O Östman & J. Blommart (eds.), *Handbook of Pragmatics,* Amsterdam: John Benjamins.

Wodak, R.: 1996, *Disorders of Discourse,* London: Longman.

JOHN BAUGH

LINGUISTIC DISCRIMINATION IN EDUCATIONAL CONTEXTS

Many nations provide a combination of public and/or private education for (some?) children who represent their future citizens, and many of these schools have classrooms of different sizes that also vary considerably in their linguistic composition. Some schools, or classes within schools, may be linguistically homogeneous – while other schools, or classes within them, may be dissimilar from a linguistic point of view.

Most schools advocate the dominant literate and linguistic norms of a given society, and some students will not acquire the most influential linguistic standards. The preceding point is especially the case in socially stratified speech communities where access to the best education is only available to a small elite population who have sufficient wealth. Children born into these wealthy families are also likely to be native speakers of the dominant standard language(s).

This review begins with a reintroduction of Ferguson's (1959) "Diglossia", with emphasis on educational implications and prospects for linguistic discrimination in educational contexts. Bernstein's (1971) formulation of elaborated and restricted codes is then surveyed, along with related socially stratified linguistic analyses by Labov (1972a). The social importance of education and literacy is either explicit or implied in these developmental studies, and they lead us to consider contrasts between oral and literate discourse (Chafe 1987; Ong 1991; Tannen 1984), as well as social issues that are tied more directly to forms of linguistic discrimination (Kontra 1995; Kontra & Baugh 1994; Skutnabb-Kangas & Phillipson R. 1994; Smitherman & van Djik 1988; Wodak 1989).

Beyond linguistic observations lie the educational policies that relate to teaching that supports language planning and development in countries throughout the world. Readers of this review may be familiar with the trend to view the United States and Switzerland as representing opposite extremes regarding official policies that either thwart or enhance multilingual coexistence (along with the related social, political, historical, and economic dimensions that reinforce language boundaries); a few examples from different countries are presented for illustrative purposes, and they provide frames of reference for a model of diverse educational opportunities.

A brief survey of recent scholarship from around the world is then presented that focuses on matters of language development and language

R. Wodak and D. Corson (eds), Encyclopedia of Language and Education,
Volume 1: Language Policy and Political Issues in Education, 33–41.
© *1997 Kluwer Academic Publishers. Printed in the Netherlands.*

policies. Implications for future research and possible educational policies are also explored with primary emphasis on equitable education for
students from diverse cultural and linguistic backgrounds. Toward this
end vital recent scholarship regarding the importance of language rights
is introduced (Kontra 1995; Skutnabb-Kangas 1994), as are matters of
language awareness (Fairclough 1992), as well as issues regarding gender,
language, and minority education (Corson 1993).

DEVELOPMENTAL FOUNDATIONS

Ferguson's (1959) "Diglossia" has been chosen as the preliminary work
for this review for two main reasons: Diglossia was originally described
in global terms, and each exemplary speech community included a written
literary tradition. Ferguson described (H)igh and (L)ow dialects of Arabic,
Modern Greek, Swiss-German, and Haitian Creole, as well as the social
circumstances under which each is used. For educational purposes it is
important to recognize that (L) forms are acquired naturally (i.e. through
child language acquisition and development), and (H) forms are introduced
in schools. (H) is not the normal mode of vernacular discourse, and is
therefore not acquired through natural first-language acquisition processes;
rather, (H) is learned through formal education.

Bernstein's (1971) introduction of elaborated codes (EC) and restricted
codes (RC) of British English drew international attention to class differences in socially stratified dialects of a language. Inspired greatly
by the Whorfian hypothesis, Bernstein's observations explored class differences in relationship to the relative magnitude of different levels of
cognitive abstraction that correspond, in turn, to linguistic codes that are
conditioned by social class. These issues took on racial connotations in
the United States (Labov 1972a), as illustrated in the educational controversy over Ebonics – which is overtly linked to the racial classification
of African Americans. Labov, perhaps more than any other sociolinguist,
demonstrated important linguistic characteristics of vernacular African
American English (AAE) at the same time that he developed procedures to
quantify linguistic variation across dialects of the same language, that is,
without any a priori cognitive assumptions regarding the speech produced
by speakers from different social, regional, sexual, or racial backgrounds.

Racial differences in Europe vary from one nation to another, that is,
as more nonwhite residents migrate to various European countries. This
linguistic and educational picture has been made more complicated in
western Europe due to political circumstances that triggered large influxes
of eastern Europeans to the west. Additional tensions have grown as a result
of an unfortunate rise of antisemitic rhetoric from conservative politicians
and journalists in major urban centers throughout Europe (Wodak 1989;
Mitten & Wodak 1994).

Before turning to the incontrovertible role of political considerations that influence linguistic discrimination in schools and the societies that contain those schools, we should first consider important differences between orality and literacy (i.e. talking vs. reading and writing). Chomsky (1957, 1965) affirmed that the miracle of child language acquisition is uniquely human, and Ong (1991) stressed the conceptual difference between oral language and literate language. Chafe (1987) and Tannen (1984) provide excellent illustrations of these distinctions as well. For the present purpose, however, it is perhaps most important to note that all normal children acquire their first language orally without the aid of formal instruction, and it is only through a combination of luck, opportunity, and personal ability that individuals are taught to read and write.

While it may be true that some exceptional people have taught themselves to read and write without any external help whatsoever, these rare individuals do not compare with the vast majority of students who are instructed how to read. Writing is a wonderful symbolic representation of speech, but the determination of which mode of writing comes to represent the "standard" is always determined by political circumstances that have absolutely nothing to do with linguistic content. As such, those who control political power within a given society have typically inherited linguistic norms that also reflect that stature (see the review by Corson: 99–109).

As we shall see momentarily, an important caveat must be added to this observation, because the influential dialects in post-colonial countries vary considerably from the linguistic standards of former colonizers. British English differs from American, Australian, and Indian English; so too does Parisian French differ from Canadian or Haitian French; Brazilian Portuguese differs from that spoken in Lisbon; and Peninsular Spanish is distinctive when compared to Spanish in Cuba, Mexico, Peru, and Puerto Rico. Other examples would demonstrate that linguistic discrimination and its educational consequences must ultimately be viewed in local ethnographic terms.

DIVERSE EDUCATIONAL OPPORTUNITIES

Four dimensions having a direct impact on educational opportunities throughout the world are briefly described to place education within a global comparative framework. The first dimension is linked to funding, particularly with reference to the source of that educational funding: in short, are the schools in question operated by public funds (i.e. typically obtained through some form of taxes) or private funding (i.e. acquired through some form of tuition)? The second dimension is linked more directly to educational policies; some nations have centralized educational policies while others – like the US – have decentralized educational policies. So, in addition to public and private funding lie the dictates of (de?)centralized educational policies. Another dimension could easily consider former colonial status; education in lands that were never colonized can differ considerably from education in nations that were once colonized, although economic standing plays a formidable role in this regard. Wealthy former colonies have considerable economic options in comparison to impoverished former colonies with minimum economic resources.

In the case of former colonies it is equally important to determine the extent to which liberated citizens either maintain or reject the languages of former colonizers. Often those who retain and maintain the colonial language are members of the elite classes, that is, within the former colony; less fortunate residents may not reap the benefits of a superior education or the corresponding linguistic exposure it could afford. These matters are not free from political influence. On the contrary, schools and educational policies have been used to support and deter language development and literacy through forms of language planning and linguistic engineering that are either explicit or benign in their effort to lend political and educational legitimacy to those who have the most political and economic influence within a sovereign nation. Many other authors confirm these facts elsewhere in other reviews throughout these volumes.

SOME RELEVANT EXAMPLES

Ogbu (1992) points to one of the more interesting cases regarding linguistic and cultural discrimination in two different countries; namely, that of Korean students who live in the US and Japan. Like many other Asian immigrants to America, Koreans have often been included in the "model minority" category that has been made popular in efforts to attack affirmative action programs that (in the US context) have been developed to help women and minorities gain greater access to improved educational and professional opportunities. In Japan many Korean students have not fared as well, and Ogbu (1978) attributes this diversity – at least in part – to his research on "caste-like minorities" in various communities throughout the world. His work will be of interest to educators and others who seek to improve education for students in nations where social stratification is marked by linguistic sedimentation.

Bernstein's studies and those of Labov (1972a, 1972b, 1994), tend to concentrate on variation among dialects within a single language. Trudgill (1986), Giles and Powesland (1975), and Chambers (1995) have added considerably to our understanding of how dialects vary, and how speakers come to acquire the particular types of dialects and styles of speaking that they use.

Krashen (1991), Cummins (1978), Valdés (1996), van Dam van Isselt (1993), Hakuta (1981), and Koschat and Wagner (1994) focus more specifically on bilingual concerns; that is, the education of students who know – or need to know – more than their primary (i.e. first) language; that is, in order to become successful students in the schools which they attend (i.e., schools that utilize languages with which they are unfamiliar).

Thus, we draw contrasts here between students who are privileged and learn the standard dialect (SD) of the dominant language(s) natively, from those who encounter linguistic discrimination based on their use of non-standard dialects (NSD) of the dominant languages, or students for whom the dominant language(s) are not native (DLNN). Students from NSD and DLNN linguistic backgrounds are at clear disadvantages when compared to children who are born into well educated families where the dominant dialect is native (i.e., SD).

These linguistic groupings, as well as the stages of linguistic transition that may gradually lead to the eventual acquisition of the dominant linguistic norms are illustrated by bold print below, including (SD) standard speakers, (NSD), nonstandard speakers, and (DLNN) those who are not native speakers of the dominant language:

SD → **Those who speak the standard dialect(s) of dominant Lg.(s)**
NSD → **Those who speak nonstandard dialects of dominant Lg.(s)**
DLNN → **Those for whom the dominant languages are not native**

These illustrated differences have obvious limitations, however, and a brief global comparison of Black English illustrates this point. Fordham and Ogbu (1985) have observed that many Black students in the US actively resist the acquisition of the dominant (i.e., standard) dialect(s) because of racial pride and an overt desire to avoid any possible accusation of "acting white". Edwards (1986) and Sutcliff (1982) have considered the linguistic and educational plight of Blacks who live in England, and a very different sociolinguistic picture emerges there. Many Blacks in England do master the educated linguistic norms of the upper classes, but they are less likely to experience upward social mobility in ways that many wealthy African Americans have. This may be due, in part, to a host of cultural and social differences. This is especially evident when we look at Black English in South Africa, where the indigenous languages of the majority population were suppressed for so long under racialized apartheid. At this point in history, however, South Africa is actively promoting new educational and language policies that are designed to help include those Blacks who were previously excluded prior to the abolition of comprehensive racist social policies.

By coincidence, the original definition of "Ebonics", which was first coined by an African American social psychologist is based precisely on the kind of international comparison of "Black English" that is described above. Despite global coverage of the Ebonics controversy in the United States early in 1997, few journalists recognized that its use was initially concerned with the international linguistic consequences of the African

slave trade. Readers are therefore advised to survey the international literature on linguistic discrimination in educational contexts with careful
attention to ethnographic relativity; that is, linguistic discrimination and
educational opportunities – or lack of them – are ultimately local matters,
and the vast majority of scholars who work on these issues look very
closely at a given society at a clearly delineated point in history. Kress's
(1989) studies under the title of *Language as Ideology* are especially relevant in this regard, because they demonstrate that linguistic behavior
is often closely aligned with political ideology, and dogmatic linguistic
enlightenment seldom advances greater social harmony or the important
educational benefits that greater linguistic tolerance and awareness might
otherwise accrue.

CRITICAL LANGUAGE AWARENESS

The procedures that Labov developed in association with the formulation
of quantitative sociolinguistics differs considerably from Critical Language Awareness (CLA) theorists because their research intentionally blurs
conceptual lines between individuals who might otherwise be evaluated
apart from the social group (or groups) to which s/he or they belong. Fairclough (1992) provides a comprehensive review of this orientation, and
Lantolf (1996) challenges some idealistic linguistic assumptions, particularly regarding the teaching of official standard languages.

Educators would benefit considerably from familiarity with these topics,
because they offer insights into more effective ways to approach students
from diverse linguistic backgrounds.

GENDER DIFFERENCES AND LANGUAGE MINORITY EDUCATION

Corson (1993) complements the preceding CLA studies through discussion
and analyses of the educational abyss that confronts many females and
minorities who lack the combination of influence or political clout to
demand educational improvements that will be effective for students who
previously have been under served. Related discussion by Corson and
Lemay (1996) focuses squarely on the justice of language policies in
linguistically diverse communities, and has a direct bearing upon the education of students that similarly live in communities where multifarious
linguistic norms thrive simultaneously. Often social tensions are reinforced
by linguistic differences, along sexual or racial lines, and educators must
be extremely mindful of this fact if they are to break the cycles of social
preference that have far too often perpetuated educational inequities.

SCHOLARLY CONTRIBUTIONS

Few scholars have concentrated explicitly on matters of linguistic discrimination in schools, but many of the following citations are more-or-less related to various forms of linguistic discrimination. For example, *Women and Language in Transition* (Penfield 1987), and *Feminist Language Planning and Language Change* (1991) both direct attention to the special plight of women and their unique linguistic status. Walters (1989) has likewise shown that Arabic women in Tunisia do not have the same linguistic and educational opportunities as do men from similar backgrounds, and much of this discrimination is embedded in long-standing cultural and religious practices. These texts reveal that women may be linguistically victimized along with other forms of sexual discrimination.

Many researchers have concentrated on the linguistic climate within particular countries or regions, and O'Coileain (1988), Kirkwood (1989), Bortoni (1985), Conseil de la langue francaise (1990), Swanepoel and Pieterse (1993), are just a few examples of important scholarship that exists with specific national foci. Within some nations others have looked to contrasts between urban and rural speakers such as Blom and Gumperz (1972), and Robinson (1996); each of these works are illustrative of linguistic studies that acknowledge linguistic discrimination against members of rural speech communities. Wolfram and Christian (1976) and Robinson (1996) concentrate specifically on matters of linguistic discrimination, indeed, *Discrimination through Language Planning in Africa* (1995) attempts to place these issues within the political contexts of social and economic change across the African continent.

IMPLICATIONS FOR FUTURE RESEARCH AND EDUCATIONAL POLICIES

One of the fundamental tenets of linguistic science is the recognition that all languages and dialects of the world are considered to be equal, but it is equally obvious that social evolution has resulted in forms of linguistic Darwinism that have come to favor some languages over others, and some dialects within those surviving languages are also favored over subordinate dialects (i.e. NSD). Because linguistic attitudes occur within the ecological context of changing political circumstances, future research may wish to explore linguistic discrimination comparatively and, perhaps, longitudinally.

Under favorable circumstances these analyses could lead to enlightened social and educational policies that serve to diminish forms of linguistic discrimination, but studies of violations of linguistic human rights have alerted concerned scholars and citizens that hostile discrimination against minority groups is not merely confined to language. Fishman (1966) has observed the competing influences between the linguistic foundations of social strife and language loyalty for many years, and future research may serve to identify instances of linguistic discrimination, and through that effort, eventually come to support social and linguistic liberation. This review has therefore been written with an acknowledged bias, one that advocates prospects to enhance greater equality among all people.

Stanford University
USA

REFERENCES

Bernstein, B.: 1971, *Class, Codes and Control*, Routledge and K. Paul, London.
Blom, J.P. & Gumperz, J.: 1972, 'Social meaning in linguistic structures: Code-switching in Norway', in D. Hymes & J. Gumperz (eds.), *Directions in Sociolinguistics: the Ethnography of Communication*, Holt, Rinehart & Winston, New York.
Bortoni, S.: 1985, *The Urbanization of Rural Dialect Speakers*, Cambridge University Press, Cambridge.
Chafe, W.: 1987, *Properties of Spoken and Written Language*, Center for the Study of Writing, Berkeley, CA.
Chambers, J.K.: 1995, *Sociolinguistic Theory*, Blackwell, London.
Chomsky, N.: 1957, *Syntactic Structures*, Mouton, The Hague.
Chomsky, N.: 1965, *Aspects of the Theory of Syntax*, M.I.T. Press, Cambridge, MA.
Clayton, Vic.: 1991, *Feminist Language Planning and Language Change*, AILA Commission on Language and Gender, Australia.
Conseil de la langue francaise: 1990, *Dix etudes portant sur l'amenagement de la langue au Quebec*, Conseil de la langue francaise, Quebec Province.
Corson, D.: 1993, *Language, minority education and gender: Linking social justice and power*, Multilingual Matters, Clevedon, Avon UK.
Corson, D. & Lemay, S.: 1996, *Social Justice and language Policy in Education: The Canadian Research*, OISE Press, Toronto.
Cummins, J.: 1978, 'Educational implications of mother tongue maintenance in minority-language groups', *Canadian Modern Language Review* 34, 395–416.
Edwards, V.: 1986, *Language in a Black Community*, Multilingual Matters, Ltd., Clevedon.
Fairclough, N. (ed.): 1992, *Critical Language Awareness*, London: Longman.
Ferguson, C.: 1959, 'Diglossia', *Word* 15, 325–40.
Fishman, J.: 1966, *Language Loyalty in the United States*, Mouton, The Hague.
Fordham, S. & Ogbu, J.: 1985, 'The burden of acting white', *Urban Review* 18, 176–206.
Giles, H. & Powesland, P.G.: 1975, *Speech Style and Social Evaluation*, Academic Press, New York.
Hakuta, K.: 1981. *Mirror of Language*, Basic Books, New York.
Kirkwood, M. (ed.): 1989, *Language Planning in the Soviet Union*, Macmillan, University of London.
Krashen, S.D.: 1991, *Bilingual Education*, National Clearinghouse for Bilingual Education, Washington, D.C.
Kontra, M.: 1995, 'No CARE-packages, please – We're Hungarians', in J. Harlig and D. Pléh (eds.), *When East Met West: Sociolinguistics in the Former Socialist Block*, Berlin: Mouton De Gruyter.
Kontra, M. & Baugh, J.: 1994, 'Should they give up their language and culture voluntarily?', in Z. Fejos (ed.), *Regio: A review of Minority and Ethnic Studies*, Teleki Foundation, Veszpr'm, Hungary.

Koschat, F. & Wagner G.: 1994, *Bilinguale Schulen: lernen in zwei Sprachen*, Bundersministerium fur Unterricht und Kunst, Wien.
Kress, G.R.: 1989, *Linguistic Processes in Sociocultural Practices*, Oxford University Press, Oxford.
Labov, W.: 1972a, *Language in the Inner-City: Studies of the Black English Vernacular*, University of Pennsylvania Press, Philadelphia.
Labov, W.: 1972b, *Sociolinguistic Patterns*, University of Pennsylvania Press, Philadelphia.
Labov, W.: 1994, *Principles of Linguistic Change*, Blackwell, Oxford.
Lantolf, J.: 1996, 'SLA theory building: letting all the flowers bloom!', *Language Learning* 46, 4.
O'Coileain, A.: 1988, *The Irish Language in a Changing Society: Shaping the Future*, Bord na Gaeilge, Dublin.
Ogbu, J.: 1978, *Minority Education and Caste*, Academic Press, New York.
Ogbu, J.: 1992, 'Understanding cultural diversity and learning', *Educational Researcher* 21: 8, 5–15.
Ong, W.: 1991, *Orality and Literacy*, Routledge, London.
Penfield, J. (ed.): 1987, *Women and Language in Transition*, State University of New York Press, Albany.
Putz, M. (ed.): 1995, *Discrimination Through Language in Africa? Perspectives on the Namibian Experience*, Mouton de Gruyter, Berlin.
Robinson, C.: 1996, *Language Use in Rural Development*, Mouton de Gruyter, Berlin.
Skutnabb-Kangas, T.& Phillipson, R. (eds.): 1994, *Linguistic Human Rights: Overcoming Linguistic Discrimination*, M. de Gruyter, Berlin.
Smitherman, G. & van Dijk, T. (eds.): 1988, *Discourse and Discrimination*, Wayne State University Press, Detroit.
Sutcliff, D.E. (ed.): 1982. *British Black English*, Blackwell, Oxford.
Swanepoel, P.H. & Pieterse, H.J.: (eds): 1993, *Perspektiewe op taalbeplanning vir Suid-Afrika*, Universiteit van Suid-Afrika, Pretoria.
Tannen, D.(ed.): 1984, *Coherence in Spoken and Written Discourse*, Ablex, Norwood, N.J.
Trudgill, P.: 1986, *Dialects in Contact*, Blackwell, London.
Valdés, G.: 1996, *Con Respecto*, Teachers College Press, New York.
Van Dam van Isselt, H.R.: 1993, *Her Name is – Uh Dat Week Ik Niet*, Universiteit van Amsterdam, Amsterdam.
Walters, K.: 1987, Linguistic variation and change in Kobra, a small Tunisian Town. Unpublished Ph.D. Dissertation. Austin: University of Texas.
Wodak, R. (ed.): 1989, *Language, Power, and Ideology: Studies in Political Discourse*, J. Benjamins, Philadelphia.
Wodak, R. & Mitten, R.: 1994, 'On the discourse of racism and prejudice', *Folia Linguistica* XXVII/3–4, 191–215.
Wolfram, W. & Christian, D.: 1976, *Appalachian Speech*, Center for Applied Linguistics, Washington, D.C.

DUNCAN WAITE

POWER AND TEACHER-ADMINISTRATOR DISCOURSE

This review concerns the discourse between teachers and administrators. 'Teacher' and 'administrator' are used here in an all-inclusive sense – teachers being taken to include practicing teachers and student teachers; and administrators as including supervisors and administrators, unless specifically noted otherwise.

Discourse here means the spoken word and texts of various sorts. Additionally, in the various senses of discourse used by Foucault and Bourdieu, discourse involves systems of thought and the discursive norms operant within and between discursive communities.

Power is here used in its broadest significance, where 'social power is usually indirect and operates through the "minds" of people' (van Dijk 1989: p. 20). Power is enacted by groups or individuals in social interactions of various sorts, presupposes an ideological framework, conscious or unconscious, and occasions its own resistance.

EARLY DEVELOPMENTS

Early work in the field of teacher-administrator discourse was done by Blumberg (1970, 1980), Blumberg and Amidon (1965), Kyte (1971) and Weller (1971). As is to be supposed, the work in this field has demonstrated continued methodological sophistication. Blumberg adapted Flanders' (1965) classroom observation instrument of 'interaction analysis' to the study of teacher-supervisor verbal interaction. Blumberg sampled tape recordings of actual supervision conferences at three second intervals. He coded supervisor verbal behavior in ten separate categories and teacher verbal behavior in four separate categories. He also coded silence or confusion. Blumberg found that supervisors talked 45 percent of the time and in conference contexts did 'little to encourage teachers to discuss their feelings' (1970: p. 2), 'rarely made statements which would help build a healthy climate between themselves and teachers', and did 'not seem to communicate the desire to understand the teachers with whom they work, nor [did] . . . supervisors strive to develop a collaborative, problem-centered relationship with teachers' (p. 3).

Weller (1971) likewise employed a coding system, his M.O.S.A.I.C.S. system (Multidimensional Observational System for the Analysis of Interaction in Clinical Supervision). As a result of his study into clinical supervision, Weller concluded that 'supervisors speak almost twice as much as

R. Wodak and D. Corson (eds), Encyclopedia of Language and Education,
Volume 1: Language Policy and Political Issues in Education, 43–52.
© 1997 Kluwer Academic Publishers. Printed in the Netherlands.

individual teachers' (p. 137) in formal conferences, and that 'the supervisor commonly assumes an initiatory role in the conference. . . . Teachers
tend to assume a reflexive role, asking few questions but answering many'
(p. 137), a finding later corroborated by Waite (1995a). Weller stated
that 'in general, clinical supervision in the . . . Harvard-Newton Summer
School is definitely not a one-sided affair in which the supervisor transmits
information and advice to novice teachers' (p. 139). Weller recognized the
limitations of the coding system he developed and encouraged other types
of research into supervisory processes: While the M.O.S.A.I.C.S. protocol, argued Weller, 'permits the study of interrelationships between and
among these dimensions of meaning, thus increasing the potentialities
of the instrument for investigating the "fine structure" of these complex
interactions. This focus, however, essentially neglects the affective or
social-emotional aspects of supervision which might in the last analysis be
the most crucial factors' (p. 141). These shortcomings, he suggested, might
only be remedied through the conduct of 'participant observer techniques'
(p. 142), because, as he recognized, his 'instrument also focuses on formal
supervision as carried out in structured conference settings. Much actual
supervision is carried out informally, and the supervisor's major impact on
the supervisee may frequently occur in such unstructured settings' (p. 142).

Kyte (1971) reported upon a teacher-supervisor conference using a
conference transcript. Kyte's interpretations of conference occurrences
accompanied the transcript. This case study of Kyte's was one of the
earliest, if not the earliest, use of naturally occurring talk in the analysis
of teacher-administrator discourse. However, every study conducted up to
this time was firmly entrenched in the process-product research paradigm,
intended to demonstrate the so-called effectiveness of the phenomena under
study.

MAJOR CONTRIBUTIONS

The 1980s saw a further refinement of the research methods and analyses used to examine teacher-administrator discourse. Some exemplary
work of this period was that done by Gronn (1983, 1984), who examined
how school administration is accomplished through discourse. His analysis of naturally occurring discourse dealt with the dynamics of power in
dyadic and group interactions, such as a school council setting, employed
a sophisticated transcription protocol, and included discussion of the contexts within which the discourse occurred.

Other notable work of this decade was done by Hargreaves (1984) and
Kilbourn (1982). As a result of a case study of supervision, Kilbourn
wrote that one of the primary goals of supervision is autonomy, to work
'toward developing [the teacher's] abilities to function autonomously so
that teachers can be "self-supervising"' (p. 3).

Citing the dearth of interactional studies until that time, a point also made by Gronn (1984), Hargreaves (1984) stated how contrastive rhetoric in school settings, especially when used by heads and deputies, draws boundaries between the acceptable and the unacceptable. 'The success of contrastive rhetoric', wrote Hargreaves, 'in screening out undesirable alternatives is therefore contingent on the kind of knowledge, assumptions and interpretive schemes that teachers bring to the interaction, and on the capacity of its users – the head and deputy – to trade on these components of teachers' culture' (p. 223). Contrastive rhetoric serves as a centripetal force, consolidating the boundaries of existing practice. Citing extremist talk as counter-hegemonic, Hargreaves noted how it acts as a centrifugal force, serving to extend the boundaries of existing practice. However, 'differential access to the cultural resources underlying decision-making ... means that the head and deputy hold not only *de jure* institutional power, but also tend to possess *de facto* interactional power' (p. 225) in face-to-face meetings with teachers. These observations corroborated those of Gronn.

At about the same time, and though not the central focus of their work, others contributed to the overall understanding of teacher-administrator discourse (Hunter 1980; Ross 1980). Hunter described decision making in schools, particularly from teachers' perspectives, as 'autocratic, though presented as nominally democratic', where despite the many meetings, 'staff did not feel that they could influence events' (p. 223). Hunter contrasted the relative openness of the staff within the 'semi-privacy of small groups in the staff room' (p. 223) with the 'apathy, timidity and caution' (p. 223) they demonstrated in open meetings. Meetings, and staff participation in them, according to Hunter, simulated a participative democracy, in order 'to foster the involvement and commitment of the participants, and to legitimate the resultant decisions' (p. 226). Hunter concluded that 'these more indirect forms of control used by the Head ... [were a] more effective means of control in that they reduce resistance through calls to collective responsibility' (p. 226). These processes were found to be still operant in another study conducted 15 years later (Wodak 1995).

Within the classroom, and as concerns classroom occurrences, Ross (1980: p. 220) stressed 'the invulnerability of teachers to administrative control', claiming that 'decisions at the classroom level may be informed by decisions at other levels, but only in particular sets of circumstances'. Further, he asserted that 'modern principals ... ensure that they are not placed in the position of issuing an unambiguous directive in the face of visible teacher resistance. Principals are most likely to couch their instructions in the language of request if their instructions impinge upon the self-contained classroom of the individual teacher' (p. 221). Ross found that a principal can influence teacher norms 'to the extent that he functions as a definer of what is best for children' (p. 226).

In a study of the control structure of two schools, Packard (1976) differentiated five different decision-making processes in which teachers and administrators took part: discretionary decisions of teachers; collegial decisions between teachers; principal-directed decisions; conjoint decisions; and bounded decisions, in which the principal collaborated with an individual teacher about an instructional matter. Packard found that principals were *not* involved in most decisions affecting teachers and their instruction: In conventional schools, these decisions were made most often by other administrators in the district; in the team school, colleagues were more likely to influence decisions.

Zeichner and Liston (1985) and Zeichner, Liston, Mahlios and Gomez (1988) explored the quality and variety of discourse in supervisory conferences. Though firmly lodged in the process-product line of research – eschewing transcriptions of supervisory conferences in favor of coding 'thought units' to judge the congruence between supervisory discourse and the goals of a teacher education program – the analyses of Zeichner et al. led them to assert that attention ought to be given 'the conceptual levels of student teachers if there is a concern with promoting more complex modes of reasoning during conferences' (1985: p. 170). Zeichner and Liston found that 'the student teacher may exert a stronger influence than the supervisor in determining the level of supervisory discourse' (p. 170).

Of the four types of discourse examined by these authors – factual, prudential, justificatory, critical – factual discourse predominated in supervisory conferences. This, despite the critical, inquiry focus of one of the programs studied, caused some consternation for the researchers (Zeichner et al. 1988: pp. 357–8), who found that teacher education program goals had little or no effect on the resultant supervisory discourse. Reasons thought to account for this lack of effect were that 'student teachers may have so little authority' and that 'the university supervisor lacked any formal authority to influence the classrooms in which students were placed' (p. 358).

The studies cited above (Packard 1976; Hunter 1980; Ross 1980; Gronn 1983, 1984; Hargreaves 1984; Zeichner & Liston 1985; Zeichner, Liston, Mahlios & Gomez 1988) are difficult to reconcile, especially as regards the power dynamic in teacher-administrator discourse. One possible line of reasoning would suggest that administrators can and do exercise power over teachers in face-to-face interactions, in dyads and in groups. They do so through recourse to interactional processes – that is, activating norms of power and privilege in setting agendas and distributing turns at talk, for instance. Administrators also can and do influence school culture and their operant norms.

It must be kept in mind that teachers are not powerless, even in face-to-face interactions with administrators, and, as Hargreaves (1984), Ross (1980) and others have since demonstrated, teachers can activate 'counter-discourses' (Waite 1995a: p. 84) with which to counter or resist administrative imposition. Also, administrators, especially principals or heads, are not omnipotent (Packard 1976). They most certainly contribute to the power dynamics between teachers and administrators, but in turn are subject to certain power dynamics themselves.

WORK IN PROGRESS

Present research on power and teacher-administrator discourse reflects a continuing methodological and theoretical sophistication. For instance, notions of power employed by researchers have become much more complex and dynamic, as have issues of gender.

Some researchers have applied Habermas' concepts of distorted communication and ideal speech situations to the study of teacher-administrator discourse. Corson (1995b) analyzed a school's Board of Trustee's meeting, comparing it with Habermas' ideal speech situation. He found how 'easily distorted communication can arise in formal administrative discourse when the interests of those with some stake in the matter under discussion are not represented among the participants in the discourse' (p. 99).

Retallick (1990) employed Habermasian concepts in a project designed to overcome the technocratic rationality of supervision and hierarchical supervisory relationships between teachers and school executives (supervisors); trying to replace those relationships with more symmetrical structures of communication. He reported only limited success. The constraints which prevented a more successful attainment of the ideals envisioned for the project included: 'an inadequacy in the reconstructive method [used in the project] which, in focussing specifically on the structure of communication in hierarchical relationships, failed to intervene sufficiently into other critical areas of life in schools' (p. 21); and, the biographies of the participants and 'the social context of their work [which] have them firmly implanted in technical and bureaucratic modes of thinking and acting' (p. 24).

Understanding the mutual influences of gender, power, and language has benefitted from more dynamic views of each in regards to the other. In 1992, Corson provided a critical review of the work done up to that time on language, gender, education, social justice and power. As a result of his review, Corson developed recommendations by which schools could work to eliminate 'undesirable discursive practices' (p. 248). Several of these recommendations promise to positively affect teacher-administrator discourse:

- reducing the use of impersonal or bureaucratic language in official communications;
- softening formal messages with more humour, less pomposity, less condescension, and a use of vivid metaphors linked to the real world of the organisation;
- sending messages to staff and students which personalise the recipient;
  . . .
- introducing a language of institutional symbols and mottos that express collaboration rather than competition, co-operation for shared rewards rather than winning for personal glory . . . (p. 248)

Corson advocated a type of administration where 'effective solutions to the problems of organisations are found in discovering the intentions and interests of participants and . . . trying to either change some of those intentions or work in harmony with them' (p. 248). His ideal view of administrative power was of one that manifests 'an interactive and collaborative use of power [which] overshadows the exercise of power through authority and hierarchy' (p. 248).

Wodak's (1995) research into female leadership styles produced some striking results. Her study focused solely on female school leaders and, thus, she was able to avoid the tender trap of comparing the leadership styles of males with those of females. Wodak found that 'purely organizational issues predominated in all settings in all schools' (p. 38) studied and that these women leaders were 'convinced that a completely open atmosphere existed in their school' (p. 46). Still, Wodak's conclusion was that the women leaders she studied 'applied controlling and authoritarian strategies to achieve their aims' (p. 54).

Waite (1995b) examined discourse and power, specifically a teacher's counter-discourse, in laying open a teacher's resistance strategies in face-to-face interaction with her supervisor. The teacher resistance strategies he found included the teacher's breaking the frame of the conference, activation of a counter-discourse – including invocation of shared teacher norms which countered supervisory/administrative norms and desires, and use or manipulation of the interactional strategies and rights pertaining to the interactants, the teacher in this case. This study exploded the myth of a supervisor's power in face-to-face interaction.

PROBLEMS AND DIFFICULTIES

There seem to be at least five major problems which confront and/or are operant in the study of teacher-administrator discourse:
- the persistence of democratic rhetoric about schools and school processes, especially teacher-administrator discourse, when the evidence fails to support such claims;

- the sometime lack of systematic, rigorous analysis, including explicit discussion of evidentiary claims, with presentation of data;
- problems of essentialism;
- the continuing, perhaps intractable problem of reconciling macro and micro levels of analysis; and
- the limited impact of the extant research upon practice.

Some of the authors cited in this review refer to a simulation of democratic processes in schools, school meetings or teacher-administrator discourse, a process of self- or group-delusion. Is a democratic ideal unrealizable? What might be the dynamic necessary to edge teacher-administrator discourse toward this ideal? (This is, of course, related to the last problem mentioned above, that of the limited impact of research upon practice.)

Given the myriad of approaches possible for the study of teacher-administrator discourse, it is no wonder that some studies would be more rigorous, more methodologically satisfying than others. More rigorous, complete studies inspire more confidence in their findings and results. From the present vantage point, earlier studies are suspect, if not entirely dismissible, due to their seeming lack of methodological rigor, unsophisticated analysis, or because process-product research has fallen into disrepute (e.g., Blumberg 1970; Packard 1976). Likewise, the growing acceptance and practice of qualitative research methods have caused researchers and readers alike to expect more close-grained analysis in a study, more depth of study and analysis, a more complete contextualization of a study in order to allow for generalization by the reader, and more access or recourse to the author's raw data. The research community, both its writers and readers, today is more sophisticated and more cynical. That is to say, unlike in previous times and with previous conventional research, where by simply following the established research protocols the author could be assured of gaining the readers' confidence, under today's evidentiary standards readers are more likely to question an author's analysis and interpretation. Studies which seem not to meet the criteria above are still being conducted and reported, even though they offer little by way of understanding.

Problems of essentialism persist in the study of teacher-administrator discourse. Perhaps the most likely place such a problem might appear is in the study of gender and gender differences in leadership styles or leaders' discourse styles. Such studies fall prey to essentialistic thinking when, in effect, they idealize one group's style and trivialize or demonize another's, often on flimsy empirical grounds. (It is possible that the second and third problems in the study of teacher-administrator discourse can often operate simultaneously.) That these problems persist make all the more welcome studies which do not exhibit such essentialism (e.g., Wodak 1995).

Problems having to do with the reconciliation of micro and macro levels of analysis are unlikely to disappear. As a general rule, micro level analysis permits more close-grained analysis; whereas macro level analysis, by its very nature, aims for a more global analysis and seeks application to larger populations. Recent work in the field of sociology, especially, has attempted to solve this particular dilemma (e.g., Hall 1991), though not specifically in the area of discourse. Corson (1995a) advocated critical ethnography and critical discourse analysis as candidates to ameliorate problems posed by macro and micro distinctions. It is a commonsense understanding that extra-contextual factors have an impact upon proximate environments, yet there has been little or no research illuminating the effects of these relations upon the power dynamics of teacher-administrator discourse.

The problem of application remains. Though, undoubtedly, professors of educational administration employ the research literature in their teaching, what of practitioners?

FUTURE DIRECTIONS

That researchers are aware of some of the problems discussed is promising; just as it can be assumed that there will continue to be further refinement and sophistication of research theory and method. Essentialism has come under attack by feminist theorists of educational administration (Hammett 1996). Other promising theories are just beginning to be applied to the study of teacher-administrator discourse. Some promising lines of inquiry involve the application of Bakhtinian concepts (Fairclough 1995; Waite 1995a) and those of Basil Bernstein (Tyler 1995) to the study of teacher-administrator discourse. Though each of these lines of inquiry have begun to be developed theoretically, they have yet to be pursued empirically.

Another promising avenue of inquiry would be the examination of teacher-administrator discourse from a cross-cultural perspective along the lines suggested by Scollon and Scollon (1995). These authors provide insights into how power operates in sociocultural contexts. If, as has been suggested, teachers and administrators operate from within two distinct cultures, then teacher-administrator discourse could be examined as intercultural communication. This line of inquiry promises to bridge macro and micro levels of analysis and to provide an initial glimpse into the discursive norms of and between each 'culture' that contribute to forms of language, thought, power, and control.

The University of Georgia
USA

REFERENCES

Blumberg, A.: 1970, 'Supervisor-teacher relationships: A look at the supervisory conference', *Administrator's Notebook* 19, 1–4.

Blumberg, A.: 1980, *Supervisors & Teachers: A Private Cold War* (second edition), Mc-Cutchan Publishing, Berkeley.

Blumberg, A. & Amidon, E.: 1965, 'Teacher perceptions of supervisor-teacher interactions', *Administrator's Notebook* 14, 1–4.

Corson, D.: 1992, 'Language, gender and education: A critical review linking social justice and power', *Gender and Education* 4, 229–254.

Corson, D.: 1995a, 'Critical perspectives in leadership and educational administration', paper presented to the American Educational Research Association annual meeting, New York.

Corson, D.: 1995b, 'Ideology and distortion in the administration of outgroup interests', in D. Corson (ed.), *Discourse and Power in Educational Organizations*, Hampton Press, Cresskill NJ, 87–110.

Fairclough, N.: 1995, 'Critical language awareness and self-identity in education', in D. Corson (ed.), *Discourse and Power in Educational Organizations*, Hampton Press, Cresskill, NJ, 257–272.

Flanders, N.: 1965, *Teacher Influence, Pupil Attitudes, and Achievement* (Cooperative Research Monograph No. 12 OE-25040), U. S. Department of Health, Education, and Welfare, Washington, D.C.

Gronn, P.C.: 1983, 'Talk as the work: The accomplishment of school administration', *Administrative Science Quarterly* 28, 1–21.

Gronn, P.C.: 1984, ' "I have a solution . . . ": Administrative power in a school meeting', *Educational Administration Quarterly* 20, 65–92.

Hall, P.M.: 1991, 'In search of the meso domain: Commentary on the contributions of Pestello and Voydanoff', *Symbolic Interaction* 14, 129–134.

Hammett, R.: 1996, 'Changing leadership styles', paper presented to the American Educational Research Association annual meeting, New York.

Hargreaves, A.: 1984, 'Contrastive rhetoric and extremist talk', in A. Hargreaves & P. Woods (eds.), *Classrooms & Staffrooms: The Sociology of Teachers & Teaching*, Open University Press, Milton Keynes.

Hunter, C.: 1980, 'The politics of participation – With specific reference to teacher-pupil relationships', in P. Woods (ed.), *Teacher Strategies: Explorations in the Sociology of the School*, Croom Helm, London.

Kilbourn, B.: 1982, 'Linda: A case study in clinical supervision', *Canadian Journal of Education* 7, 1–24.

Kyte, G.C.: 1971, 'The supervisor-teacher conference: A case study', *Education* 92, 17–25.

Packard, J.S.: 1976, 'Supervision as administration: The control structure of the school', Center for Educational Policy and Management, Eugene OR.

Retallick, J.A.: 1990, 'Clinical supervision and the structure of communication', paper presented to the American Educational Research Association annual meeting, Boston.

Ross, A.J.: 1980, 'The influence of the principal on the curriculum decisions of teachers', *Journal of Curriculum Studies* 12, 219–230.

Scollon, R. & Scollon, S. W.: 1995, *Intercultural Communication*, Blackwell, Oxford.

Tyler, W.: 1995, 'Decoding school reform: Bernstein's market-oriented pedagogy and postmodern power', in A.R. Sadovnik (ed.), *Knowledge & Pedagogy: The Sociology of Basil Bernstein*, Ablex Publishing Corporation, Norwood, NJ, 237–258.

van Dijk, T.A.: 1989, 'Structures of discourse and structures of power', in J.A. Anderson (ed.), *Communication Yearbook 12*, Sage, Newbury Park, CA, 18–59.

Waite, D.: 1995a, *Rethinking Instructional Supervision: Notes on Its Language and Culture*, The Falmer Press, London.

Waite, D.: 1995b, 'Teacher resistance in a supervision conference', in D. Corson (ed.), *Discourse and Power in Educational Organizations*, Hampton Press, Cresskill, NJ, 71–86.

Weller, R.H.: 1971, *Verbal Communication in Instructional Supervision*, Teacher's College Press, New York.

Wodak, R.: 1995, 'Power, discourse, and styles of female leadership in school committee meetings', in D. Corson (ed.), *Discourse and Power in Educational Organizations*, Hampton Press, Cresskill, NJ, 31-54.

Zeichner, K.M. & Liston, D.: 1985, 'Varieties of discourse in supervisory conferences', *Teaching & Teacher Education* 1, 155–174.

Zeichner, K.M., Liston, D., Mahlios, M. & Gomez, M.: 1988, 'The structure and goals of a student teaching program and the character and quality of supervisory discourse', *Teaching & Teacher Education* 4, 349–362.

Section 2

Minorities and Education

TOVE SKUTNABB-KANGAS

HUMAN RIGHTS AND LANGUAGE POLICY IN EDUCATION

Many people have struggled throughout history to get *language rights* for themselves (and others). Language rights have been discussed and written about for quite some time, before and, especially, during the era of the League of Nations, and often by lawyers writing constitutions. *Human rights* is a much more thoroughly studied and clarified but still contested concept which has been at the centre of a whole field of study and politics, but, so far, by very few language experts.

Putting language rights *together* with human rights gives *linguistic human rights*. This topic has been approached only very recently, and a lot of work needs to be done, both scientifically and politically.

THE IMPORTANCE OF LINGUISTIC HUMAN RIGHTS IN EDUCATION

Language rights in education are central for the maintenance of languages and for prevention of linguistic and cultural genocide, regardless of whether this education happens in schools, formally, or in the homes and communities, informally, and regardless of whether and to what extent literacy is involved. Transmission of languages from the parent generation to children is *the* most vital factor for the maintenance of languages. Children must have the opportunity of learning their parents' idiom fully and properly so that they become (at least) as proficient as the parents. Language learning in this sense has to continue at least into young adulthood, for many functions throughout life. When more and more children get access to formal education, much of their more formal language learning which earlier happened in the community, happens in schools. If an alien language is used in schools, i.e. if children do not have the right to learn and use their language in schools, the language is not going to survive because children educated through the medium of an alien language are not likely to pass their own language on to their children and grandchildren. "Modernization" has accelerated the death/murder of languages which without formal education had survived for centuries or millennia.

When the United Nations worked on the final draft of what was to become The Convention on the Prevention and Punishment of the Crime of Genocide (E 794, 1948), a definition of *linguistic genocide* was included in Article III.1:

R. Wodak and D. Corson (eds), Encyclopedia of Language and Education,
Volume 1: Language Policy and Political Issues in Education, 55–65.
© 1997 Kluwer Academic Publishers. Printed in the Netherlands.

Prohibiting the use of the language of the group in daily inter-
course or in schools, or the printing and circulation of publications in the language of the group.

In the final vote in General Assembly, Art. III was voted down, and
is NOT part of the final Convention. Still, the definition can be used. If
we accept the claim that "prohibition" can be direct or indirect, it follows
that if the minority language is not used as a medium of education in the
preschool/school and if there are no minority teachers in the school, the
use of the language is *indirectly* prohibited in daily intercourse/in schools,
i.e. it is a question of linguistic genocide.

For maintenance and development of languages, educational linguistic rights, including the right to mother tongue medium education, are
absolutely vital. I would not hesitate in calling *educational language
rights the most important linguistic human rights* if we are interested in
maintaining linguistic and cultural diversity on our planet.

EARLY DEVELOPMENTS

Charters produced during the American and French Revolutions, forerun-
ners of today's human rights charters, contained no clauses on the rights
of minorities and did not guarantee minorities any language rights in education. Before 1815 language rights were not covered in any *international*
treaties. The Final Act of the Congress of Vienna 1815 had clauses safe-
guarding national minorities who of course also were linguistic minorities.
Several constitutions and bi- and multilateral treaties in the 19th century
also had similar clauses. Some also gave educational language rights (e.g.
the Austrian Constitutional Law of 1867).

The Peace Treaties that concluded the First World War attempted to guarantee minority rights, including language rights in education, in Central
and Eastern Europe, but Britain, France and the United States, signato-
ries to the Treaties, did not offer equivalent rights to their own minority
group citizens. Several countries (e.g. Latvia 1922; Lithuania 1925;
Poland 1932, 1933, 1934) proposed universal minority protection within
the League of Nations, but all the drafts were rejected.

MAJOR CONTRIBUTIONS

The period from 1945 to the 1970s implied a relative neglect of minority
and therefore also language rights, with the exception of broad formulations
outlawing discrimination. It was thought that human rights instruments in
general provided enough protection for *every individual* and that specific
rights to minorities were thus unnecessary. Proposals to include a provision on minorities in the Universal Declaration of Human Rights did not
succeed.

In many of the human rights instruments, language is mentioned in the preambles and in general clauses, as one of the characteristics on the basis of which individuals are not to be discriminated against in their enjoyment of human rights and fundamental freedoms. The other original characteristics (from the joint Art. 2, Universal Declaration of Human Rights, and Art. 2.1, International Covenant on Civil and Political Rights) are "*race, colour, sex, religion, political or other opinion, national or social origin, property, birth or other status*". Later instruments have added *disability, economic status or any other social condition, ethnic origin, conviction, nationality, age* and *marital status*. The original and basic four (in the United Nations Charter, Art. 13) are "*race, sex, language, or religion*". This shows that language has been seen as one of the most important characteristics of humans in terms of their human rights.

When we move from the non-duty-inducing phrases in the preambles, to the binding clauses, and especially to the educational clauses, something very strange happens.

Often *language disappears completely*. This happens in *The Universal Declaration of Human Rights* (1948): the paragraph on education (26), does not refer to language at all. Often there is still a list which has all or most of the others – but language is no longer there. *The International Covenant on Economic, Social and Cultural Rights* (adopted in 1966 and in force since 1976) mentions language on a par with race, colour, sex, religion etc in its *general* article (2.2), but then omits any reference to language in the *educational* Article 13, even if the Article *does* explicitly refer to "racial, ethnic or religious groups" – but not "linguistic" groups.

In 1970, The United Nations appointed a Special Rapporteur on Minorities, Francesco Capotorti whose report (1979) still is one of the most thorough existing treatises of minority rights (only Thornberry 1991; de Varennes 1996 have superseded it). Capotorti saw a clear need for more international legislation to protect minorities. Several Declarations and Conventions to protect minorities and/or minority languages have been passed in the 1990s. But even in the new instruments strange things are happening in relation to the Articles about language rights in education.

If language indeed *is* included, the Article with language-related rights is so weak and unsatisfactory that it is virtually meaningless. All or many of the other human characteristics are still there and get proper treatment and detailed, positive rights. The clauses about them create obligations and contain demanding formulations, where the states are firm dutyholders and '*shall*' do something positive in order to ensure the rights; there are few modifications, few opt-out clauses and few alternatives on a gliding scale. Many of the other characteristics get their own specific conventions (e.g. conventions to prevent racism or sexism, or to guarantee freedom of religion). But not so for language, especially in education.

Compare the *demanding formulations* relating to other characteristics
(1.1, 1.2), with the treatment, with the many *opt-outs, modifications and
alternatives*, that language in education (4.3) gets in The *UN Declaration
on the Rights of Persons Belonging to National or Ethnic, Religious and
Linguistic Minorities*, adopted by the General Assembly in December 1992
(my emphases):

1.1. States *shall protect* the existence and the national or ethnic, cultural,
religious and linguistic identity of minorities within their respective
territories, and *shall encourage* conditions for the *promotion* of that
identity.

1.2. States *shall* adopt *appropriate* legislative *and other* measures *to
achieve those ends*.

4.3. States *should* take *appropriate* measures so that, *wherever possible*,
persons belonging to minorities have *adequate* opportunities to learn
their mother tongue *or* to have instruction in their mother tongue.

Clearly such a formulation as in Art. 4.3 raises many questions. What
constitute "appropriate measures" or "adequate opportunities", and who
is to decide what is "possible"? Does "instruction in" the mother tongue
mean "through the medium of the mother tongue" or does it only mean
instruction in the mother tongue as a subject?

We can see the same phenomenon in the *European Charter for Regional
or Minority Languages* (22 June 1992). A state can choose which para-
graphs or subparagraphs it wants to apply (a minimum of 35 is required).
The formulations in the education Article 8 include a range of modifications
like "*as far as possible*", "*relevant*", "*appropriate*", "*where necessary*",
"*pupils who so wish in a number considered sufficient*", "*if the number
of users of a regional or minority language justifies it*", and a number of
alternatives as in "to allow, encourage *or* provide teaching in *or* of the
regional or minority language at all the *appropriate* stages of education".

While the Charter demonstrates how difficult it is to write binding formulations which are sensitive to local conditions (and this is, we certainly
have to admit, a real problem), just like in the UN Declaration above, its
opt-outs and alternatives permit a reluctant state to meet the requirements
in a minimalist way which it can legitimate by claiming that a provision
was not "possible" or "appropriate", numbers were not "sufficient" or did
not "justify" a provision, and that it "allowed" the minority to organise
teaching of their language as a subject, outside school, at their own cost.

Also in a new Council of Europe *Framework Convention for the Protection of National Minorities* (adopted by the Committee of Ministers of
the Council of Europe on 10 November 1994), again the Article (14.2)
covering the medium of education is more heavily qualified than anything
else in the Framework Convention:

In areas inhabited by persons belonging to national minorities traditionally or in *substantial* numbers, *if there is sufficient demand*, the parties shall *endeavour* to ensure, *as far as possible* and *within the framework of their education systems*, that persons belonging to those minorities have *adequate* opportunities for being taught in the minority language *or* for receiving instruction in this language (my emphases).

There is a hierarchy, with different rights, between different groups whose languages are not main official languages in the state where they live (see Human Rights Fact Sheets from the UN Centre for Human Rights in Geneva for these). *Traditional/territorial/autochthonous/national minorities* have *more language rights* than other groups and most human rights instruments pertain to them. *Immigrant/guest worker/refugee minorities* have practically *no language rights* in education in relation to their own language, and only few in relation to learning the official language. The UN International Convention on the Protection of the Rights of All Migrant Workers and Members of Their Families, from December 1990 but not yet in force because of lack of signatures, in its assimilation-oriented educational language Article (45) accords minimal rights to the mother tongues and is even more vague than the instruments mentioned before. *Indigenous peoples* have on paper some rights and more are suggested in the UN *Draft Universal Declaration on Rights of Indigenous Peoples* – see below.

WORK IN PROGRESS

A more recent attempt to promote language rights, a Universal Declaration of Linguistic Rights, accepted in Barcelona in June 1996 and handed over to UNESCO, also suffers from similar shortcomings even if it for several beneficiaries (*language communities* and, to some extent, *language groups*) represents great progress in relation to the other instruments described. Still, indirectly its education section forces all others except those defined as members of *language communities* (which roughly correspond to national territorially based minorities) to assimilate. For all others, only education in the language of the territory is a right, i.e. not education in their own language (see below). There are many states which claim that they do not have minority language communities, or which do not want to give these communities any rights. Since *self-determination* is not an unconditional right in international law, neither internally (autonomy of some kind) nor externally (secession, independence), a Declaration which gives most of the rights to linguistic *communities*, without firm dutyholders, makes these communities completely dependent on the acceptance of their existence by states, an acceptance that many states are not willing to grant. This makes individual rights enormously important in the Declaration. But these individual rights are the weakest part of the Declaration.

The new Universal Declaration does not give any positive *educational* language rights to *all* individuals, regardless of which category they belong to – and this is exactly what individual human rights are supposed to do. If something is to be seen as an individual *human right*, it means, per definition, a right which *every individual* in the world has, simply because that individual is a human being. It means an unconditional, fundamental right that no state is allowed to take away. In addition, the new Declaration seems to be in many ways completely unrealistic – few if any states in the world would be willing to accept it in its present form.

This will probably be the fate of the UN *Draft Universal Declaration on Rights of Indigenous Peoples* also, according to its chair, Erica Irene Daes (1995). Despite the careful negotiations over a decade, several countries, most importantly the United States, are probably going to demand substantial changes which undermine the progress achieved in the Declaration (Morris 1995).

The conclusion is that we are still to see the right to education through the medium of the mother tongue become a human right. We are still living with basic language wrongs in human rights law, especially in education policy. Denial of linguistic human rights, linguistic and cultural genocide and forced assimilation through education are still characteristic of many states, notably in Europe and Neo-Europes.

DEVELOPMENT OF THE DENIAL

States seem to have three main reasons for denying linguistic human rights, one more economic, two more political.

The *economic* reason has to do with (falsely) seeing homogenization (including monolingualism or subtractive learning of official or "world" languages) and standardization as necessary prerequisites for industrialisation, "modernization", consumerism, efficiency and large single markets.

The principle of the territorial integrity and political sovereignty of contemporary states is often presented as being in conflict with another human rights principle, that of self-determination, both important principles in human rights law. The first *political* reason for the denial of linguistic human rights is to try to "solve" this conflict. Minorities with educational linguistic rights, reproducing themselves as distinct minorities, are seen as a threat to the present states because they are expected by the states to demand first internal then external self-determination. Therefore, many states strive, through homogenizing forced assimilation, towards eradicating distinct groups which could demand self-determination. By denying them linguistic human rights and by committing linguistic and cultural genocide in education and otherwise, the states seem to hope that there will eventually not be any distinct groups left to demand self-determination: the states will be homogenized as a result of the forced assimilation. Language plays here a multiple role from a collective point of view (Skutnabb-Kangas 1997a).

The second *political* reason has to do with the changing forms of power and control. Physical violence as a means of control is already increasingly seen as unacceptable *between* states (but not yet *within* states – most of today's wars are intra-state wars). Physical violence is in the process of being replaced by carrots and ideas (remuneration and persuasion, Galtung 1980; symbolic violence, Bourdieu 1992) which are more efficient and cheaper to use for the power-holders, both economically and psychologically. In order for people to accept common norms which are a prerequisite for seeing at least symbolic remuneration, for instance status-related rewards and benefits, as remuneration, hegemonic ideas have to be spread and consent manufactured.

Ideas are spread mainly through the *consciousness industry* (most importantly education, mass media and religions). Even if visual and audio-images are important, ideas are mainly spread via language.

In order for everybody to understand the power holders' language (and to prevent people from the analyses needed for counterhegemonies), indigenous peoples, minorities and dialect-speakers have to be forcefully assimilated (Skutnabb-Kangas & Phillipson 1994, 1996), and everybody in the world has to learn (some) English (Phillipson 1992). A common language, preferably learned in a subtractive way, is the most important prerequisite for ruling and control via ideas. Again, this can be achieved by denying linguistic human rights. And this is in fact what is done in education (Skutnabb-Kangas 1997b).

PROBLEMS AND DIFFICULTIES

From a research point of view, there are several conceptual challenges to be tackled. Some of the most urgent ones are:

A. Most language rights are related to "minorities", but there is no commonly accepted definition of the concept "minority" (see Andrýsek 1989; Capotorti 1979; Gromacki 1992; Packer 1993; Thornberry 1991; de Varennes 1996 for discussions).

B. Many other concepts needed for language rights are equally unclear. What does it mean to "learn/acquire a language", or to learn it "fully" or to be "proficient" in it? How should "mother tongue" be defined for language rights purposes? What are the consequences for concept definitions of including sign languages (so far, only Uganda and Finland seem to grant them constitutional rights). What is the borderline between "language" and "dialect" or "standard variety" (see reviews by Corson on non-standard varieties in this volume and in volume 6) and other varieties? Does an entity called "language" really exist, or is it a Western myth? (see Mühlhäusler 1996 for discussions).

C. The legitimacy of hierarchies between rights of various groups needs clarification. So far, (im)migrant minorities have not had any linguistic rights in education to use and maintain their languages. *The European Charter for Regional and Minority Languages*, for example, explicitly excludes immigrant minority languages. So do the *OSCE* (Organisation on Security and Cooperation in Europe) and several other non-binding documents. Some of the UN documents (e.g. the *UN Declaration on the Rights of Persons Belonging to National or Ethnic, Religious and Linguistic Minorities*) are unclear/open to different interpretations as to whether (im)migrant minorities count as minorities. Should they have rights? When do they cease to be immigrants and become minorities? So far Hungary seems to be the only country which has defined this in law (after 100 years).

It makes little sense, though, to differentiate between the language rights of majorities, indigenous peoples and autochthonous or immigrant minorities *in education* – the needs of every child to learn their own and at least some other languages are similar. The only distinction one might make is that between *necessary rights* on the one hand (the right to one's mother tongue and to an official language if it is not the mother tongue) and *enrichment-oriented rights* on the other hand (the right to learn any foreign languages). For instance in the *Draft Universal Declaration on Linguistic Rights* (see above), members of *language communities* have *more* rights, when they want to learn any foreign language in the world, than individuals not defined as members of language communities, when these want to learn their *own* language. This means that the most important right of *everyone*, the linguistic *human* right that is *necessary* for the maintenance of linguistic diversity, is NOT in the Declaration, while a strongly formulated positive *enrichment-oriented* but not necessary rights to foreign languages is there for language community members. To those who have, shall more be given.

D. Is there a conflict between *individual rights* and *collective rights*, and if so, how can it be solved?

E. How should the rights and duties of both *beneficiaries* and *duty-holders* be defined so that they are firm and clear (instead of vague and conditional) but at the same time flexible and sensitive to local conditions?

FUTURE DIRECTIONS

Three promising developments should be mentioned. The UN ICCPR (International Covenant on Civil and Political Rights) Article 27 still grants the best legally binding protection to languages:

"In those states in which ethnic, religious or linguistic minorities exist, persons belonging to such minorities shall not be denied the right, in community with other members of their group, to enjoy their own culture, to profess and practise their own religion, or to use their own language".

In the customary reading of Art. 27, rights were only granted to individuals, not collectivities. "Persons belonging to ... minorities" only had these rights *in states which accepted that the minorities exist.* So far, the Article has been interpreted as

- excluding groups (even if they are citizens) which are not recognised as minorities by the State;
- only conferring some protection from discrimination (= "negative rights") but not a positive right to maintain or even use one's language;
- not imposing any obligations on the States;
- excluding (im)migrants (who have not been seen as minorities).

In 1994 the *UN Human Rights Committee* adopted a *General Comment* on Article 27 which interprets it in a substantially more positive way than earlier. The Committee sees the Article as

- stating that the existence of a minority does not depend on a decision by the State but requires to be established by objective criteria;
- recognizing the existence of a "right";
- imposing positive obligations on the States;
- protecting all individuals on the State's territory or under its jurisdiction (i.e. also immigrants and refugees), irrespective of whether they belong to the minorities specified in the Article or not.

What might be the possible implications of the General Comment on the educational linguistic human rights of (im)migrant minorities, we do not know yet. It remains to be seen to what extent this General Comment will influence the State parties. If the Committee's interpretation ("soft law") becomes the general norm, and if the Western European countries where migrant and refugee minorities live start observing this norm, the educational linguistic rights might improve.

The second positive development is the new educational guidelines from the *OSCE High Commissioner on National Minorities*, Max van der Stoel, *The Hague Recommendations and Explanatory Notes* (October 1996). These guidelines were worked out by a small group of experts on human rights and education (including the undersigned). According to them, the genocidal language policy in education

   ... [s]ubmersion-type approaches whereby the curriculum is taught exclusively through the medium of the state language and minority children are entirely integrated into classes with children of the majority are not in line with international standards.

Thirdly, the work of UNESCO to revise the Draft Universal Declaration on Linguistic Rights began in autumn 1996. Despite many shortcomings the Declaration represents, together with several Articles in the UN Draft Universal Declaration on Rights of Indigenous Peoples, the most fargoing suggested protection so far for some of the groups needing language rights in education.

Still, other protection is needed for the groups which are outside the rights described in these. Besides, Declarations are usually not binding. But the greatest hurdle of all is the fact that none of the linguistic human rights in education included in these Declarations, nor other types of protection seem to be easily (if at all) acceptable to many states. Several Western states (notably Britain, France, Greece, Turkey, the USA) have during this century not only *not promoted* but in fact *tried to prevent* the acceptance of positive language rights in education (see Skutnabb-Kangas 1996 for an analysis).

Just as *absence* of economic and social rights in the period *between* the world wars *promoted* the emergence of totalitarian regimes according to Asbjørn Eide (1995: pp. 29–30) of the UN Human Rights Commission, it seems that *absence or denial of linguistic and cultural rights* are *today* effective ways of *promoting* the "ethnic conflict" and "ethnic tension" which are seen as the most important possible reasons for unrest, conflict and violence in the world. These conflicts which have multiple causes *can* take ethnically and linguistically defined or articulated forms in situations where groups *lack* linguistic rights *and/or* political/economic rights, and where at the same time political and/or economic power and material resources are unevenly distributed along linguistic and ethnic lines. There are, therefore, strong reasons why states should *support* rather than try to kill linguistic and cultural diversity. The elites of the world should thus support linguistic rights *for egoistic reasons*, not only for human rights reasons.

Roskilde University
Denmark

REFERENCES

Andrýsek, O.: 1989, *Report on the Definition of Minorities*, Utrecht: Netherlands Institute of Human Rights, Studie- en Informatiecentrum Mensenrechten (SIM), SIM Special No 8.

Bourdieu, P.: 1992, *Language & Symbolic Power*, Edited and Introduced by J. B.Thompson, Polity Press, Cambridge.

Capotorti, F.: 1979, *Study of the Rights of Persons Belonging to Ethnic, Religious and Linguistic Minorities*, United Nations, New York.

Daes, E.-I.: 1995, 'Redressing the balance: The struggle to be heard', paper to the Global Cultural Diversity Conference, Sydney, 26–28 April 1995.

Eide, A.: 1995, 'Economic, social and cultural rights as human rights', in A. Eide, C. Krause & A. Rosas (eds.), *Economic, Social and Cultural Rights. A Textbook*, Martinus Nijhoff Publishers, Dordrecht, Boston & London, 21–40.

Galtung, J.: 1980, *The True Worlds. A transnational perspective*. The Free Press, New York.

Gromacki, J.P.: 1992, 'The protection of language rights in international human rights law: A proposed draft declaration of linguistic rights', *Virginia Journal of International Law* 32, 471, 515–579.

Morris, G.T.: 1995, '12th session of UN working group on indigenous peoples. The declaration passes and the US assumes a new role', *Fourth World Bulletin. Issues in Indigenous Law and Politics*. University of Colorado at Denver. 4, 1–2, 1ff.

Packer, J.: 1993, 'On the definition of minorities', in J. Packer & K. Myntti (eds.), *The Protection of Ethnic and Linguistic Minorities in Europe*. Èbo Akademi University. Institute for Human rights, Èbo, 23–65.

Phillipson, R.: 1992, *Linguistic Imperialism*, Oxford University Press, Oxford.

Phillipson, R. & Skutnabb-Kangas, T.: 1996, 'English only worldwide, or language ecology', *TESOL Quarterly*, Special-Topic Issue: Language Planning and Policy, eds. Thomas Ricento & Nancy Hornberger, 429–452.

Skutnabb-Kangas, T.: 1996, 'Promotion of linguistic tolerance and development', in Legér, S. (ed.), *Vers un agenda linguistique: regard futuriste sur les Nations Unies / Towards a Language Agenda: Futurist Outlook on the United Nations*, Canadian Center of Language Rights, Ottawa, 579–629.

Skutnabb-Kangas, T.: (1997a), 'Language, racism and linguistic human rights', *Global Cultural Diversity Conference, Strength in Diversity – an Investment in Our Future*, Conference to celebratate the 50th Anniversary of the United Nations, organised by the Australian Prime Minister's Office, Sydney 26–28 April 1995.

Skutnabb-Kangas, T.: (1997b), *Linguistic Genocide in Education*, Contributions to the Sociology of Language, Mouton de Gruyter, Berlin & New York.

Skutnabb-Kangas, T. & Phillipson, R.: 1994, 'Linguistic human rights, past and present', in T. Skutnabb-Kangas & R. Phillipson (eds.), in collaboration with M. Rannut, *Linguistic Human Rights. Overcoming Linguistic Discrimination*, Contributions to the Sociology of Language 67, Mouton de Gruyter, Berlin and New York, 71–110.

Skutnabb-Kangas, T. & Phillipson, R.: (1996). Linguicide and Linguicism, Article nr 80, Chapter VI, Central Issues in Contact Linguistics, for Handbücher zur Sprach- und Kommunikationswissenschaft, Kontaktlinguistik / Handbooks of Linguistics and Communication Science, Contact Linguistics / Manuels de linguistique et des sciences de communication, Linguistique de contact, Hans Goebl, Peter Hans Nelde, Zdeněk Stáry, Wolfgang Wölck (eds.), Walter de Gruyter, Berlin & New York, 667–675.

Smolicz, J.J.: 1979, *Culture and Education in a Plural Society*, Curriculum Development Centre, Canberra.

Stavenhagen, R.: 1995, 'Cultural rights and universal human rights', in A.Eide, C.Krause & A.Rosas (eds.), *Economic, Social and Cultural Rights. A Textbook*. Martinus Nijhoff Publishers Dordrecht, Boston & London, 63–77.

Thornberry, P.: 1991, *International Law and the Rights of Minorities*, Clarendon Press, Oxford.

UN Human Rights Fact Sheet.: 1992, *Minority Rights*, Fact Sheet No. 18, Centre for Human Rights, United Nations Office at Geneva.

de Varennes, F.: 1996, *Language, Minorities and Human Rights*, Martinus Nijhoff, The Hague, Boston, London.

INTERNATIONAL LAW AND EDUCATION IN A MINORITY LANGUAGE

The Statute of the International Court of Justice sets out three principal (and two subsidiary) sources of international law. They are treaties, customary international law as evidenced by the practice of countries accepted as law, general principles of law recognised by all countries, and as subsidiary sources, judicial decisions and the writing of "highly qualified publicists". The literature on the international law of minority language education is thus not a primary source of the law, but it serves as both a subsidiary source and as a record of discussion of the primary sources. This chapter discusses the international law concerning the right to an education in a language that is not the majority language of the state providing the education. The definition of "minority language" used in this chapter is the language spoken by

> a group numerically inferior to the rest of the population of a State, in a non-dominant position, whose members – being nationals of the State – possess ethnic, religious or linguistic characteristics differing from those of the rest of the population and show, if only implicitly, a sense of solidarity, directed towards preserving their culture, traditions, religion, or language (Capotorti 1979).

Consistent with this definition, this chapter will not focus on the international law concerning the rights of non-nationals to the provision of minority language education. The discussion will concern international law relevant to a state's own nationals.

EARLY DEVELOPMENTS

International law relating to minority language education can be found in general principles and in specific sources. General principles include equality, non-discrimination and self-determination. Specific sources include treaties and state practice which explicitly provide for the recognition by the provider state of a right possessed by its own nationals to minority language education. Until the creation of the League of Nations, minorities were only sporadically protected to varying degrees by treaties arising mostly from peace settlements. Minorities were generally defined by either religious or national affiliation. The League of Nations established a comprehensive, mostly multilateral, treaty-based minorities pro-

R. Wodak and D. Corson (eds), Encyclopedia of Language and Education,
Volume 1: Language Policy and Political Issues in Education, 67–76.
© *1997 Kluwer Academic Publishers. Printed in the Netherlands.*

tection system in Europe which combined both general principles and
specific treaty provisions. These treaties guaranteed equality of treatment
of all nationals before the law and the equal enjoyment of civil and political rights. They also contained provisions specific to minorities, including
the provision of public state-funded and private minority language education. States were obligated to treat these provisions as superior to any
contrary national law or administrative act. The minorities provisions were
also guaranteed internationally by a petition procedure to the Council and
actions in the Permanent Court of International Justice. Both the Council and the Court were often concerned with minority language education
rights (Permanent Court of International Justice 1928, 1935).

The League system began to fail well before the Second World War. The
reasons most often given are that the states subject to the system resented
the infringement of their sovereignty caused by League interventions;
states not subject to the system often contained minorities who wanted
rights similar to those guaranteed by the League system which created
internal instability; the minorities were not often content with League
petition procedures and were encouraged to demand greater autonomy;
and of course the rise of Hitler and sympathetic regimes in other states
subjected the League to intense destabilisation (Thornberry 1980).

MAJOR CONTRIBUTIONS

The major contributors to the modern international law of minority language education rights are bodies within the United Nations, and the
International Labour Organisation. Of most interest in the United Nations
is the work of the Sub-Commission on the Prevention of Discrimination
and Protection of Minorities. Following the creation of the United Nations, there was a general shift in legal discourse from "minority rights"
to "human rights" (see the review by Skutnabb Kangas in this volume).
Perhaps because of a desire to distance new instruments from the failure
of the League system, there was a tendency to submerge minority rights
in human rights until the creation of the International Covenant on Civil
and Political Rights and the International Covenant on Social, Economic
and Cultural Rights in 1960. The modern international law relevant to
minority language education rights is discussed in chronological order of
creation. The trend from very general and often negative phrasing towards
greater specificity should be noted.

In 1948 the General Assembly adopted the Universal Declaration of
Human Rights. Although the Declaration is contained in a General Assembly Resolution and not a treaty, it is now regarded as an authoritative
statement of the customary international law of human rights. There is no
provision in the Universal Declaration specifically related to minorities.
Instead, it states in Article 2 that "[e]veryone is entitled to all the rights and

freedoms set forth in this Declaration, without distinction of any kind, such as . . . language . . . ". One of those rights is the right to education in Article 26 which states that "[e]veryone has the right to education. Education shall be free, at least in the elementary and fundamental stages.... " Article 7 also provides that "[a]ll are equal before the law and are entitled without any discrimination to equal protection of the law . . . ". Any claim to specific minority language education rights using the Universal Declaration must be found in these statements of more general principles.

In 1960, the Sub-Commission on the Prevention of Discrimination and Protection of Minorities succeeded in obtaining a provision specifically related to minorities in Article 27 of the International Covenant on Civil and Political Rights. It was the first such provision in a general multilateral treaty since the demise of the League system. Article 27 states that "[i]n those States in which ethnic, religious or linguistic minorities exist, persons belonging to such minorities shall not be denied the right, in community with the other members of their group, to enjoy their own culture, to profess and practise their own religion, or to use their own language". Articles 2 and 26 largely repeat the provisions of Articles 2 and 7 of the Universal Declaration relating to equality and non-discrimination on various grounds including language. Although the phrase "shall not be denied" at first glance does not seem to impose a positive obligation on a state to provide opportunities, including educational opportunities, to use a minority language (Lannung 1968; Lebel 1974), it has been argued that to recognise a right to use a minority language implies a positive obligation that the right is made effective (Capotorti 1979). When Article 27 is read with the equality and non-discrimination provisions of Articles 2 and 26, the latter argument is strengthened (Hastings 1988).

The right to an education is specifically recognised in Article 13 of the International Covenant on Economic, Social and Cultural Rights, 1960. It states that "[t]he States Parties to the present Covenant recognise the right of everyone to education . . . They further agree that education shall enable all persons to participate effectively in a free society, promote understanding, tolerance and friendship among all nations and all racial, ethnic and religious groups . . . ". Article 2 requires that the right to education "will be exercised without discrimination of any kind as to . . . language". Article 4 allows states to limit the right to education "only in so far as this may be compatible with the nature of these rights and solely for the purpose of promoting the general welfare of a democratic society". In light of the effect on learning ability and potential societal stratification of those to whom a minority mother language education is denied discussed elsewhere in these volumes, it is possible to interpret Articles 13, 2 and 4 to mean that to enable the right to an education to be exercised without discrimination on language grounds, any student should be able to derive as much individual benefit from the exercise of the right as any other student. A student would not be able to benefit from the right to education if she were taught in a language not her mother tongue. A discrimination on language grounds would have occurred which prevented full benefit from the exercise of the right to education, and which could be remedied with mother tongue instruction.

The UNESCO Convention Against Discrimination in Education, 1960 defines "discrimination" by referring to "equality of treatment in education" in Article 1:

1. For the purposes of this Convention, the term 'discrimination' includes any distinction, exclusion, limitation or preference which, being based on ... language ... has the purpose or effect of nullifying or impairing equality of treatment in education and in particular:

   (a) Of depriving any person or group of persons access to education of any type at any level;

   (b) Of limiting any person or group of persons to education of an inferior standard;

   (c) Subject to the provisions of Article 2 of this convention, of establishing or maintaining separate educational systems or institutions for persons or groups of persons;

The Convention goes on to provide for the establishment or maintenance, for linguistic reasons, of separate schools provided attendance is optional and the education is up to state standards (Article 2(b)). Article 5 states that

(1)(c) It is essential to recognise the right of members of national minorities to carry on their own educational activities, including the maintenance of schools and, depending on the educational policy of each State, the use or the teaching of their own language, provided however:

   (i) That this right is not exercised in a manner which prevents the members of these minorities from understanding the culture and language of the community as a whole and from participating in its activities, or which prejudices national sovereignty;

   (ii) That the standard of education is not lower than the general standard laid down or approved by the competent authorities; and

   (iii) That attendance at such schools is optional.

Article 5(2) then binds states to "undertake all necessary measures to ensure the application" of the principles set out above.

WORK IN PROGRESS

Apart from regional developments in the period from 1961 to 1985, language and education rights in international law remained embedded in the general human rights instruments discussed above. Many domestic constitutions and statutes recognised to varying degrees minority language rights in education (de Varennes 1996). Minority language education rights are now often found in the context of an emerging discourse on the right to development (Paul 1995), indigenous rights, and children's rights. While the instruments discussed above continue in force, they must now be interpreted in new contexts.

The Declaration on the Right to Development was adopted by the United Nations General Assembly in Resolution 41/128 on 4 December 1986. As a General Assembly Resolution it cannot bind states. It may however record existing customary international law which is binding. Article 8 provides that states "shall ensure, *inter alia*, equality of opportunity for all in their access to basic resources, education, health services, food, housing, employment and the fair distribution of income". It also provides that states "should co-operate with a view to promoting, encouraging and strengthening universal respect for and observance of all human rights and fundamental freedoms for all without any distinction as to ... language ...". The international law of development is evolving and must be "harmonised with, indeed reinforced by, the promotion of universal [human] rights' (Paul 1995: p. 312). Once referred to as "soft" law because of the normative, non-binding nature of the instruments containing principles of development law, there is evidence of a steady trend towards recognition of the need for institutional and procedural change to "harden" the binding nature of the various development rights. Resistance to this trend arises from state sovereignty because many development rights impinge on what many states continue to regard as domestic policy. On the other hand, the slow but continuous hardening of development rights can be seen as a sign of the decline of state sovereignty.

The International Labour Organisation's Convention No. 169 Concerning Indigenous and Tribal Peoples in Independent Countries done at Geneva on 27 June 1989 partly revises the Tribal Populations Convention of 1957. The 1957 Convention emphasised assimilation as a desirable aim of indigenous peoples' development. The 1989 Convention reflects a reversal of thought on this issue and as such is consistent with both the rise of the international law of development and with the decline of state sovereignty. Articles 26 to 31 set out indigenous minority education rights in detail uncharacteristic of previous treaties containing education rights. Article 26 provides that "[m]easures shall be taken to ensure that members of the peoples concerned have the opportunity to acquire education at all

levels on at least an equal footing with the rest of the national community".
Article 28 is specifically aimed at indigenous minority language education
rights:

1. Children belonging to the peoples concerned shall, wherever practicable, be taught to read and write in their own indigenous language
   or in the language most commonly used by the group to which they
   belong. When this is not practicable, the competent authorities shall
   undertake consultations with these peoples with a view to the adoption
   of measures to achieve this objective.
2. Adequate measures shall be taken to ensure that these peoples have
   the opportunity to attain fluency in the national language or in one of
   the official languages of the country.
3. Measures shall be taken to preserve and promote the development
   and practice of the indigenous languages of the peoples concerned.

The language of this part of Convention 169 indicates a recognition of both
the benefits of minority language education and the need to reconcile these
benefits with the practical resource cost of providing such education and the
need to be able to participate fully in the whole national community. The
Convention also places minority language education rights in the context
of eliminating prejudice against, and promoting an accurate portrayal of,
indigenous cultures and societies.

Also concerned with the development of indigenous rights is the Working Group on Indigenous Populations established by the Sub-Commission
on Prevention of Discrimination and Protection of Minorities in 1981. The
working group is chaired by Ms Erica-Irene Daes, has met annually for
fourteen years, and has developed a Draft Declaration on the Rights of
Indigenous Peoples. Article 15 of the Draft Declaration states that:

> Indigenous children have the right to all levels and forms of ed-
> ucation of the State. All indigenous peoples also have this right
> and the right to establish and control their educational systems
> and institutions providing education in their own languages, in
> a manner appropriate to their cultural methods of teaching and
> learning.
> Indigenous children living outside their communities have the
> right to be provided access to education in their own culture and
> language.
> States shall take effective measures to provide appropriate re-
> sources for these purposes.

The Working Group is also exploring the possibility of establishing a permanent forum for indigenous people. This work will include discussion of
minority language education rights in the context of emerging indigenous
rights law.

Finally, the United Nations Convention on the Rights of the Child,
done at New York on 20 November 1989 recognises "the right of the

child to education" in Article 28. Article 29 provides that states parties to the Convention "agree that the education of the child shall be directed to the development of respect for the child's parents, his or her own cultural identity, language and values ... ". Particular focus on children in international law is not new. Indeed, much of this Convention can be seen as a specific application to children of the general principles of the Universal Declaration of Human Rights and the two International Covenants. The Convention does however incorporate many aspects of development rights and indigenous and minority self-determination, and must be read in these contexts.

PROBLEMS AND DIFFICULTIES

There are persistent challenges inherent in claiming a right to education in a minority language. From the point of view of the claimant minority, the right to an education in a minority language can be a double-edged sword. On one hand, the main purpose of the right is to engender minority individual and group dignity by preserving the minority language. This is made possible by ensuring that the minority language can continue to be a useful medium for conveying culture and thought. On the other hand, if the result of such an education is to make thought and communication in the majority language difficult, the benefit to the linguistic minority of minority language preservation could be offset by all the detriments of language ghetto-isation. In this scenario, education in a minority language would cease to be of any benefit and could contribute as much to the decline of minority language as any programme of assimilation would. The more modern instruments of international law discussed above attempt to safeguard against this scenario by placing minority language education rights in a broader context of development and indigenous rights law.

Another persistent challenge to minority language education rights is the (in)ability to marshal, or give priority to, adequate resources. Indeed, unwillingness to commit resources to minority language education was arguably one of the reasons why such rights were characterised as "soft law". However, the decline of state sovereignty has meant that there is increasing opportunity for international education rights, along with other international social and economic rights, to play a role in the decisions of states to allocate resources and develop policy. The increasing realignment of political borders along ethnic boundaries, itself a sign of the decline of traditional state sovereignty, has also often resulted in an allocation of resources more in accordance with the social, economic and cultural needs of former minorities. This further increases the importance of minority language education rights as expressed in the modern context of hardening international commitment to development and indigenous rights law.

FUTURE DIRECTIONS

As discussed above, the decline of state sovereignty has provided the opportunity for, and has been in some ways caused by, a new discourse that locates the international law relating to minority language education firmly in the context of international development law and the law concerning indigenous self-determination or autonomy. Another challenge is arising that mirrors these developments. It is caused by recent successful exercises of self-determination resulting from the decline of mid-twentieth century state sovereignty. It is the "double minority" problem (Hanneman 1995). This has arisen as the result of the secession of a minority which forms itself into a state. The former minority becomes the new majority in the new state, and the former majority becomes the new minority. Both groups identify and present aspects of majority and minority characteristics at once. This creates a tension between the right of self-determination and the right to protect language and culture against the "other". It also raises a question inherent in international law between 1945 and 1985 about whether minority group rights can be given full effect through general provisions concerning equality and non-discrimination, and since 1985, whether minority group rights can be adequately dealt with in the broader context of international development law or by analogy with the international law of indigenous rights. Finally, these new directions will continue to be influenced by the extent to which international law can form part of the decision-making within states or state-like entities with respect to the resources to be committed to minority language education in light of other competing needs.

Victoria University of Wellington
New Zealand

REFERENCES

Capotorti, F.: 1979, *Study on the Rights of Persons Belonging to Ethnic, Religious and Linguistic Minorities*, United Nations, Human Rights Commission, Sub-Commission on Prevention of Discrimination and Protection of Minorities, E/CN.4/Sub.2/384/Rev.1.
Deschènes, J.: 1985, *Promotion, Protection and Restoration of Human Rights at the National, Regional and International Levels: Prevention of Discrimination and Protection of Minorities,* United Nations, Human Rights Commission, Sub-Commission on Prevention of Discrimination and Protection of Minorities, E/CN.4/Sub.2/1985/31.
Dinstein, Y.: 1976, 'Collective human rights of peoples and minorities', *International and Comparative Law Quarterly* 25, 102.
Dinstein, Y. & Tabory, M. (eds.): 1992, *The Protection of Minorities and Human Rights*, M. Nijhoff, Dordrecht.
European Court of Human Rights: 1968, 'Case relating to certain aspects of the laws on the use of languages in education in Belgium (Merits)' (the 'Belgian Linguistic Case'), *Year Book of the European Convention on Human Rights* 11, 832.

Foucher, P.: 1987, 'Language rights and education', in M. Bastarache (ed.), *Language Rights in Canada*, Y. Blais, Montréal, 257.

Gotlieb, A.E.: 1970, *Human Rights, Federalism and Minorities*, Canadian Institute of International Affairs, Toronto.

Gromacki, J.: 1992, 'The protection of language rights in international human rights law: A proposed draft declaration of linguistic rights', *Virginia Journal of International Law* 32, 515–579.

Hanneman, A.J.: 1995, 'Independence and group rights in the Baltics: A double minority problem', *Virginia Journal of International Law* 35, 485–527.

Hastings, W.K.: 1988, *The Right to an Education in Maori: The Case from International Law*, Institute of Policy Studies, Wellington.

International Labour Organisation: 1989, Convention 169, *Convention Concerning Indigenous and Tribal Peoples in Independent Countries*, International Labour Conference, Geneva, reprinted in B.Weston, R. Falk & A. D'Amato (eds.), *Basic Documents in International Law and World Order* (second edition), West Publishing Co, St. Paul, 489–497.

Lannung, H.: 1968, 'The rights of minorities' in *Mélanges Offerts à Polys Modinos*, Éditions A. Pedone, Paris, 181–195.

Lebel, M.: 1974, 'Le choix de la langue d'enseignment et le droit international', *Révue Juridique Thémis* 9, 211–237.

Magnet, J.E.: 1982, 'Minority-language educational rights', *Supreme Court Law Review* 4, 195–216.

Martínez Cobo, J.R.: 1986, *Study of the Problem of Discrimination Against Indigenous Populations*, United Nations, Human Rights Commission, Sub-Commission on Prevention of Discrimination and Protection of Minorities, E/CN.4/Sub.2/1986/7.

McDougal, M.S., Lasswell, H.D. & Chen, L-C.: 1980, 'Claims for freedom from discrimination in choice of language', in M.S. McDougal, H.D. Lasswell, & L-C. Chen, *Human Rights and World Public Order*, Yale University Press, New Haven, 713–736.

Minority Rights Group (ed.): 1994, *Education Rights and Minorities*, Minority Rights Group, London.

Paul, J.C.N.: 1995, 'The United Nations and the creation of an international law of development', *Harvard International Law Journal* 36, 307–328.

Permanent Court of International Justice: 1928, *Rights of Minorities in Upper Silesia (Minority Schools)*, P.C.I.J. Reports, Series A, No. 15.

Permanent Court of International Justice: 1935, *Minority Schools in Albania*, P.C.I.J. Reports, Series A/B, No. 64.

Tabory, M.: 1980, 'Language rights as human rights', *Israeli Yearbook on Human Rights* 10, 167.

Thornberry, P.: 1980, 'Is there a Phoenix in the ashes? – International law and minority rights', *Texas International Law Journal* 15, 421–458.

Thornberry, P.: 1990, *International Law and the Rights of Minorities*, Clarendon Press, Oxford.

Réaume, D. & Green, L.: 1989, 'Education and linguistic security in the *Charter*', *McGill Law Journal* 34, 777–816.

United Nations Economic and Social Council: 1993, *Draft Declaration on the Rights of Indigenous Peoples*, E/CN.4/Sub.2/1993/29/Annex I, reprinted at http://www.halcyon.com/FWDP/.

United Nations Educational, Scientific and Cultural Organisation: 1960, *Convention Against Discrimination in Education*, UNESCO, Paris, reprinted in *United Nations Treaty Series* 429, 93.

United Nations General Assembly: 1966, Resolution 2200 (XXI), *International Covenant on Economic, Social and Cultural Rights*, United Nations, New York, reprinted in *International Legal Materials* 6, 360.

United Nations General Assembly: 1966, Resolution 2200 (XXI), *International Covenant on Civil and Political Rights,* United Nations, New York, reprinted in *International Legal Materials* 6, 368.

United Nations General Assembly: 1986, Resolution 41/128, *Declaration on the Right to Development,* United Nations, New York, reprinted in Weston, B., Falk, R. & D'Amato, A (eds.), *Basic Documents in International Law and World Order* (second edition), West Publishing Co, St. Paul, 1990, 485–488.

United Nations General Assembly: 1989, Resolution 25 (XLIV), *Convention on the Rights of the Child,* United Nations, New York, reprinted in Weston, B., Falk, R. & D'Amato, A (eds.), *Basic Documents in International Law and World Order* (second edition), West Publishing Co, St. Paul, 1990, 498–512.

de Varennes, F.: 1996, *Language, Minorities and Human Rights*, M. Nijhoff, Dordrecht.

DAVID CORSON

LANGUAGE POLICIES FOR INDIGENOUS PEOPLES

Indigenous, aboriginal peoples inhabit modern nation states on every continent. As well as the differences of race or cultural origin that distinguish
them from the dominant populations of their countries, indigenous peoples
also differ in having endured a long history of colonial exploitation and
repression, usually involving invasion and conquest. In every case the languages of these peoples show the marks of this history of oppression that
their speakers have experienced. So where these indigenous languages
are not extinct or on the verge of extinction, they survive in language
contact situations where dominant invasion languages threaten to swamp
the aboriginal languages. Only recently have governments in some places
introduced formal language policies to protect and promote the use and
development of their countries' indigenous languages. Elsewhere the linguistic repression of the past continues through tacit language policies that
are little different in effect from the policies of repression that operated in
earlier centuries.

EARLY DEVELOPMENTS

The history of contact between indigenous peoples and their colonizers
has been a steady escalation of pressures on the aboriginal peoples to
conform to the imposed cultures. Alien cultures and languages, imposed
on aboriginal peoples by invasion and conquest, became institutionalized
for them when a system of schooling based solely in the alien culture and in
its languages became their only route to education. Until as recently as the
1970s, policy makers everywhere believed that their indigenous peoples
were better off learning and using the languages of the colonizers, since
this seemed to give them access to the cultural and economic goods of
the dominant cultures while moving them away from their own aboriginal
sociocultural contexts, which were widely regarded as inferior to those of
the invaders.

Today these views seem a mixture of ignorance and racism. But their
impact on educational policy lingers. For more than a century of compulsory education, aboriginal languages have usually been ignored in schools
and they have been replaced with the dominant language or languages
of education. Often educational authorities have done more than simply
ignore the aboriginal languages. There are many documented accounts
of injustices regularly inflicted upon indigenous minorities in an attempt

R. Wodak and D. Corson (eds), Encyclopedia of Language and Education,
Volume 1: Language Policy and Political Issues in Education, 77–87.
© *1997 Kluwer Academic Publishers. Printed in the Netherlands.*

to eradicate their languages through schooling. Many of these accounts are quite recent and they make harrowing reading (Skutnabb-Kangas & Cummins 1988; Romaine 1989, 1991).

These pressures on entire indigenous peoples to conform linguistically were partly justified in the minds of policy makers because there was little evidence available confirming the desirability of bilingualism as a human achievement. The advantages of having a bilingual education were not widely known and often the evidence was even suppressed in the face of competing ideologies (Cummins 1984). But in 1951 a new direction was suggested by a UNESCO 'committee of experts' who ruled that "it is axiomatic that the best medium for teaching a child" is the child's mother tongue (UNESCO 1953: p. 11). The committee claimed that this was the case on psychological, sociological and educational grounds. Yet, as recently as the early 1980s, conclusive research evidence for or against the UNESCO claim had not appeared. From this lack of evidence many were ready to conclude that aboriginal language medium instruction, aimed at making children bilingual in both their aboriginal language and the dominant language, might not really be worthwhile for indigenous children. Language policies in education remained unchanged.

MAJOR CONTRIBUTIONS

Changes in attitude to bilingual education and to bilingualism itself began to arrive along with the evidence from many studies in many countries that supported a revision in policy priorities for minority languages of all kinds (for summaries see Skutnabb-Kangas 1984; Cummins & Swain 1986; Skutnabb-Kangas & Cummins 1988; Corson 1993). Gradually in those countries where social justice had some political priority, policy makers became more receptive to the longstanding demands from indigenous peoples that their languages receive more protection against the inroads of dominant languages, and that bilingual and bicultural forms of education were appropriate ways to do this.

In several places, notably in parts of the United States and Australia, policy makers were also persuaded to follow this new course because it seemed consistent with meeting other, fiscal policy aims (see reviews by Harris & Devlin, and by McCarty in Volume 5). Reducing the long-term costs of social programs that targeted the indigenous poor provided a real inducement. It had long been argued, for example, that the loss of their languages was a major contributing factor to the loss of community self-esteem among indigenous peoples. After the middle years of the twentieth century, the decline in indigenous language usage increased sharply when an international culture of capitalism, carried by a ubiquitous mass media, created pressures on aboriginal peoples everywhere to assimilate to outside norms and to conform, especially in their language usage and preferences.

The growing social anomie experienced by aboriginal peoples in many places, especially in remote settlements and in inner urban areas (see the review by Heimbecker in Volume 5), is clearly linked to the destructive and destabilizing inroads made into their cultures by a culture of capitalism promulgated through the mass media. But by treating this loss of self-esteem and social anomie only with costly social welfare programs, policy makers were ignoring the real causes of these conditions.

The demands for cultural and linguistic revival, along with the trend towards political devolution down to indigenous peoples, clans, tribes, and bands, gave policy makers some hope that the costs of social programs for aboriginal peoples might be gradually reduced in the long-term. On the evidence from several countries, policy makers may be correct in this aspiration. The once disempowered communities do begin to rise in esteem, in political influence, and also in economic self-sufficiency at the same time as the strengthening of their languages and cultures. Higher educational success rates follow, along with a concomitant increase in life chances. Where the local community becomes more in charge of the schooling process, and where their language is valued and used as a vehicle of instruction in their school, the entire program of schooling is directed towards elevating the status of the community and questioning the role of formal education in that process. Language questions become subsumed under much more important issues (Corson 1998).

In 1990 the various policies for bilingual and bicultural education developed in different countries received international support in the ILO convention on indigenous peoples. Articles 27 and 28 concern rights to independent forms of education and general language rights: "govern-ments shall recognise the right of these peoples to establish their own educational institutions and facilities . . . Children belonging to the peoples concerned shall, wherever practicable, be taught to read and write in their own indigenous language or in the language most commonly used by the group to which they belong" (ILO 1990: p. 16). This convention gave strong encouragement to governments to act more rigorously and justly in their language policies for indigenous peoples. But there are many places where the discriminatory language policies of the past continue, largely unchanged.

Some countries even repeat the worst and most shameful policies of the past. In the late twentieth century, the Kurdish peoples suffer various forms of linguistic oppression in the five countries that they inhabit as homelands. These include attempts in Iraq to eliminate the Kurds entirely as a people, even though they speak an official language of the country; and also legislation in Turkey forbidding the public use of the Kurdish languages and punishing that use in education (McDowall 1994; Skutnabb-Kangas & Bucak 1995; Havrest, 1997). Elsewhere tacit language policies that are tantamount to linguistic repression continue. In the Chiapas region of

Mexico, the Mayan peoples receive little official support for their languages in education even though more than 80% of the indigenous people speak their traditional languages and many speak nothing else.

Elsewhere in South and Central America, the languages of indigenous peoples get more supportive treatment in educational policies. Some Quechua-speaking children in the Peruvian Andes, for example, receive bilingual education in Quechua and Spanish. Their classroom opportunities and their general attitudes to schooling seem to contrast favourably with other Quechua children who are educated only in the dominant Spanish language (Hornberger 1988a, 1988b). Also, spanning national borders, indigenous children in the Amazon basin receive formal and informal bilingual and bicultural education aimed at meeting the linguistic and cultural rights of people largely ignored in the official policies of their respective governments (Trapnell 1996).

But other countries go much further in their policies. In Greenland, for example, the relatively greater autonomy and collective rights of the Inuit affect the relative strength and development of the Inuktitut language in that country. Because of the long and relatively balanced history of intercultural contacts in Greenland, its indigenous education system offers an important language policy model for aboriginal educational development elsewhere (Dorais 1992). The next section of this review examines other recent and current developments in countries that are exemplary in some way in their language policies for aboriginal peoples: Norway, New Zealand, Canada, and Australia.

WORK IN PROGRESS: PROBLEMS AND DIFFICULTIES

The four countries fall into two categories for discussion purposes: Norway and New Zealand are both countries where the indigenous people are relatively homogeneous in culture and language. But Canada and Australia are countries where there is great heterogeneity in the cultures and the languages of the indigenous peoples. So these two countries are rather constrained in their language policy development by the great diversity of the aboriginal languages that are still widely spoken or understood.

Norway's language policies, developed at national level for the Sámi peoples, are among the most comprehensive and the most effective in the world. Legislation giving major language and cultural rights to the Sámi, was enacted in 1992 (Magga 1995). Following Norway's ratification of the ILO convention on indigenous peoples (see above), its Parliament acted to strengthen official use of the three Sámi languages and to declare the Sámi languages and Norwegian as equal languages with equal status. The Sámi Language Act's stated purposes are to enable the Sámi to safeguard and develop their languages, culture, and way of life; and to give equal status to Sámi and Norwegian in all the countries laws and in all its people's social relations. A specific administrative area for the Sámi languages has been declared. A Sámi Language Council is being created. This will complement the work of the Sámi Education Council which already plays a major role in Sámi language education. Both bodies are to be administered by the Sámi Parliament, which in Norway has great independence of action in directing all Sámi affairs.

The Sámi Language Act provides the following for children living inside the Sámi area: the right to receive instruction in Sámi, or through the medium of Sámi in all subjects; parent or student choice in deciding whether pupils will receive instruction in or through Sámi; and the pos-sibility for children with Sámi as their mother tongue to be taught using the languages for all nine compulsory years of education (see the review by Balto & Todal in Volume 5). Outside the Sámi area, the following laws apply: instruction in or through Sámi is guaranteed for pupils with a Sámi background; anyone, regardless of background, has the right to be taught Sámi; and Sámi history and culture are included in national cur-riculum guidelines as topics that all children should become familiar with. As a result of these legal changes and the longstanding work of the Sámi Education Council, Norwegian schools offer a great range of bilingual education provisions that are already producing school graduates in the Sámi regions who are fully bilingual in their aboriginal language and in the national language. The status of the indigenous languages has risen noticeably, especially inside the areas officially declared as Sámi areas (Corson 1995). These formal provisions in Norway offer a guide to other countries planning similar developments.

New Zealand is a country without an official national policy for its Maori people and their language. The Maori language has been an official language of the country since 1987, and Maori is spoken with only minor dialectal differences throughout the country. Also Maori students make up 20% of the elementary school population, but few have Maori as their first language. While all these things would seem to allow for the easy drafting of a single language-in-education policy, only a draft discussion language policy has been developed and circulated (Waite 1992). The country's policy makers seem reluctant to endorse or give much recognition to this draft policy. Instead, New Zealand's language policies in education have evolved along with changes to education policies in general. These have gradually allowed many bilingual Maori/English elementary schools and monolingual Maori schools to develop. Maori communities and tribal groups have been quick to take advantage of these changes. Indeed most of the positive developments in Maori language policies in education have come from the efforts of the indigenous people themselves (see the review by Durie in Volume 5).

There are three developments in New Zealand education that are most significant for Maori language policy (Corson 1993). The first is the 'kohanga reo' or 'language nests' pre-school movement which began and developed with virtually no government sponsorship. Many Maori children begin in early infancy, and continue in these kohanga until they start school. The kohanga reo aims to recreate the atmosphere of a traditional Maori home. It has no formal structures except opening prayers, regular meal breaks, and occasional ceremonies to greet guests. While the kohanga has no structured curriculum and little equipment, there is plenty of singing and movement. The children create their own games but they are able to stay close to adults if they choose to, because there are always lots of adults taking part in activities, interacting with the children, and providing language and culture models. Beginning in the 1980s, the hundreds of kohanga reo send thousands of their graduates into state elementary schools. Many of the children are well on the way to active bilingualism and biculturalism, since they inevitably acquire English and the majority culture outside the language nests, where that culture's dominance is unchallenged.

The second response to Maori language rights was the creation of multi-ethnic schools that incorporate the values of various minority cultures into dominant culture educational values. Some of them have kohanga reo operating on the school premises (May 1994). In these elementary schools, the Maori language is used as the vehicle of instruction for some major part of the school day for children from Maori backgrounds or others who want a bilingual education in Maori and English. These schools are still few in number and do not always meet the language and culture demands of the Maori people themselves. New arrangements allow the establishment of separate Maori language and culture state-funded schools. These are becoming an integral part of the national pattern of schooling, spreading rapidly across New Zealand wherever Maori communities exist.

So the third important development is these 'kura kaupapa Maori' or 'Maori philosophy elementary schools'. National reforms in educational policy lent impetus to this movement by allowing small groups of people to establish their own state-funded schools. The kura respond to a passionately felt belief among many Maori that the European-style school system that has been their sole avenue to formal education for over a century within the state provided system, is not appropriate organizationally or pedagogically to the sustenance and the development of a Polynesian culture. For the pupils, being Maori in these schools is the norm. The school and classroom environment connects with the Maori home. Maori culture and language are central. At the same time, these schools are concerned to teach a modern, up-to-date, and relevant curriculum following national guidelines set by the state, whose outcome is the graduation of fully bilingual and bicultural students (Hingangaroa Smith 1995). Similarly patterned secondary schools will follow, and perhaps a Maori language and culture university on an equal footing with other universities in the country.

Canada is an officially bilingual country, but its two official languages are the languages of the colonizers: the French and the English. The many languages that give Canada's aboriginal peoples their identity have no official status in the country. Many of these languages are dying out, or they are already extinct. Only two Indian languages, Cree and Ojibway, and the Inuit language, Inuktitut, seem likely tó survive for much longer as widely used community languages. Quebec is the only province where a pattern of decline in aboriginal languages has been reversed. So its model of cooperation between aboriginal, federal, and provincial authorities seems to offer an important guide to other provinces. Elsewhere about a third of schools report an aboriginal language offered as a subject. But less than 4% of schools report using an aboriginal language as a medium of instruction. Most of these are inside the Arctic Circle where Inuktitut is used, but only in the elementary grades with the gradual introduction of English in later years (Kirkness & Bowman Selkirk 1992).

Because so much bilingual education research, looking mainly at French/English bilingualism, has been carried out in Canada, the country also offers important models for designing and implementing programs using aboriginal languages as vehicle and subject of instruction (see Corson & Lemay 1996). While these models are exemplary, they are also rather isolated and spread across the country. In general, they receive little coordination at provincial or national levels, depending often on the efforts of local aboriginal peoples themselves. There are few reports of evaluations of language-in-education programs developed as management tools to improve the quality and range of other programs across the country. An Aboriginal Language Policy Study (Assembly of First Nations 1988) called for the creation of policies to ensure the survival and revitalization of aboriginal languages across Canada. It mentions the desperate need for more resources and the need to develop a means for sharing information and materials, like an aboriginal language foundation to provide funds for language and education initiatives and to oversee developments.

Canada has a great need for careful and systematically managed language planning aimed at aboriginal language revival. At present the country has no such facility and none is in the planning stages, in spite of the release of the Report from the 'Royal Commission on Aboriginal Peoples' in 1996. This Report cost tens of millions of dollars to produce following extensive consultations over a five year period. Although that Report says much about language matters, its language recommendations are likely to be ignored because of the political priority that the French/English debate has in Canada.

Like Canada, Australia's language policies in education need to address many very different indigenous languages and huge distances that have to be dealt with in implementing educational reforms. The problem of the federal nature of both countries has been solved in Australian language policy making by having a single national coordinating body to oversee developments. And for a generation, an underlying trend in Australian language policy has been towards granting more formal recognition and implicit language rights to the country's Aboriginal peoples.

Much of the groundwork for this development was laid in the work of the National Aboriginal Languages Program (NALP) which raised expectations for more enduring reforms through its disbursement of funds for the preservation and development of Aboriginal and Torres Strait Islander languages. In the first four years of this program, more than 90 languages benefited, directly or indirectly. A formal review of the NALP was very positive about the program's overall benefits and its role in redressing the serious neglect of these languages. Its reported achievements included raising consciousness among teachers of the problems experienced by aboriginal first language speakers; increasing the self-esteem of aboriginal language speakers; winning greater public recognition for aboriginal languages; and improving student retention rates among first language speakers themselves (AACLAME 1990).

After the implementation of the National Aboriginal Education Policy in 1990, the disbursement of these NALP funds is now managed under the Aboriginal Education Assistance Act. But in Australia, as in Canada, there is no Commonwealth legislation giving some form of 'official language' status to Aboriginal and Torres Strait Islander languages, so the protection and development of the languages within their home territories is not easily guaranteed or promoted. This means that school policies are rather piecemeal in this area and vary greatly from district to district. Walsh observes of Australia's response to the decline of traditional languages: "Bilingual education is one possible solution to this legitimate concern. Regrettably there has been too little and most of it too late" (1991: pp. 47–48). There are notable successes, like "the outstandingly successful [Kriol/English] programme at Barunga school" (Harris 1991: p. 202). But where aboriginal first language schools do exist, mainly in parts of Northern Australia, the languages are used exclusively in the primary grades, with progressive transition to English as the goal (Romaine 1991; Fesl 1988).

In spite of national planning, very little is being done in Australia to remedy this situation at local levels (see the review by Harris & Devlin in Volume 5). The National Languages and Literacy Institute of Australia (NLLIA) does internationally noted work in many areas. But its mandate to provide for Aboriginal and Torres Strait Islander languages at the same time as meeting all its other functions, inevitably marginalizes that important function and takes it out of the hands of people with a real stake in the languages and the cultures that they support. Handicapped by the remoteness of the NLLIA in Canberra, and by the narrowness of the goals set for it in relation to aboriginal languages by politicians (NLLIA 1993), its future achievements can never approach the potential for unity of aboriginal educational purpose that the Sámi Education Council is realising, nor the legislated effectiveness and emancipatory reform already achieved by the Sámi Language Act. While the NALP tried to link its support for the strongest aboriginal languages with support for the most neglected, there has been a rapid and alarming decline in aboriginal language retention. While a few languages can be characterised as 'healthy', most of the surviving languages are 'weakening' or 'dying' (Dixon 1989).

FUTURE DIRECTIONS

Below I present some broad research and policy recommendations in point form. These suggest future policy directions that are already available in countries that lead the world in their indigenous language policy provisions:

- as overriding policy-making norms, nation states need to designate their aboriginal languages as official-languages, perhaps within appropriately specified districts, areas, or territories (as in Norway)
- aboriginal teacher education in purpose-designed colleges (on the Sámi model) needs to accompany extensions of bilingual and bicultural education
- aboriginal languages should be introduced as vehicles of instruction in schools wherever student numbers warrant
- as part of these reforms, the control of implementation processes should devolve down to local communities, boards, and schools
- where the languages are not the languages of daily communication, local aboriginal communities may need to begin the process of language revival by creating language and culture preschools (perhaps on the Maori model) staffed by fluent speakers of the language, where children are surrounded by an environment that is thoroughly congruent with the aboriginal culture
- within a few years of the successful introduction of preschool bilingual and bicultural education, local communities could move quickly towards creating aboriginal language monolingual, or bilingual and bicultural elementary schools with the eventual aim of extending these reforms to secondary and higher levels of education
- policy research evaluating the effectiveness of aboriginal language-in-education implementation needs high priority in countries with indigenous populations, so that the results can be used by communities elsewhere as models to learn from

86   DAVID CORSON

• coordinated language planning and officially supported policies are
  needed at national level to help revitalize those aboriginal languages
  that are under threat, to maintain and develop those capable of survival, and to foster and promote mother tongue education (perhaps
  using the model of the Sámi Education Council in Norway)

Ontario Institute for Studies in Education
University of Toronto
Canada

REFERENCES

AACLAME: 1990, *The National Policy on Languages: Report to the Minister for Em-
ployment, Education and Training by the Australian Advisory Council on Languages
and Multicultural Education*, Canberra.
Assembly of First Nations: 1988, *The Aboriginal Language Policy Study,* Assembly of
First Nations, Ottawa.
Corson, D.: 1993, *Language, Minority Education, and Gender: Linking Social Justice and
Power*, Multilingual Matters, Clevedon, Avon.
Corson, D.: 1995, 'Norway's "Sámi Language Act": Emancipatory implications for the
world's aboriginal peoples', *Language in Society* 24, 493–514.
Corson, D.: 1998, *Changing Education for Diversity*, Open University Press, London.
Corson, D. & Lemay, S.: 1996, *Social Justice and Language Policy in Education: The
Canadian Research*, OISE Press, Toronto.
Cummins, J.: 1984, *Bilingualism and Special Education: Issues in Assessment and Peda-
gogy*, Multilingual Matters, Clevedon, Avon.
Cummins, J. & Swain, M.: 1986, *Bilingualism in Education: Aspects of Theory, Research
and Practice*, Longman, London.
Dixon, R.: 1989, 'The original languages of Australia', *Vox* 3, 26–33.
Dorais, L.-J.: 1992, 'La situation linguistique dans l'arctique'. *Études Inuits Studies* 16,
237–255.
Fesl, E.: 1988, *Language Policy Formulation and Implementation: An Historical Per-
spective on Australian Languages*, PhD thesis, Monash University, Melbourne.
Harris, J.: 1991, 'Kriol - the creation of a new language', in S. Romaine (ed.), *Language
in Australia,* Cambridge University Press, Sydney.
Havrest, L.: 1997, *Sprachenpolitik für das Kurdische*, Passagenverlag Vienna.
Hingangaroa Smith, G.: 1995, 'Whakaoho Whanau: New formations of Whanau as
an innovative intervention into Maori cultural and educational crises', *He Pukenga
Korero: A Journal of Maori Studies* 1, 18–36.
Hornberger, N.: 1988a, 'Misbehaviour, punishment and put-down: Stress for Quechua
children in school', *Language and Education* 2, 239–253.
Hornberger, N.: 1988b, *Bilingual Education and Language Maintenance: A Southern
Peruvian Quechua Case*, Foris, Dordrecht.
International Labour Office (ILO): 1990, *ILO Convention Number 169 Concerning Indige-
nous and Tribal Peoples in Independent Countries*, The Hague.
Kirkness, V. & Bowman Selkirk, S.: 1992, *First Nations and Schools: Triumphs and
Struggles*, Canadian Education Association, Toronto.
Magga, O. H.: 1995, 'The Sámi Language Act', in T. Skutnabb-Kangas & R. Phillipson
(eds.), *Linguistic Human Rights: Overcoming Linguistic Discrimination*, Mouton de
Gruyter, Berlin, 219–233.

May, S.: 1994, *Making Multicultural Education Work*, Multilingual Matters, Clevedon, Avon.

McDowall. D.: 1994, *A Modern History of the Kurds*, I.B. Tauris, London.

NLLIA: 1993, *Workplan '93*, National Languages and Literacy Institute of Australia, Canberra.

Romaine, S.: 1989, *Bilingualism*, Basil Blackwell, Oxford.

Romaine, S.: 1991, *Language in Australia,* Cambridge University Press, Sydney.

Skutnabb-Kangas, T.: 1984, *Bilingualism or Not: The Education of Minorities*, Multilingual Matters, Philadelphia.

Skutnabb-Kangas, T. & Bucak, S.: 1995, 'Killing a mother tongue: How the Kurds are deprived of linguistic human rights', in T. Skutnabb-Kangas & R. Phillipson (eds.), *Linguistic Human Rights: Overcoming Linguistic Discrimination*, Mouton de Gruyter, Berlin, 347–370.

Skutnabb-Kangas, T. & Cummins, J.: 1988, *Minority Education: From Shame to Struggle,* Multilingual Matters, Clevedon, Avon.

Trapnell, L.: 1996, 'Brought together: Informal and formal education in an indigenous programme in the Amazon Basin', *International Jubilee Conference in Guovdageaidnu*, Sámi Education Council. Norway.

UNESCO: 1953, *The Use of Vernacular Languages in Education*, UNESCO, Paris.

Waite, J.: 1992, *Aoteareo: Speaking for Ourselves*, Learning Media, Wellington.

Walsh, M.: 1991, 'Overview of indigenous languages of Australia', in S. Romaine (ed.), *Language in Australia,* Cambridge University Press, Sydney.

JAN BRANSON AND DON MILLER

NATIONAL SIGN LANGUAGES AND LANGUAGE POLICIES

The development of national sign languages and of language policies
associated with national sign languages are both relatively recent, and
are products of the spread of nationalism, spurred on by national and
international movements in the fields of human rights and education. There
have, however, always been policies towards sign languages, policies
which have overtly or covertly been influenced by wider attitudes towards
language in general. These policies have often denied sign language the
status of languages and have in turn denied their users their full humanity.
The impact of philosophers of language on these policies towards sign
languages has often been profound, especially where speech has been
assumed to be synonymous with language.

Pre-Enlightenment policies towards sign languages were frequently
linked to religious practice. Membership of a community was almost
invariably membership of a religious community and that membership
hinged on effective religious practice. Where speech was assumed to be
central to this practice – for example saying the creed or taking confession
– and where signing was not regarded as the equivalent of speech, the
Deaf were often denied full communal membership and thus denied their
complete humanity. In the post-Enlightenment period, as detailed below,
although the impact of religious groups on the use of sign language has remained important, the primary focus of these language policies has shifted
to the sphere of education. Language policies in relation to education have
both overtly and covertly impacted on the use of sign language not only in
the education of the Deaf but in the wider community. Educational policies
have operated at times to accept the use of sign languages and to accord
them the status of languages, but have more often than not denigrated
these languages either by banning their use altogether or by transforming
them radically to serve as manually coded versions of the dominant spoken
language.

The key political issue in relation to policies on sign languages both in
education and beyond, continues to be a battle, on the one hand, between
signing and oralism (oralism referring to the position taken by those who
believe that all deaf people should learn to speak, lip-read and "hear"
[through the use of aids such as hearing aids or cochlear implants] in the
dominant language to the exclusion of sign language), and on the other
between the use of sign language and the use of manually coded versions

R. Wodak and D. Corson (eds), Encyclopedia of Language and Education,
Volume 1: Language Policy and Political Issues in Education, 89–98.
© 1997 Kluwer Academic Publishers. Printed in the Netherlands.

of the dominant spoken language. It must be added, however, that there are still sign languages which are not affected by these educationally-based policies, since one country may have many indigenous sign languages used by communities which have not come under the impact of national or even regional language policies (see, for example, Branson, Miller & Marsaja 1996).

Sign languages, like all fully-fledged languages, are natural languages that develop through their use for communication within communal contexts. Signing communities might be residential localised communities or dispersed networks of people, and, since sign languages are unwritten languages, the boundaries of their sign languages are defined by the boundaries of their communal activity. The concept of a national sign language is therefore, with a few exceptions where nations are small enough or young enough for their communities to be at the same time national communities, primarily a political concept, possibly a political aspiration. The degree to which sign language users within a nation state use a common sign language will depend on the effectiveness of national networks within the Deaf community, on the impact of national sign language based education, and on the impact on Deaf communities of formal research into, and the associated standardisation of and teaching of, a national sign language.

The promotion and indeed the development of national sign languages, as distinct from more localised community sign languages, is associated with four basic movements: the development of national associations of Deaf people; the drive for the achievement of linguistic rights as an aspect of human rights; the development of formal language policies; and the drive for national education systems with sign language as the medium of instruction. This nationalism is manifested in the drive for the publication of national sign language dictionaries. As the World Federation of the Deaf report on the status of sign languages reveals, no country has a dictionary for more than one sign language. Of the 43 countries surveyed, only six did not have sign language dictionaries, but all the rest had only one, a national sign language dictionary. The dictionaries themselves embody not only the symbolic representation of a language and thus its recognition, but also the standardisation of language, the move towards linguistic purity that is a feature of literate languages (see Edwards 1985: p. 27ff). Assumptions about the unitary nature of national spoken and written languages are transferred to the way that sign languages are in turn conceptualised. National sign languages are not only formally standardised and developed through the publication of dictionaries and sign language teaching manuals but are also assumed to exist. An understanding of the concept of a national sign language and of the social, cultural and linguistic dynamics involved in their development, therefore requires reference to literature on nationalism itself. Here the work of Ben Anderson (1991) is particularly pertinent, with its focus on the forces that have created these "imagined communities". As Anderson points out, the nation assumes the status of a community, encompassing and transforming traditional communities, claiming the loyalties and orientations that were formerly afforded the village, the lineage, the clan, the tribe, the neighbourhood.

SIGN LANGUAGES AND EDUCATIONAL POLICIES

As indicated above, since the Enlightenment, it has been educational policy which has exerted the greatest influence on policies towards sign languages. The development of national sign languages and the history of language policies associated with those languages is therefore an integral part of the history of the education of deaf people in the West. It is also through an examination of the use of sign languages in deaf education that the impact of dominant hearing communities and their languages on the use of "signing" is revealed, initially in the late nineteenth century through the overt banning of sign language use in school, associated with the denial of the linguistic status of sign languages, as well as later, from the 1960s, through the development and promotion of manually coded versions of national spoken and written languages in formal education. Manually coded versions of national spoken and written languages – such as Signed English, Signed Swedish, Signed French, Signed Thai, and Signed Indonesian – have been, and still often are, promoted as national sign languages, particularly by hearing professionals associated with the education of the deaf, who believe that the acquisition of literacy in the national (spoken and written) language occurs most effectively through the use of manually-coded versions of that national (spoken and written) language.

These signed versions of dominant languages are neither fully fledged languages of communication nor natural languages, but rather manual codes based on written forms of language, using "frozen signs" – a single unchanging sign for each word or morpheme – and thus making little use of the dynamic and creative features of sign languages. While some signs in natural sign languages are "frozen signs", much of the lexicon is a productive lexicon – signs change and develop in response to the meaning being generated, utilising a range of conventions of transformation based on handshapes, the use of space, the face and body. Associated with the use of a productive lexicon is the extensive use of classifiers. These dynamic aspects of sign language lexicons contrast starkly with manually coded versions of sound-based languages.

In those non-Western countries which have developed Western-style educational systems, educational policy has also been the forum in which national policies towards sign languages have been developed. In these cases policies have often been strongly influenced by Western experts, especially Western teachers of the deaf, who have taken a direct role in the development of national policies towards sign languages, frequently in the development of manually-coded versions of the national spoken language, for example, Signed Thai and Signed Indonesian, which are then assumed to be the national sign language.

EARLY DEVELOPMENTS

Most early policies developed by default. While there is evidence of the Deaf being taught through the medium of natural sign languages to read and write, first in Latin and later in the languages of everyday life, from well before the so-called Enlightenment, it is from the sixteenth century that educators emerge throughout Europe intent on teaching "the Deaf and Dumb" (privileged children of merchants and the nobility) not only to read and write but to speak. They paid little attention to existing sign languages but rather developed systems of fingerspelling designed for the purposes of speech training. Fingerspelling increasingly became associated with the manual representation of the dominant written language, rather than with the normal processes of borrowing between languages.

As the education of the Deaf moved beyond the very exclusive instruction of the nobility to the development of education for the poor deaf, the impact of national languages on the Deaf became more extreme. In the mid-eighteenth century, in 1755, the Abbé de l'Epée established a school for poor Deaf children in Paris (see Lane 1988). While teaching the deaf children to speak was one of his educational aims, particularly in the beginning, he moved away from speech training as central to the education of the deaf towards the use of signing as a means for teaching the deaf pupils to read and write. But he did not use the two-handed alphabet in use among the Parisian Deaf communities and did not use existing sign languages with their distinctive syntax as the language of instruction. Rather he used the one-handed alphabet and developed a system of signed French. The die had been cast. While other educators in other times and places – Castberg in Denmark, Bébian in France later – used natural sign languages to a greater or lesser degree – often with a lot of fingerspelling – and did not necessarily develop manually coded versions of the written language, hearing educators constantly tampered with the signing traditions of their pupils, subordinating and severely restricting their lexicon to the demands of spoken and written languages, some insisting on the possibility of signing and speaking at the same time. The widespread use of signing of various kinds throughout the eighteenth and nineteenth centuries, gave way on an almost universal scale from the late nineteenth century to the partial or complete banning of signing in schools and a dedication to oralism – teaching deaf people to speak and lip read the dominant spoken language. In Milan in 1880, an international conference of teachers of the deaf voted overwhelmingly to ban the use of sign language in the education of the deaf (see Lane 1988). By this single vote, the national policies of virtually all Western countries towards sign languages were effectively determined – sign languages were banned and their linguistic status denied. The climb back to linguistic and educational rights for the Deaf was a hard one.

From the late 1960s, the use of signing, albeit often manually coded versions of the dominant spoken language, emerged again in opposition to oralism. Today, the drive throughout much, but by no means all, of the world, is for the use of natural sign languages in a bilingual educational system (see in particular Ahlgren & Hylenstam 1994 and also the review by Gibson, Small & Mason in Volume 5). These bilingual policies are again linked to the transformation of national policies. Where bilingual deaf education is promoted, the wider national recognition of sign languages as viable communal languages tends to be found. In Sweden, Denmark, Finland, Venezuela and Uruguay, for example, bilingual education with sign languages as the primary mode of instruction are national policy, supported by state-run programs for the teaching of sign language to pre-school children and their families. Comprehensive international data on national policies towards sign languages has yet to be collected and collated. A survey by Gloria Pullen and Lesley Jones (1990) of policies towards Deaf people in eleven European countries clearly showed that government policies towards Deaf people and their languages were, with the exception of the one Scandinavian country in the survey, Denmark, governed by their perception of Deaf people as disabled rather than as a linguistic minority.

WORK IN PROGRESS

Most of the current research into, and commentary on, national sign languages and language policies is conducted under the auspices of international and national associations of the Deaf. Examples are discussed below. The best known work on the history of policies and practices relating to the use of sign language in the education of the Deaf in Western societies, with a particular focus on France and the United States, is Harlan Lane's *When the Mind Hears* (Lane 1988), complemented by Lane's treatment of the marginalization of the Deaf in the West in his *The Mask of Benevolence* (Lane 1992). Comprehensive linguistic research into sign languages is relatively recent, and is associated with a small but very active international community of scholars, with research results published through a few specialised journals and in books based on international conferences (for details of linguistic research see the review by Branson & Miller in Volume 8). Much current writing on the relationship between language policies and educational policies, as they relate to the Deaf, is to be found in proceedings of national and international conferences of teachers of the deaf. International Congresses on Education of the Deaf are held every five years and although they have moved far beyond the complete intolerance of sign languages evident at their congress in Milan in 1880, they still include very few Deaf people. A large proportion of the papers reprinted in their proceedings are still devoted to papers advocating either pure oralism in deaf education or the use of manually coded versions of the national spoken and written language (for example see Taylor 1988).

Linguistic research has played an important part in questioning the use of manually coded versions of spoken languages in Deaf education (see in particular Johnson, Liddle & Erting 1989), providing support to the demands of Deaf communities for the use of their natural sign languages. Examples of this process are well documented for Sweden in Bergman and Wallin (1990), particularly the interweaving of research and the Deaf community organisations in the development and promotion of Swedish Sign Language, to the point where the right of Deaf people to education through Swedish Sign Language was officially recognised by the Swedish parliament in 1981. The current issue of bilingual education for the Deaf with a sign language as the prime medium of instruction is the focus for an increasing amount of research (see in particular Bouvet 1990; Hansen 1990; Ahlgren & Hylenstam 1994; Branson & Miller 1991, 1993; Lewis 1995; Mahshie 1995; Heiling 1995). Specific discussion of the policies and practices relating to the use of sign languages in Canada, with reference also to the United States, is to be found in Corson and Lemay (1996).

SIGN LANGUAGES AND LINGUISTIC RIGHTS

Today, as throughout much of their history, Deaf communities themselves are the prime movers in the establishment of linguistic rights for the Deaf, particularly in education, and are, in the process, the driving force for the recognition not only of sign languages but of national sign languages. These principles and orientations are succinctly stated in the "Recommendations of the Commission on Sign Language" of the World Congress of the World Federation of the Deaf held in Tokyo in 1991 (*Proceedings of XI World Congress of the World Federation of the Deaf* (nd): pp. 50–53). They call for:

- the recognition and right to use sign languages;
- the right of Deaf children to have access to and education through sign languages as their first languages;
- the teaching of sign languages to parents of Deaf children and to all teachers of the Deaf with the national sign language (sic) as an academic subject;

- the promotion and funding of sign language research by governments with the active involvement at all stages of Deaf people;
- the expansion of sign language instruction;
- the promotion of effective sign language interpreting and of effective access to interpreting for Deaf people;
- and for governments to support the availability of the media through sign language.

In relation to the rights of Deaf children to sign language as a first language and to education through sign language, the Commission on Sign Language states:

A. A Sign language should be recognized and treated as the first language of a Deaf child.

   a) The Sign language in question must be the national Sign language, that is, the natural Sign language of the adult Deaf community in that region. (Proceedings . . . : p. 50)

They continue, in relation to the education of Deaf children:

B. Deaf children have the right to be educated, particularly with regard to reading and writing, in a bilingual (or multilingual) environment.

   a) The national Sign language should be the language of instruction for most academic subjects. (Proceedings . . . : p. 50)

PROBLEMS AND DIFFICULTIES

Recommendations, like the policies they stimulate, are therefore framed in terms of "national" sign languages. The pressures for the development of national sign languages are well illustrated by the example of the recently compiled Dictionary of Southern African Signs for Communication with the Deaf (Penn 1992). The signs illustrated there come from at least twelve cultural regions, from twelve distinct communities with distinct natural sign languages, and yet, in one of the prefaces to the first volume, Timothy Reagan states,

   A beginning has now been made to record the beauty and diversity of South African Sign Language . . . Needed as well are studies of the syntax of South African Sign Language in its many forms, . . . This is a formidable challenge, but it is one that the South African Deaf community is more than capable of meeting. (Penn 1992: p. xi).

The slip from the recognition of the diversity and multilingual nature of the South African Deaf, of the many Deaf communities in South Africa, into a unitary orientation towards "South African Sign Language" and "the South African Deaf community", both in the singular, is symptomatic of the approach taken by governments, linguists, and linguistic rights activists alike. Linguists in particular are involved in the standardisation of sign languages towards "national" variants – British Sign Language, American Sign Language, South African Sign Language, etc. – each with a dictionary.

The drive for the recognition of sign languages as "national" sign languages thus poses a conundrum. The recognition of sign languages involves:

- the assertion by national Deaf associations of the existence of national sign languages;
- the drive for formal recognition of these languages as national sign languages; and
- the demand for and the development of education through these respective languages for all Deaf people nationally.

But the assertion and recognition of national sign languages can lead to the failure to recognise the existence of minority sign languages in precisely the same way as the assertion and promotion of national spoken and written languages leads to the oppression and suppression of minority spoken and written languages (see the review by Corson on policies for non-standard varieties, in this volume). And yet the recognition of the sign languages of the majority is an enormous and vital, even revolutionary, step forward for Deaf communities throughout the world. This is a conundrum posed by nationalism itself.

FUTURE DIRECTIONS

The search for a solution to this conundrum demands the integration of research on sign languages with current research on minority language rights (see Skutnabb-Kangas & Phillipson 1994 and the reviews by Skutnabb-Kangas, and by Phillipson in this volume). Multilingual solutions involving national and local sign languages as well as literacy in the dominant national spoken language must be considered. Moves of this kind are under way in some countries, especially where they are asserting the need for the use of local sign languages in education rather than the use of imported Western sign languages such as American Sign Language, as has frequently been the case (see for example, de Carpentier 1995). Models of bilingual education which assume that a national sign language does or can exist need to be complemented with multilingual models which recognise that sign languages are both natural and face to face languages and that it is local languages that must be used. Whether or not national sign languages will emerge is dependent on the networks of effective communication that can also be developed. Towards this end, the sociolinguistics of sign languages is moving towards the study of localised rather than national sign languages, studied within their distinct social and cultural contexts (Johnson 1994; Branson, Miller & Marsaja 1996).

La Trobe University
Australia

and

Monash University
Australia

REFERENCES

Ahlgren, I: 1990, 'Sign language in deaf education', in S. Prillwitz & T. Vollhaber (eds.), *Sign Language Research and Application: Proceedings of the International Congress, Hamburg, 1990*, Signum Press, Hamburg, 91–94.

Ahlgren, I & Hylenstam, K. (eds.): 1994, *Bilingualism in Deaf Education*, Signum Press, Hamburg.

Anderson, B: 1991, *Imagined Communities: reflections on the origin and spread of nationalism*, Verso, London.

Bergman, B. & Wallin, L.: 1990, 'Sign language research and the deaf community', in S. Prillwitz & T. Vollhaber (eds.), *Sign Language Research and Application: Proceedings of the International Congress, Hamburg, 1990*, Signum Press, Hamburg, 187–214.

Bouvet, D.: 1990, *The Path to Language: Bilingual Education for Deaf Children*, Multilingual Matters, Clevedon.

Branson, J. & Miller, D.: 1991, 'Language and identity in the Australian deaf community: Australian sign language and language policy. An issue of social justice', in T. Liddicoat (ed.), *Language planning and language policy in Australia, Australian Review of Applied Linguistics* S8., 135–176.

Branson, J. & Miller, D.: 1993, 'Sign language, the deaf, and the epistemic violence of mainstreaming', *Language and Education* 7(1), 21–41.

Branson, J., Miller, D., & Marsaja, G: 1996, 'Everyone here speaks sign language too: A deaf village in Bali, Indonesia – An initial report', in C. Lucas (ed.), *Multicultural Aspects of Sociolinguistics in Deaf Communities*, Gallaudet University Press, Washington D.C.

Corson, D. & Lemay, S.: 1996, *Social Justice and Language Policy in Education: The Canadian Research*, OISE Press, Ontario.

de Carpentier, A. L.: 1995, 'Deaf education in developing countries', paper presented at the *18th International Congress on Education of the Deaf*, Tel Aviv.

Edwards, J.:1985, *Language, Society, and Identity*, Basil Blackwell, Oxford.

Hansen, B.: 1990, 'Trends in the progress towards bilingual education for deaf children in Denmark', in S. Prillwitz & T. Vollhaber (eds.), *Sign Language Research and Application: Proceedings of the International Congress, Hamburg, 1990*, Signum Press, Hamburg, 51–62.

Heiling, K.: 1995, *The Development of Deaf Children: Academic Achievement Levels and Social Processes*, Signum Press, Hamburg.

Johnson, Robert E. (1994) 'Sign language and the concept of deafness in a traditional Yucatec Mayan village', in C. Erting et. al. (eds.), *The Deaf Way*, Gallaudet University Press, Washington, D.C., 102–109.

Johnson, R., Liddle, S., & Erting, C.: 1989, *Unlocking the Curriculum: Principles for achieving access in deaf education*, Gallaudet University Press, Washington, D.C.

Lane, H.: 1988, *When the Mind Hears: A History of the Deaf*, Penguin Books, Har-
    mondsworth.
Lane, H.: 1992, *The Mask of Benevolence: Disabling the Deaf Community*, Alfred A.
    Knopf, New York.
Lewis, W. (ed.): 1995, *Bilingual Teaching of Deaf Children in Denmark – Description of
    a Project 1982–1992*, Døveskolernes Materialecenter, Aalborg.
Mahshie, S.N.: 1995, *Educating Deaf Children Bilingually – with Insights and Applications
    from Sweden and Denmark*, Gallaudet University, Washington D.C.
Penn, C.: 1992, *Dictionary of Southern African Signs for Communicating with the Deaf*,
    Human Sciences Research Council.
*Proceedings of XI World Congress of the World Federation of the Deaf, Tokyo, Japan 2–11
    July 1991* (nd), World Federation of the Deaf, Tokyo.
Pullen, G. & Jones, L.: 1990, 'Social policy survey of deaf people in Europe', in J. Kyle
    (ed.), *Deafness and Sign Language into the 1990's: Ongoing Research Work in the
    Bristol Programme*, Deaf Studies Trust, Bristol.
Skutnabb-Kangas, T. & R. Phillipson (eds.): 1994, *Linguistic Human Rights: Overcoming
    Linguistic Discrimination*, Mouton de Gruyter, Berlin.
Taylor, I.G. (ed.): 1988, *The Education of the Deaf: Current Perspectives. Papers Pre-
    sented at the International Congress on Education of the Deaf 4–9 August, 1985
    University of Manchester*, Croom Helm, London.
World Federation of the Deaf: 1994, *Report on the Status of Sign Languages*, World
    Federation of the Deaf.

DAVID CORSON

NON-STANDARD VARIETIES AND EDUCATIONAL POLICY

Formal educational policies for the treatment of non-standard varieties in schools are conspicuous by their absence in most educational systems. Where they do exist, their net effect is usually to strengthen the position of the standard variety in formal education (see Poulson, Radmor & Turner-Bisset 1996). Yet in any language community, including all monolingual societies, there is a range of non-standard varieties that is used by closely knit social or ethnic groups. These varieties are brought into the work of the school in one way or another. Children coming from these backgrounds often possess two or more varieties which they use in their everyday language, perhaps one variety used in the home, another in the peer group, and a third in the school. Largely as a result of the school's influence, this last variety may come to be very close to the standard variety.

At the same time, many children arrive in schools with little or no contact with the more standard variety used as the language of formal education. Often these children are penalized for having a language variety that is different from the linguistic capital that has high status in the school (Corson 1998). So the absence of formal policies supporting non-standard varieties actually creates a tacit language policy that legitimizes the standard variety, creating a paradoxical situation for non-standard language users: They come to believe that non-possession of the standard variety is no excuse for not using it.

The non-standard language of socially marginalized people is also often used unjustly as 'a mirror' to their potential for achievement and to their worth as human beings. This occurs in any stratified society where many variations in vocabulary, syntax, accent and discourse style are socially marked, so that even a basic communicative exchange between individuals gives evidence that other people tend to use stereotypically to judge people's place in the social structure. In this review, I use the term 'language variety' to cover any standard or non-standard form of a language, whether a geographical or social dialect, a patois, a creole, or some other code of a language. I examine the roots of the common prejudices about non-standard varieties and suggest policy directions that schools and school systems might take in softening this form of linguistic discrimination that affects non-standard users everywhere.

R. Wodak and D. Corson (eds), Encyclopedia of Language and Education,
Volume 1: Language Policy and Political Issues in Education, 99–109.
© *1997 Kluwer Academic Publishers. Printed in the Netherlands.*

EARLY DEVELOPMENTS

The history of prejudice against the users of non-standard varieties of a dominant language is probably as long as the history of language itself. It is certain that the Ancient Greeks used the evidence of different Greek dialects as a way of stereotyping other Greeks. In fact, their wars with one another tended to be fought by armies allied by dialect, in spite of the fact that all the Greek city states used different varieties of the same language. At the same time, foreigners living as immigrants in Athens were often the target of public mockery for the different regional varieties of Greek that they brought with them, or for the different social varieties that they developed while learning Attic Greek as a second language. Aristophanes, the comic playwright, regularly drew his humour from poking fun at different dialects, in much the same way as modern music hall performers and less sophisticated television comedians still do.

"Speech is a mirror to the soul: As a people speak, so are they". This harsh judgment, made by the playwright Publilius Cyrus in the Roman world, did not die with that world. The prejudice against the non-standard varieties of marginalized groups continues today. In some places it is supported by official policies. For example, over several centuries in France, the Académie Française has directed its efforts towards maintaining the 'purity' of the French standard variety. And this has a direct impact on French schooling (see the review by Christ on pages 1–11 of this volume). Claudine Dannequin (1987) describes very young students who are non-standard speakers of French as 'gagged children' in their own classrooms ('les enfants bâillonnés'). Through its purifying practices, the Académie has lent institutional support in French education to what I call an 'ideology of correctness' (Corson 1993). Elsewhere, standard Spanish and Portuguese varieties are similarly elevated (Telles 1996; Bortoni-Ricardo 1985), sometimes with negative consequences for the speakers of kindred varieties. Also in eastern and central Europe, the role of national or other dominant varieties, especially varieties of German, has received much attention in the literature (Ammon 1972; Oevermann 1972; Pollack 1973; Wodak 1975; Wodak & de Cillia 1995). And the speakers of aboriginal languages, in many places, often develop under-valued new varieties to facilitate communication with the users of more dominant languages (see the reviews by Khubchandani, and by Harris & Devlin, both in Volume 5).

The role of the State has been central in maintaining an ideology of correctness. It is governments that legitimize a particular form of language by making it obligatory on official occasions and in official settings, like schools, public administration, and political institutions. This prestigious form of language, as Pierre Bourdieu (1981) has pointed out, then becomes the standard variety against which all other linguistic practices are measured, including especially the practices sanctioned in schools. Although similar practices are put in place by nation states almost everywhere, in the wider societies of the English-speaking world, except in England itself, this ideology of correctness has been declining in recent decades (Herriman & Burnaby 1996), especially in those countries where non-standard varieties have never been stigmatized or socially marked to the degree that they are in Britain. At the same time official documents for England and Wales have given renewed status in education to the standard variety, on grounds deriving less from the class prejudices of the past and more from other arguments (DES 1985, 1988, 1989). Moreover discrimination against a range of non-standard varieties is easily disguised in other countries, even in a country like Canada that prides itself on its reputation for linguistic tolerance (Corson & Lemay 1996).

MAJOR CONTRIBUTIONS TO NON-STANDARD/STANDARD POLICY THEORY

Three key theorists have contributed to our understanding of the place of non-standard varieties in educational policy: Pierre Bourdieu, Basil Bernstein, and William Labov (Corson 1995). Bourdieu's earlier experiences as an ethnographer (in francophone parts of North Africa) inform all his work and his conclusions. He argues that all forms of power that impose meanings in such a way as to legitimate those meanings and conceal the relations that underlie the exercise of power itself, add their own specifically symbolic force to those relations of power. In this way, dominant ideas reinforce the power of the same forces exercising it. He sees the culture of education as a creation of the dominant culture, which is a culture that automatically works to sanction its own language varieties.

Bourdieu's special term 'habitus' names a system of rather durable dispositions at the core of a person's behaviour. He argues that the habitus shared by members of dominant groups permeates every aspect of formal education. This limits the educational opportunities of people from non-dominant groups, because the school demands competence in the dominant language and culture which can readily be acquired only through family upbringing. While education might not openly stress this culture, it implicitly demands it through its definitions of success. So groups who are capable of transmitting through the family the habitus necessary for the reception of the school's messages, come to monopolize the system of schooling. Those with alternative dispositions have little purchase on the culture of education, or on the social rewards that that culture makes available.

Bourdieu's ideas here rest not on some notion of linguistic deficit that can be linked in turn to levels of syntactic or verbal complexity of utterances. Rather he argues from the different types of relations to their sociocultural backgrounds that different sociocultural groups possess, relations which are themselves embedded in different sets of dispositions and attitudes towards the material world and towards other people. He introduced the phrase 'cultural capital' (Bourdieu 1966) to describe those culturally esteemed advantages that people acquire as a part of their life experiences, their peer group contacts, and their family backgrounds: such things as 'good taste', 'style', certain kinds of knowledge, abilities, and the presentation of self. Bourdieu sees 'linguistic capital' as the key part of the cultural heritage. But this linguistic capital is more than the competence to produce grammatically well formed expressions and language forms. It also includes the ability to utilize appropriate norms for language use, including the language variety and style considered 'appropriate' in a given setting, and to produce the 'right' expressions at the right time for a particular context of situation.

Bourdieu argues that while the cultural or linguistic capital that is valued in education is not equally available to people from different backgrounds, education everywhere still operates as if everyone had equal access to it. By basing its assessments of success and failure on people's possession of this high status capital, education reproduces the sociocultural arrangements that create the situation in the first place. And the members of some sociocultural groups come to believe that their educational failure, rather than coming from their lowly esteemed sociocultural status, results from their natural inability: their lack of giftedness. They wrongly come to believe that social and cultural factors are somehow neutralized in the educational selection process and that the process itself is a fair one, based on objective educational criteria.

Bernstein's position within this sociology of language has similarities to Bourdieu's position, and he also offers a complex sociological and philosophical argument. Like Bourdieu too, his theories have been misinterpreted by some who take pieces out of the theories and critique them away from their original meaning system. In fact, Bernstein's early work seemed to lend itself to this kind of misinterpretation, and it had a largely unhelpful impact on educational debates. Yet he says that his project was always a clear one (Bernstein 1990): He tried to show how people from different class positions differ in the ways that they categorize and conceptually order the world. And it is only within this essentially sociological theory that Bernstein became concerned with language. His interest in contexts, meaning systems, and the different orientations to the world that go with them, encouraged him to look for linguistic evidence of these differences. This led to the famous misunderstanding that he has been at pains to correct:

> What is at stake is not the issue of the intrinsic nature of different varieties of language but different modalities of privileged meanings, practices and social relations which act selectively

upon shared linguistic resources ... Educational failure (official
pedagogic failure) is a complex function of the official transmission system of the school and the local acquisition process of the
family/peer group/community (1990: p. 114).

This position seems very close to Bourdieu's. As far as non-standard
varieties are concerned, the linguistic evidence that Bernstein and his
associates gathered was used only illustratively to present his central idea
of 'code': "a regulative principle, tacitly acquired, which selects and
integrates relevant meanings, forms of realizations, and evoking contexts"
(1990: p. 101).

Although Bernstein's concern with standard and non-standard varieties
of language was only an incidental interest at most, his work attracted the
ire of linguists in particular. Linguists tend to believe, as a logical principle,
that all languages and language varieties are equal. Since he seemed to offer
evidence of 'inequality between varieties', Bernstein earned the hostility
of linguists who found their rallying point in the work of the American
descriptive linguist, William Labov.

Labov's studies comparing Black American and Puerto Rican vernaculars of English, and other varieties (1966, 1972a), offered many original
insights. In particular, he found that people from different sociocultural
backgrounds speak different kinds of English that in all important respects
deviate systematically and regularly from each other. His findings helped
overturn the common stereotype that these and many other varieties of language are incorrect forms of a language. Rather, he was able to show that
non-standard varieties have their own norms and rules of use. Accordingly
they deserve respect and valuation, although the institution of education
itself, as a standard and routine practice, disvalues varieties that are very
different from the dominant norm.

Labov (1972b) successfully argued that there is no real basis for attribut-
ing poor performance to the grammatical and phonological characteristics of any non-standard variety of English. But the status of vocabulary
in Labov's account is left open. He explicitly allowed that certain key
aspects of words and their meanings, including mastery of the very different morphosemantic features of Latinate words in English, may be
critical attainments for educational success (1972b). Studies of the lexico-
semantic range of adolescents from different sociocultural and language
backgrounds suggest that Labov's guardedness on the matter of vocabulary
was justified (Corson 1995). Clearly educational experience, and language
experience itself, are vital factors in shaping lexico-semantic range and
access to the cultural meaning systems that schools try to disseminate.

Labov was also a protagonist in a celebrated court case that took place
in Ann Arbor, Michigan. As part of its judgment in favour of parents, the
court required teachers of minority children to take a course of in-service
training in sociolinguistics (Labov 1982). In this case, the parents of

African American children had brought an action against a school, alleging that their children were failing because they were wrongly labelled 'educationally disabled' on the basis of their use of an African American non-standard variety. But it was found that the language variety used by the children, in itself, was in no sense an obstacle to their success. Rather, the expectations of pupil success that teachers held, based on their stereotypes about that variety (see my review in Volume 6), led the school as a whole to misperceive the children's real potential, thus causing them to fail. The children were deemed to be deficient in educational potential because their language variety was wrongly judged to be deficient in the context of the school (see reviews by Baugh in this volume and in Volume 8). Generalising on this point, much of the blame for misjudgments of this kind is due to simple ignorance among people about the range of varieties that can and do co-exist in a single linguistic space.

FUTURE POLICY DIRECTIONS: PROBLEMS AND DIFFICULTIES

The work of language-in-education theorists (Barnes, Britton & Rosen 1969; Britton 1970; and Rosen & Rosen 1973), coupled with Labov's findings, prompted official recognition of the need to give fairer treatment to non-standard varieties in education. This is best evidenced in the Bullock Report (DES 1975) in Britain. This policy document recommended that schools should begin to value whatever language variety children bring with them to school, while adding to it, in every case, those other forms, functions, styles, and registers that are necessary acquisitions for educated people to make. This watershed document prompted a search for ways to make teachers more aware of their own prejudices about non-standard varieties, and more aware of the range of varieties that do co-exist in monolingual societies. More recently the idea emerged that students and teachers need to become much more *critically* aware of language varieties, especially of their role in activating prejudices and stereotypes.

Yet most policy recommendations offered about the difficult issue of valuing non-standard varieties in the classroom are either statements about what not to do, or statements that side-step the issue entirely. For example, the Kingman Report into the Teaching of English (DES 1988) in Britain places a proper stress on 'historical and geographical variation' but curiously ignores social and cultural variation, perhaps in the vain hope that these latter varieties of English will disappear if they are ignored. And schools almost everywhere still uncritically uphold the ideology of correctness. Moreover both beginning and experienced teachers admit that they deliberately exclude non-standard varieties from their classrooms as a routine practice (see Blair [1986] for Canada and Australia; Telles [1996] for Brazil; but see Smitherman [1992] for the United States, and also my review in Volume 6).

As a result children who use non-standard varieties still often see the standard variety that is valued in schools as the model of excellence against which their own varieties are measured. It is 'correct', while their own varieties are 'less correct' (or more commonly 'just do not exist'). This readiness of non-standard language users to stigmatize their own variety means that as children and later as adults, they often condemn themselves to silence in public settings for fear of offending norms that work against them in ways that they themselves sanction. Using Bourdieu's metaphor, there are many linguistic markets in which they assign a limited value to their own speech. They are either silent within those 'markets' or they withdraw from them. In the middle and upper levels of education, both of these responses from children of low-income and socially marginalized backgrounds are common.

So what should the policy be? Can school systems justify maintaining a ubiquitous but largely tacit policy that gives high status to the standard variety? If so, can the obvious inequities of that policy be softened in some way? Many do argue for a guaranteed central place for the standard variety in education. It is also clear that teachers themselves agree that all children should have access to standard forms of the language (Poulson, Radmor & Turner-Bisset 1996). In fact most teachers rarely associate the standard variety with any particularly privileged section of society. For them, it is no more than the standard language of the school, whose actual mastery is a correlate of school success. While people disagree about how this mastery of the standard variety might be provided, the standard increasingly gets preference not because of its 'correctness' but because of what many see as its more general 'appropriateness'.

Christopher Winch (1989) distinguishes criteria of 'appropriateness' in language use from the criteria of 'correctness' that firm rules provide. In defending the use of the standard variety for teaching purposes, school policy makers have a better case, according to Winch, if they argue from the appropriateness of the standard variety, across a wide range of contexts, rather than from its correctness. On the other hand, Norman Fairclough (1992) asks teachers and others to think carefully about what people mean when they use this word 'appropriateness' to discuss the respective place of standard and non-standard varieties in schools. He sees the idea of 'appropriateness' itself as a compromise that allows the standard variety to maintain its position of prestige, thus confusing sociolinguistic reality with ideology. There is real merit to Fairclough's view, but while its pros and cons are debated in local contexts, schools still have to get on with the job of teaching a language-based curriculum that uses a language variety as its pedagogical vehicle. The choice of the standard variety is very largely determined for teachers by the practices that they inherit from their pedagogical predecessors and by the policy decisions of their political masters. Often at most, they can work to reform systemic injustices in language policies by nudging them in more socially just directions. I suggest ways of doing this below, and more fully in my review in Volume 6.

While an argument based on correctness would seem to fail, the appropriateness argument has some logical support, and in most contexts is supported by justice claims, as well as on the following more pragmatic grounds. A standard variety of a language that is really widely used seems to provide a more effective means of communication than non-standard varieties because it has appropriateness across a much greater range of contexts and people. It is far more acceptable from a practical viewpoint, in that it meets the acquired interests and expectations of many groups, rather than just the interests of its more particular speakers. There are other practical advantages identified by Winch (1989) and by Gramsci (1948: cited in Corson [1995]). If the standard variety is associated historically with the written language, access to it is empowering for individuals in the acquisition of literacy. If it has traditionally been the language of higher and technical education, access to it may give easier access to the technical registers of scientific and academic discourse. If that standard variety is both a national and an international variety, access to it is empowering in all those contexts where it provides a medium of communication across national boundaries. Note, however, that different international varieties of English are appearing all the time (see the review by Pakir in Volume 4) and every one of these is a non-standard variety. In fact, the standard variety of a language seems to be little more than its written version. And even this variety will vary orthographically, semantically, and increasingly (as in the case of the written variety of English now in use in North America) syntactically too.

But if the standard variety of a language is a necessary acquisition for 'educated' speakers of that language to make, because its possession meets the objective interests of speakers as individuals and as a group, what is to be done about the rights of non-standard speakers in schools and about the objective sociolinguistic fact that non-standard varieties exist in everyone's world? I believe that the difficulty can be minimized by taking the language policy that the Bullock Report (DES 1975) recommends much further. Like other critical language awareness theorists, I would want to add a necessary rider to the Bullock recommendation: For the 'valuing' of language diversity that Bullock recommends to really count, it needs to be carried out in a genuinely *critical* context. In other words, all children need to become critically aware of the social and historical factors that have combined to make one variety of the language more appropriate in contexts resonant with power and prestige, while allotting non-standard varieties a status of appropriateness only in marginalized contexts. Clearly for this to happen, school systems need policies of professional development that promote much greater teacher awareness of language diversity (see my review in Volume 6).

Valuing non-standard varieties is not an easy thing for many people to do, especially if they are only vaguely aware that non-standard varieties exist. For teachers, it may be contrary to a professional lifetime of tacit prejudice. Clearly the attitudes of teachers themselves are important variables here. Helping school staff members become clearer about the risks of stereotyping children is an early step which needs to be taken at whole school and system level, so that staff can support one another in making the necessary changes in attitude. The Ann Arbor experience offers a lead that policy makers at system level might consider: In-service education of practitioners in the sociolinguistics of schooling would certainly be helpful in identifying undesirable prejudices and eliminating the practices that result from them. Assessment policies are also a key area for urgent attention.

Ralph Fasold (1990) reviews work on the importance of the non-standard/standard issue in language testing procedures. Clearly test developers do not use criteria of 'appropriateness' as benchmarks when putting together their instruments. Instead they routinely use standards of 'correctness' in language. But these test norms based uncritically on the standard variety will always disadvantage non-standard users. This seems to follow inevitably from the fact that non-standard varieties are systematically and regularly different from the standard variety. Even when non-standard speakers have wide access to the standard variety, their possession of two varieties can mean that they have to draw on an intricate and ambiguous web of suppositions in correcting their own written texts. Fasold argues that there are similar difficulties for non-standard users in reading and answering a language test using the standard variety:

- non-standard speakers cannot rely on what 'sounds right', since what sounds right will sometimes be non-standard and therefore will be wrong in the context
- non-standard speakers cannot always rely on a 'sounds right so it must be wrong' strategy, since in most cases this will be misleading too
- while even standard speakers have instances of confusion between formal and informal uses of the standard variety (i.e. 'may' versus 'can'), non-standard speakers have many more instances of these differences to remember, and therefore many more of them to get wrong

These ambiguities significantly affect scores recorded on language tests. To counteract this, various assessment policy alternatives are possible in testing the language of non-standard speakers. The best alternative may be for test administrators always to use tests compiled by sociolinguistically competent designers. But while this policy may already be widespread, it is more difficult to ensure that sociolinguistically competent people will use language tests in schools.

Recent approaches to assessing second language competence also seem relevant to first language assessments in contexts where there are non-standard language users (Corson 1993). Instead of measuring the more visible and highly recurring features of language, like pronunciation patterns, vocabulary use, and grammatical usage, other aspects of second language learning now attract more attention. Performing a thorough observation of 'language in use' is now a common basis for assessment. When this form of 'communicative proficiency assessment' complements or replaces traditional language testing, the role of norms, statistics, and inflexible criteria of correctness lessens. The 'norm' for all children becomes a measure of observed proficiency in communicating meaning, set against an individual assessment of their potential for development. Ethnographic methods are called for here, especially participant observation in naturalistic settings where the children's language use is not inhibited by unfavourable expectations about the interaction. Labov's early work (1966, 1972b) found that individual African American children in the USA revealed a high level of verbal productivity and creativity when the research context was changed from a formal to an informal one that was more consistent with the interactional settings that the children themselves were most comfortable in. In creating a school-wide environment where non-standard varieties are really valued, there is much that schools and teachers can borrow from Labov's early findings.

Ontario Institute for Studies in Education
University of Toronto
Canada

REFERENCES

Ammon, U.: 1972, *Dialekt, soziale Ungleichheit und Schule*, Beltz, Weinheim/Basel.
Barnes, D., Britton, J. & Rosen, H.: 1969, *Language, The Learner and the School*, Penguin, London.
Bernstein, B.: 1990, *Class, Codes and Control*, Vol. 4 *The Structuring of Pedagogic Discourse*. Routledge & Kegan Paul, London.
Blair, H.: 1986, 'Teacher's attitudes toward the oral English of indigenous children in Saskatchewan and Queensland,' *Mokakit: Selected Papers from the First Mokakit Conference, July 25–27, 1984*, Vancouver, 22–35.
Bortoni-Ricardo, S.: 1985, *The Urbanization of Rural Dialect Speakers: A Sociolinguistic Study in Brazil*, Cambridge University Press, Cambridge.
Bourdieu, P.: 1966, 'L'École conservatrice', *Revue Française de Sociologie* 7, 225–26; 330–42; 346–47.
Bourdieu, P.: 1981, *Ce Que Parler Veut Dire: L'Économie des Èchanges Linguistiques*, Fayard, Paris.
Britton, J.: 1970, *Language and Learning*, Penguin, London.

Corson, D.: 1993, *Language, Minority Education, and Gender: Linking Social Justice and Power*, Multilingual Matters, Clevedon, Avon.

Corson, D.: 1995, *Using English Words*, Kluwer Academic: Boston & Dordrecht.

Corson, D.: 1998, *Changing Education for Diversity*, Open University Press, London.

Corson, D. & Lemay, S.: 1996, *Social Justice and Language Policy in Education: The Canadian Research*, OISE Press, Toronto.

Dannequin, C.: 1987, 'Les Enfants Baîllonnés: The teaching of French as mother tongue in elementary school', *Language and Education* 1, 15–31.

DES (Department of Education and Science): 1975, *A Language for Life* (The Bullock Report), HMSO, London.

DES (Department of Education and Science): 1985, *Education for All: Report of the Committee of Inquiry into the Education of Children from Ethnic Minority Groups* , (The Swann Report), HMSO, London.

DES (Department of Education and Science): 1988, *Report of the Committee of Inquiry into the Teaching of the English Language*, (The Kingman Report), HMSO, London.

DES (Department of Education and Science): 1989, *English for Ages 5–16* (The Cox Report), HMSO, London.

Fairclough, N. (ed.): 1992, *Critical Language Awareness,* Longmans, London.

Fasold, R.: 1990, *The Sociolinguistics of Language*, Basil Blackwell, Oxford.

Gramsci, A.: 1948, *Opere di Antonio Gramsci, (Quaderni del Carcere XVIII)* Vols. I–XI, Einaudi: Turin (1966 edition).

Herriman, M. & Burnaby, B.: 1996, *Language Policies in English-Dominant Countries*, Multilingual Matters, Clevedon, Avon.

Labov, W.: 1966, 'Finding out about children's language', *Working Papers in Communication* 1, 1–30.

Labov, W.: 1972a, *Language in the Inner City*, University of Pennsylvania Press, Philadelphia.

Labov, W.: 1972b, 'The logic of non-standard English', in P.P. Giglioli (ed.), *Language and Social Context*, Penguin, Harmondsworth.

Labov, W.: 1982, 'Objectivity and commitment in linguistic science: the case of the Black English trial in Ann Arbor', *Language in Society* 11, 165–201.

Oevermann, U.: 1972, *Sprache und soziale Herkunft: Ein Beitrag zur Analyse schichtspezifischer Sozialisationsprozesse und ihrer Bedeutung für den Studienerfolg*, Suhrkamp, Frankfurt/Main.

Pollack, W.: 1973, *Strategien zur Emanzipation: Bildungspolitik, Didaktik und Soziolinguistik*. Jugend und Volk, Vienna.

Poulson, L., Radmor, H. & Turner-Bisset, R.: 1996, 'From policy to practice: Language education, English teaching and curriculum reform in secondary schools in England', *Language and Education* 10, 33–46.

Rosen, C. and Rosen, H.: 1973, *The Language of Primary School Children*, Penguin, London.

Smitherman, G.: 1992, 'Black English, diverging or converging?: The view from the national assessment of educational progress', *Language and Education* 6, 47–61.

Telles, J.: 1996, *Being a Language Teacher: Stories of Critical Reflection on Language and Pedagogy [in Brazil]*, unpublished PhD thesis. Ontario Institute for Studies in Education.

Winch, C.: 1989, 'Standard English, normativity and the Cox Committee Report', *Language and Education* 3, 275–293.

Wodak, R.: 1975, *Das Sprachverhalten von Angeklagten bei Gericht*, Scriptor, Tübingen.

Wodak, R. & de Cillia, R. (eds.): 1995, *Sprachenpolitik in Mittel- und Osteuropa*, Passagen, Vienna.

Section 3

Specific Areas

NAZ RASSOOL

LANGUAGE POLICIES FOR A MULTICULTURAL BRITAIN

Since language policy for Welsh speakers has existed since 1907, parents have had the right to choose the language of instruction for their children. Although teaching hours in Welsh vary between Local Education Authorities (LEAs), different models of bilingual education exist in Wales and the overall emphasis is on developing bilingualism and bi-culturalism (Lewis 1980). Similarly, Irish has become the official language of Eire and bilingual programmes have been developed also in Ireland and Scotland (Alladina & Edwards 1991). Special language provision was made also for Polish ex-soldiers who after the second world war refused to return to a Communist occupied country. This provision was made under the Polish Resettlement Act 1947 (Tosi 1988). Similarly, European languages such as French, German, Spanish and Italian are taught as a normal part of the Modern Languages Curriculum in England and Wales. However, the situation for ethnic minority immigrant groups from former colonies is significantly different. Since no official policy has emerged to support the teaching of their languages in British schools, educational provision for their language maintenance has remained an unresolved issue. Following Lewis' (1980, ibid.) view that language policy lies at the very heart of the state, this review provides an account of the development of the debate that has surrounded language provision for immigrant groups from former colonies who have made their homes in post-colonial Britain (also see reviews by May in this volume; by Baker in Volume 5; and by Donmall in Volume 6).

EARLY DEVELOPMENTS

Britain has been a multicultural society throughout its history, with various social groups including the Irish, Picts, Welsh and English farmers living relatively discrete lives before the Norman Conquest (Lewis 1980). In the quest for an English-dominated British nationhood, Celtic culture became commonly represented as inferior, and the speakers of the Celtic languages as 'wild' and 'savage'. Historically, education has provided a primary arena in which the dominance of English could become hegemonized. As late as 1847, the Report of the Church Commissioners on schools in Wales 'viciously attacked the Welsh language on the grounds that it isolated "the masses" from the "upper portions of society", denied its speakers access to the top of the social scale and kept them "under the hatches"'

R. Wodak and D. Corson (eds), Encyclopedia of Language and Education,
Volume 1: Language Policy and Political Issues in Education, 113–126.
© 1997 Kluwer Academic Publishers. Printed in the Netherlands.

(quoted in Alladina & Edwards 1991: p. 3). Children caught speaking Welsh in school were forced to wear the notorious wooden halter called a 'Welsh not' as punishment (ibid.). Thus, although bilingualism has been a reality for different indigenous social groups living in Britain throughout the centuries, for many this followed a long process of struggle against assimilation into the English language and culture. Indeed, the notion of a monolingual, English-speaking people has remained a potent variable in shaping common understandings of British nationhood.

Social discourse centred on language in education as this relates to 'black' immigrant children first gained prominence within the aftermath of mass immigration policies in the 1950s when during a period of economic boom, workers were recruited from former colonies, and, particularly, the Caribbean to work in the service industries. Other significant migrations included those from Southern Europe, Cyprus, the Indian sub-continent as well as the Hong Kong Chinese working predominantly in the catering industry (Linguistic Minorities Project 1985). This was followed during the late 1960s by the arrival of large groups of second and even third generation 'Asians' from East Africa. Among these were refugees who had been expelled by the Ugandan regime at the time as well as Vietnamese Chinese refugees (Plowden Report 1967; Linguistic Minorities Project 1985). The languages of immigrant children, notably the dialects spoken by Caribbean pupils (then generally referred to as 'West Indians') and the lack of fluency in English amongst those from the Indian sub-continent became widely regarded as a major challenge presented to teachers. Concerns about underachievement, especially as this related to children of Caribbean origin, were based largely on notions of communication failure in classrooms. The National Foundation for Educational Research (NFER 1966: p. 173) identified three categories of 'deficit' . These included: '(1) Total language deficiency; to describe the acquisition of a foreign language but no script. (2) Partial language deficiency; to describe the acquisition of a foreign language, some English and a script which may or may not be a western alphabet, and (3) Dialect impediments; where English may be fluent but dialect or "pidgin" English was spoken. West Indian Creole was seen to be the cause of problems of listening, interpreting and later reading and writing'. Language 'deficits', associated with cognitive, cultural and social 'deficits' thus became key signifiers of immigrant children's imputed ability, or inability, to succeed in school and later in society (Carby 1982). At that time, these views were re-inforced by arguments that 'the dialect or Creole English is an immature language which is clearly inadequate for expressing the complexities of present day life, for complete understanding of human motivation and behaviour' (Jones 1963, quoted in Carby, ibid.: p. 187). Such representations of the inherent 'inferiority' of minority languages, provided a pedagogical rationale for the imperative to learn Standard English. Emphasis was placed on oral language which, according to the *Ministry of Education Pamphlet No 43. 1963* 'should be accorded priority over reading and writing'. This can be ascribed to the difficulties that teachers encountered with 'West Indian' dialects discussed above. Within the assimilationist ideology that prevailed at the time, special provision was to be made to accommodate new arrivals in language reception centres where pupils would be inducted into the language and culture of the host society for a period of at least a term. Second language teaching within this context, largely followed the pedagogic principles of English as a Foreign Language (EFL).

Amid fears of large numbers of immigrant pupils, potentially, affecting educational standards in schools adversely Sir Edward Boyle, then Minister of Education, made the recommendation that schools were not to exceed a 30% intake of immigrant pupils. A policy of dispersal was adopted in 1966 to 'bus' out those remaining children to other schools in different areas. In order to facilitate this process of dispersal, and, despite strong opposition from the National Union of Teachers (NUT) and the Community Race Commission (CRC), ethnic monitoring of pupils in school was instituted in 1966 by the Secretary of State under Section 92 of the Education Act 1944. Schools were required to provide statistics on Form 7 returns regarding the linguistic and educational status of immigrant pupils or those who had been born to parents who were first and second generation immigrants during the ten year period. In order to cater for specific conditions within local education authorities (LEAs), special funding was made available through Section 11 of the Local Government Act 1966 for the education of children from Commonwealth countries. LEAs with high numbers of immigrant pupils could now obtain Exchequer grants of 50% (later to be increased to 75%) in order to make special teaching provision for immigrant pupils. In some LEAs this amount was supplemented by monies from the Urban Aid Programme (DES 1974). This development took place at the time when Secretary of State for Education, Roy Jenkins advocated the need to move from assimilation towards integration that was defined as equal opportunity accompanied by cultural diversity within an atmosphere of mutual tolerance. Underlying the integrationist ideology was the need to maintain consensus within society by altering peoples' attitudes by promoting 'self-esteem', 'positive self-images' and to apply 'positive discrimination' to members of ethnic minority groups within the work place. Compensatory educational programmes which had been part of the social milieu at the time with regard to working class pupils, were now extended to include educational provision for black immigrant children. By thus facilitating equality of educational opportunity it was hoped to ensure social justice. Within this compensatory ethos 'Black Studies' were introduced to provide a 'relevant' curriculum particularly for children of West Indian origin. Of key significance, however, is the fact that Section 11 funding initially served the primary purpose of supporting pupils' acquisition of English in order to facilitate the process of assimilation. This was the case despite the ideological shift in discourse from assimilationism to integrationism.

MAJOR CONTRIBUTIONS

The Plowden Report *Children in their Primary Schools* (1967) which had been given the brief 'to consider the whole subject of primary education and the transition to secondary school' (Plowden Report ibid.: p. 1), took on board the recommendations made in the DES Circular 7/65 regarding the dispersal or 'bussing' of pupils in high density immigrant areas. Although emphasis on the acquisition of (Standard) English featured also in the curriculum development work of the state-funded Schools Council, in its *Working Paper No. 13* (1971) the Council did indicate an understanding of the cultural value of teaching immigrant pupils their 'mother tongue' and argued for the need to acknowledge broad issues of bilingualism and bi-culturalism. In particular, it supported the teaching of minority languages such as Italian which, it was argued, 'is generally accepted as a foreign language for school purposes in England'. However, these concessions were not extended to linguistic minority groups from the colonies. This was an issue that was to emerge again later in official discourse (see Swann Report below). Thus, despite the notional integrationism, language teaching provision for immigrant pupils from former colonies continued to take place largely in withdrawal classrooms. Many of those who originated from the Indian sub-continent were still sent to separate language centres where they were given intensive language teaching before being integrated into mainstream schools. The problem with this approach was that it decontextualized language learning and, furthermore, handicapped pupils with regard to continuity and progression in their curriculum learning. As a result of the fact that these pupils were usually integrated into mainstream classrooms without further language support, they continued to operate at a significant educational and social disadvantage.

By the mid-1970s emphasis gradually started to shift towards an acknowledgment of the validity and expressiveness of different languages and cultures of ethnic minority immigrant groups. Within this frame-work it was advocated that teachers needed to alter their attitudes towards the languages and dialects of ethnic minority immigrant groups – and to acknowledge the cultural diversity of British society. Significantly, this heralded the beginning of what became known as 'multicultural' education in Britain. Focusing mainly on altering attitudes and celebrating cultural differences, curriculum emphasis, mainly in urban schools, shifted to concerns about discriminatory attitudes, cultural stereotypes, ethnicity, religious festivals and cultural artifacts. With funding provided for community projects, different ethnic groups started to compete against one another for cultural resources. The fact that the emphasis within these projects was largely on celebrating ethnic differences contributed to the fact that the multicultural curriculum, in real terms, served to fractionalize what was previously a united black struggle against societal racism.

It was within this context of multicultural education that the Bullock Report *A Language for Life* (1975) was published. The Report foregrounded language teaching in educational debate – and, in particular, advocated the teaching of language-for-learning across the curriculum. Its argument that the child should not 'be expected to cast off the language and culture of the home as he crosses the school threshold', for the first time in official educational discourse, inserted the mother tongues of immigrant children as positive and valuable cultural and educational resources. Moreover, the Bullock Report stressed the importance of maintaining home-school links in order to bridge the cultural gap and the need to examine reading and teaching materials for racial or cultural stereotype and bias. However, other than the statement of principles, there were no guidelines on mother tongue teaching provision. As a result, immigrant children continued to be placed in intensive teaching programmes in withdrawal classrooms or language centres where the focus remained on the acquisition of Standard English *per se*. As was the case before, from here they were placed in mainstream classrooms – unsupported and educationally behind their peers in terms of the curriculum. Educationally, the Bullock Report did not address the cognitive implications of mother tongue or bilingual education regarding the importance of a first language in facilitating acquisition of the second language. Nor did it take account of the opportunity for pupils to continue to develop their knowledge within curriculum areas such as Science and Mathematics through the medium of their own languages. Moreover, monolingual criteria continued to be used to assess the achievement of second language learners – a factor which placed second language learners as a considerable educational disadvantage.

Concerns about the issue of 'mother tongue' education regarding migrant workers in Northern Europe had been raised formally first within the context of UNESCO (1976) and the Council of Europe (1975). These concerns related mainly to the need to facilitate the re-integration of the children of migrant workers into their culture of origin once their work permits have expired. This culminated in the introduction of the EC Council Directive on the education of children of migrant workers (77/486/EEC) which required member states to teach the languages of migrant groups living within their boundaries, for part of the school day. The Directive met with considerable ambivalence within the UK where concerns were expressed initially about costs, the difficulty in providing adequate numbers of 'mother tongue' teachers as well as the fact that the situation *vis a vis* Britain's immigrant groups was different to those of other member countries such as Germany and Sweden who had, predominantly, migrant workers. Although the EC Directive provided impetus to the debate on 'mother tongue' education in the UK, insufficient guidelines, information and understanding of issues resulted in mass confusion at official level. The lack of clarity with regard to definitions and approaches led to the funding of a range of un-coordinated research projects – and disparate teaching provision. Projects funded by the Department of Education and Science (DES) included: (a) the Rosen and Burgess study (1979–80) *Languages and Dialects of London School Children*. The study identified 55 languages and 24 overseas based dialects spoken in London. It drew on earlier integrationist definitions and stressed the 'vitality' and 'strength' of the languages and dialects of London's immigrant population groups. The report highlighted the significance of dialect culture and advocated bilingualism to be advanced within the framework of multicultural education; (b) *Linguistic Minorities Project (LMP) 1979–80* (extended to 1982 and published in 1983): The LMP Project aimed to assess the range of diversity of the languages spoken in Britain, patterns of bilingualism as well as the educational implications of societal bilingualism. It was hoped that the data collected would inform educational assessment and policy formulation in different parts of the country. The LMP conducted several surveys: The Adult Learning Survey (ALUS); Schools Language Survey (SLS); Mother Tongue Teaching Directory (MTTD) in collaboration with the National Council for Mother Tongue Teaching and the Secondary Pupils Survey (SPS). (c) The Bradford *Mother Tongue and Teaching Project (MOTET)* (1978–81): The sample study focused on the implementation, monitoring and evaluation of a bilingual teaching programme in the children's first year at school (d) The *EEC/Bedfordshire Pilot Project* (1976–1980) focused similarly on a bilingual teaching programme – but was abandoned by Bedfordshire LEA when the EC funding grant ran out (Tosi 1988). The LEA concluded that providing mother tongue teaching to 20% of the county's bilingual pupils was excessive and intolerable for the county (ibid.).

The next major input to the language debate came from the Swann Committee in its report *Education For All* (1985) published in the aftermath of racialized urban unrest throughout Britain. The Swann Report located its views on the education of black immigrant pupils within the ideological framework of cultural pluralism which underlines the importance of the need to socialize ethnic minority groups into the belief system of mainstream culture – whilst simultaneously maintaining links with their culture of origin. However, although the Swann Report provided a useful overview of the language debate during the previous two decades, it was unclear on the issues of language diversity and bilingual education and opposed separate educational provision for 'mother tongue' teaching. It argued that linguistic minority 'mother tongues' of black immigrant groups should not be taught in mainstream classrooms other than in the Modern Languages Curriculum. In doing so, the Swann Report lacked consideration of the distinctions between what Paulston (1981: p. 471) calls 'elitist' bilingualism which involves choice and status – and 'folk' bilingualism 'which is the result of ethnic groups in contact and competition with a single state, where one of the peoples becomes bilingual in order to survive' (see the review by Paulston in Volume 4). It also neglected to consider the negative implications that the minimal first language support, implied in its recommendations, would have on the long term educational progress of second language learners. In principle then, it continued to support a transitional model of bilingualism located within an overall assimilationist ideological framework. The underlying assumption here seems to have been the belief that assimilation would occur 'naturally' through 'benign neglect' (Grosjean 1982). As can be seen later, this position has been sustained in the continued lack of official acknowledgment of 'ethnic' minority languages as media of instruction in schools. Indeed, in advocating that provision for ethnic minority immigrant languages remained the responsibility of community groups, the Swann Report echoed earlier statements on mother tongue teaching made by the Schools Council in the 1970s (see Schools Council above).

WORK IN PROGRESS

Yet despite the lack of national policy guidelines, good educational practice was developing in many urban schools in different LEAs across the country. These developments, in many instances, were inspired by staff development work that emerged with the context of organizations such as the National Association for the Teaching of English (NATE), the Centre for Urban Educational Studies (CUES) and the English Centre based at the Inner London Educational Authority (ILEA) as well as the National Writing Project (NWP). Within the context of these largely practice-oriented research initiatives, the emphasis in many schools started to shift towards a consideration of learning conditions in schools and classrooms and the need for teaching to cater for the *process* of second language learning. Many schools, particularly in urban areas, were moving to an acceptance of curriculum entitlement for *all* pupils. In this regard they were drawing also on the principles of integration which had become part of the discourse on the education of children with special educational needs discussed in the Warnock Report (1978) *Special Educational Needs* as well as the systems approach to curriculum planning advocated in the Hargreaves Report (1981) *Improving Secondary Schools*. Some LEAs, particularly in urban areas, had appointed specialist English as a Second Language (ESL) teachers in a two-tier structure. On the first tier, a team of support teachers were allocated to schools to provide in-class support and develop curriculum materials. These support teachers linked with the ESL Department in secondary schools and in the primary sector, with a co-ordinator based in the school. On the second tier, a team of senior team co-ordinators and advisory staff monitored school-based ESL staff and provided in-service training centred on developing whole school policies on second language teaching (Rassool 1995). Within this context, the emphasis was on partner-ship teaching as a vehicle to provide access for second language learners to the mainstream curriculum. Working with mainstream staff within the subject areas enabled the support teachers to extend the range of learning experiences of second language pupils who were, erstwhile, marginalized in terms of the curriculum. Moreover, in some LEAs specialist teams were constituted to provide 'mother tongue' teaching support in schools and also incorporated some minority languages such as Bengali, Urdu, Panjabi and Greek into their Modern Languages curriculum. Within these schools the process of bilingual education had started – albeit without state policy sanction. This provides evidence of the fact that despite the absence of central policy guidelines, some schools had become involved in defin-ing their own language policy agenda in terms of the needs of the pupils within their schools (Rassool 1995). Many of these developments took place within the context of anti-racist education that had developed during the mid-1980s. Anti-racist education, grounded in a counter-hegemonic discourse, challenged racist rules and structures in institutions, curricu-lum materials and social discourse – and subsequently, provoked a strong right-wing backlash. By the late 1980s, in a discourse structured mainly within the framework of neo-Conservative 'think tanks' such as the Cen-tre for Policy Studies, the Hillgate Group and the Salisbury Review, the New Right attack on education centred on the issues of multicultural/anti-racist education and bilingual education. These, it was argued, challenged the national cultural and linguistic heritage – and contributed to 'falling standards' in schools (see Honeyford 1984; Scruton 1985).

In spite of the marginalizing discourse taking place within the New Right ideological framework, in-class support as opposed to withdrawal classes for second language learners was, nevertheless, incorporated into Section 11 funding within the framework of Home Office Circular 78/90. This showed evidence of the extent in which progressive educational develop-ments in schools had impacted on national policy frameworks. New criteria had been issued in the Home Office Circular 78/90 which stipulated that new bids for funding were to be made within a fixed time-table and were to be project-based. The changes advocated at the time by the Home Office were the outcomes of a detailed government review of Section 11 funding during the period 1988–90. Under the Educational Support Grant (ESG) system, projects requiring schools to engage in teacher partnership, were now funded for a period of 3/5years. Bids for ESGs also had to be detailed in terms of specific needs addressed, objectives, quantified targets, time scale, monitoring of results and consultation with community groups (Circular 78/90). This resulted in good examples of practice with a more coherent and co-ordinated approach within LEAs – and which was centrally monitored through funding requirements.

PROBLEMS AND DIFFICULTIES

However, despite these positive developments, Circular 78/90 marked the beginning of a heightened level of state intervention in the broad arena of second language teaching during the next few years. Both LEA and teacher accountability were increased and levels of staffing rationalized in preparation for larger changes to come. Confusion at official level reached farcical proportions when by November 1992 (less than two months after the new funding arrangements came on stream) the Government announced that the spending levels announced in April 1992 could not be sustained. Following this, and whilst pledging government support for the maintenance of teaching resources to 'overcome linguistic and cultural barriers' and to enable ethnic minorities 'to gain full access to mainstream services and facilities', the Home Office announced a series of consecutive cutbacks in the Section 11 budget to take effect from April 1994. These cutbacks were justified in terms of changing economic circumstances in the country which, it was argued, had created the imperative for the government to bring public spending 'within limits which the country can afford and to ensure adequate investment in line with the Government's strategy for sustainable growth in the economy' (Home Office letter 26.11.92). This essentially underscored monetarist fiscal policy geared to reduce public expenditure. In line with this, the earmarked national budget of £130.8 million for 1993–94 was to be cut to £110.7 in 1994–95 and to £97 million in 1995–96 (LARRIE 1993). For LEAs this amounted to a cut in funding to 57 per cent in 1994–95 and then to 50 per cent in 1995–96 – the shortfall would have to be provided by local authorities. According to a survey report published in 1993 by the Local Authorities Race Relations Information Exchange (LARRIE) only 6.7 per cent of local authorities stated that they would be able to increase their budgets beyond their 25 per cent commitment to Section 11 funding.

Significantly, by August 1993 within the framework of the amended Local Government Act (1993), the limitation placed on Section 11 funding for ethnic minority immigrants from the Commonwealth was removed. Funding was made available to all ethnic minority groups – and also, not only those who were newly arrived immigrants. To be included also were the complex psychological, linguistic and educational needs of pupils from refugee groups who had arrived recently from countries such as Zaire and Somalia. At the same time, however, it was made clear that funding would not be increased – therefore, less money had to cater for a larger number of pupils. The situation was to change further by September 1993 when LEAs were informed of new funding arrangements in the form of cash budgets as opposed to the previous approach based on percentage spending of actual costs incurred through the employment of staff. As part of the drive to rationalize spending costs LEAs were advised to prioritize projects by either scaling down or decreasing the number of projects (Home Office, September 1993). Emphasis now also started to shift to 'direct service delivery' to ethnic minority 'client' groups and LEAs were encouraged to redeploy resources by creating 'task forces' geared to make short-term inputs in a variety of schools.

By November 1993 an overall restructuring of Section 11 funding arrangements took place. The Home Office transferred 55 per cent of Section 11 funds to a new funding scheme, the Single Regeneration Budget (SRB) to be co-ordinated by the Department of the Environment and administered within nine local regions. The SRB involved the amalgamation of twenty separate budgets, from five different departments. LEAs falling within the ambit of identified Urban Priority Areas (UPAs) now had to apply for the funding of ethnic minority projects to the SRB. For these LEAs new bids catering for Section 11 type activity for 1995–6 would be made to the Department for the Environment where it would have to compete with other community programmes within the context of the Ethnic Minority Grant, Ethnic Minority Business Initiative Grants and Safer Cities (Home Office letter 4.11.93). LEAs outside the UPAs would remain within the framework of Section 11 funding to be administered by the Home Office. Bidding under the SRB scheme started in April 1994 with a deadline of September 1994. By September 1994 the overall budget for new projects was reduced to £15 million in 1995/6 and 1996/7. After public protest against 100 per cent cuts in the staffing of projects which were due to time-expire in 1995, this was increased by another £15 million through the intervention of the Home Secretary in November 1994.

FUTURE DIRECTIONS

The overall significance of the re-structuring of Section 11 funding lies in the fact that, first, the dispersal of funding 'units' has not only fractionalized community group struggle for social, cultural and linguistic resources but also set these groups in competition with one another. Secondly, the emphasis placed on funding short-term projects has placed limitations on planning in terms of what would be possible to achieve only on a long-term basis. Further erosion of LEA control and the insertion of market meanings are evident also in the transfer of LEA funds to Grant Maintained (GM) schools. As schools opt out of LEA control, the amount of money allocated to projects within such schools would be transferred from the LEA budget to the annual maintenance grant (AMG) of GM schools (Home Office letter 8.2.95). Similar reductions would be made within LEAs where demographic changes take place in terms of ethnic composition. The impact of this on long-term planning does not augur well in terms of the possibility to maintain a coherent system of second language support at LEA level.

Although the National Curriculum Council (NCC) document, 'English in the National Curriculum' (1989), acknowledged the linguistic diversity that prevailed in schools and advocated the need to value the cultural enrichment implicit in this, in reality, it did not take account of the specific needs of bilingual learners with regard to their assessment. This absence has been re-inforced in the new, revised document *English in the National Curriculum* (1995). Whilst it recommends that appropriate provision should be made for pupils with a range of special educational needs, this important document does not acknowledge the needs of second language learners either in terms of curriculum access or assessment. In consequence bilingual or rather, as is the case in reality, second language learners will continue to be assessed by the same criteria as monolingual pupils – thus, potentially, creating a cycle of underachievement amongst those second language learners who are inadequately supported in terms of gaining access to the full range of National Curriculum subjects. Many of the integrative classroom practices developed during the early to mid-1980s, the period of bottom-up policy changes aimed at empowering teachers and pupils, although notionally incorporated into the National Curriculum framework, are currently being contested and screened out by the assessment requirements contained in educational legislation. Furthermore, the cross-school competition underscored in the concept of national league tables are already encouraging some schools into streaming pupils into different ability groups for certain subjects. These factors have clear implications for children in the process of learning English as a second language. Seemingly then, the debate about second language teaching has come full circle. Despite the rhetoric of linguistic and cultural diversity previously interspersed within National Curriculum documents, the real meanings relating to ESL pupils still subscribe to the ideology of assimilationism. The debate about bilingualism for these pupils that had started amongst practising teachers in the early 1980s has once again been relegated to a marginalized discourse. The reduction in funding and staff discussed above have direct implications for the diminished range of educational choices that can be made available to pupils learning English as a second language. Since these impact later on their job-opportunities in the labour market, these disempowering strategies in education can be seen as forms of both social and structural exclusion. The needs of refugee groups often extend beyond educational and linguistic concerns to include also a consideration of psychological trauma as a result of their social displacement and, in many cases, political persecution. Lack of funding for adequate educational support to be provided to these pupils can then be seen as linking with broader issues of human rights. Moreover, the erosion of LEA control; the devolution of budgets to schools under the Local Management of Schools (LMS); the pressure on schools to produce 'good results'; the restructuring and systematic reduction in Section 11 funding – if located within the context of immigration policies within the European Union, would seem to signify decreased possibilities for developing the full potential of second language or bilingual learners. With changes taking place in terms of a culturally and economically integrated Europe, the ethnocentrism inherent in earlier discourses on multicultural and language education are in the process of being replaced with a legitimized concept of Eurocentrism. This screening out of 'alien Otherness' will consolidate the marginalization, historically, of minority languages. Since these linguistic minorities would not be able to maintain their languages, they would lose contact with their cultures of origin and thus become assimilated into a society which is fundamentally opposed to their presence. This would contribute to both cultural and social alienation. It also has implications for the social status as well as the cultural, political, economic and social needs of refugee and migrant groups. In terms of this, '. . . the issue of language maintenance cannot be discussed in relation to cultural identity without also addressing specific groups of peoples' social experience, that is to say, their civic, human and political rights as well as their social status as citizens' (Rassool 1995: p. 300). Problems of language shift could affect children from migrant and refugee families in Britain who might wish to return to their countries of origin.

Nevertheless, the concept of language policy for immigrant or migrant groups within the pluralist nation-state – and, moreover, within an era of increased globalization, is not an unambiguous one. For example, because of the relative absence of societal support and lack of co-ordinated provision, learning in their first language may create difficulties of uneven development of the two languages – at the expense of English, which is the language of power within society. Thus they would distance themselves from access to power and 'life chances'. Many would also then choose to remain within the confines of their community in their after-school years – and thus create barriers in terms of their ability to participate fully in mainstream society. In this regard, societally unsupported bilingualism would encourage ghettoization. Further research is needed to identify patterns and degrees of language maintenance and language shift for different generations of immigrants now settled in British society – and the impact of these factors on their ability to participate fully in the democratic process, as well as their social and cultural experiences. This would need to take account of hybridized identities, flexible identities, self-definition and alternative forms of cultural and individual empowerment. Self-definition here refers to racialized subjects as they are engaged in an ongoing process of critique, negotiation, self-affirmation and validation of themselves in relation to their particular experience within society. In terms of this, future research needs to take on board the issue of agency.

University of Reading
England

REFERENCES

Alladina, S. & Edwards, V. (eds.): 1993, *Multilingualism in the British Isles: The Older Mother Tongues & Europe,* Longman, London and New York.

Carby, H.: 1982, 'Schooling in Babylon' in Centre for Contemporary Cultural Studies (CCCS) (eds.) , Hutchinson & Co. Publishers , London, 183–211.

Council of Europe: 1975, *Meeting of experts on curricula for children of migrant workers. 26–27 June 1975. Strassbourg.*

Department for Education: 1995, *English in the National Curriculum,* HMSO, London.

Department of Education and Science: 1967, *Children and their Primary Schools, A Report of the Central Advisory Council for Education (England), Volume 1: Report,* HMSO, London.

Department of Education and Science: 1974, *Educational Disadvantage and the Educational Needs of Immigrants: Observations on the Report on Education of the Select Committee on Race Relations and Immigration,* HMSO, London.

Department of Education and Science: 1975, *A Language for Life, Report of the Committee of Inquiry appointed by the Secretary of State for Educational Science under the Chairmanship of Sir Alan Bullock,* HMSO, London.

Department of Education and Science: 1977, *Directive of the Council of the European Community on the Education of the Children of Migrant Workers,* Circular 77/486/EEC, HMSO, London.

Department of Education and Science: 1978, *Special Educational Needs.* Report of the Committee of Enquiry into the Education of Handicapped Children and Young People under the Chairmanship of Lady Mary Warnock [Warnock Report], HMSO, London.

Department of Education and Science: 1985, *Education For All.* Report of the Committee of Inquiry into the Education of Ethnic Minority Groups, Chairman, Lord Swann, HMSO, London.

Department of Education and Science: 1989, *English in the National Curriculum 5–16,* National Curriculum Council, HMSO, London.

Department of Education and Science:*Circular 7/65, June 1965,* London: HMSO. Home Office: 1990, Circular 78/90 *Section 11 of the Local Government Act 1966,* Home Office, London.

Home Office: 1992, *Payment of Grant Under Section 11 of the Local Government Act 1966 – Ethnic Minorities: Notification of Future Financial Provision,* Letter 26 November 1992, Home Office, London.

Home Office: 1993, *New Measures to Encourage Regeneration and economic Development in England: Implications for the payment of Grant Under Section 11 of the Local Government Act 1966 – Ethnic Minorities,* Letter 4 November 1993, Home Office, London.

Home Office: 1995, *Annual Maintenance Grant for Grant-maintained Schools and Grant-Maintained Special Schools,* Letter 8 February 1995, Home Office, London.

Honeyford, R.: 1984, 'Education and race: An alternative view', *Salisbury Review* 2(2), 30–32.

126   N A Z   R A S S O O L

Grosjean, F.: 1982, *Life with Two Languages: An Introduction to Bilingualism,* Harvard University Press, Cambridge, Massachusetts, and London, England.
Lewis, E.G.: 1980, *Bilingualism and Bilingual Education*, Pergamon Press, Oxford.
Linguistic Minorities Project: 1983, *Linguistic Minorities in England*, Institute of Education University of London, in association with Tinga Tinga, London.
Linguistic Minorities Project: 1985, *The Other Languages of England*, Routledge & Kegan Paul., London.
Local Authorities Race Relations Information Exchange (LARRIE): 1993, *LARRIE: Section 11 Survey Report, Part One,* LARRIE, London.
Local Authorities Race Relations Information Exchange (LARRIE): 1994, *LARRIE: Section 11 Survey Report, Part Two: Section 11 and the Single Regeneration Budget,* LARRIE, London.
Ministry of Education: 1963, *English for Immigrants,* Ministry of Education Pamphlet No. 43, HMSO, London.
MOTET: 1981, *Mother Tongue and English Teaching Project: Summary of the Report Vols. 1 and 2,* Bradford School of Education, The University.
National Foundation for Educational Research (NFER): 1966, *Coloured Immigrant Children: A Survey of Research, Studies and Literature on their Educational Problems and Potential in Britain,* NFER, Slough.
Paulston, C.: 1981, 'Bilingualism and education', in C. Fergusson & S. Brice-Heath (eds.), *Language in the USA,* Cambridge University Press, Cambridge, 469–485.
Rassool, N.: 1995, 'Language, cultural pluralism and the silencing of minority discourses in England and Wales' *Journal of Education Policy* 10(3), 287–302.
Rosen, H. & Burgess, T.: 1980, *Languages and Dialects of London School Children,* Ward Lock, London.
Schools Council: 1971, *English for the children of immigrants,* Working Paper No.13, HMSO, London.
Scruton, R. : 1985, *Education and Indoctrination,* Centre for Policy Studies, London.
Tosi, A.: 1983, *Immigration and Bilingual Education: a case study of movement of population, language change and education within the EEC (Bedfordshire Project),* Pergamon Press, Oxford.
Tosi, A.: 1988, 'The Jewel in the crown of the modern prince', in T. Skutnabb-Kangas & J. Cummins (eds.), *Minority Education: From Shame To Struggle,* Multilingual Matters, Clevedon, 79–102.
UNESCO: 1976, *Teaching children of migrants,* a Documentation, report of the Symposium sponsored by the World Federation of Foreign Language Teachers' Associations and UNESCO. R. Freudenstein (ed.) AIMAV, Didier, 1978.

MICHAEL CLYNE

LANGUAGE POLICY AND EDUCATION IN AUSTRALIA

This review will link the development of coherent, positive and comprehensive language policy in Australia with changes in the self-perception of
the Australian nation. It will encompass English and the other languages
of Australia and account for policy shifts. In 1991, 14.8% of the Australian
population, 26% of people in Melbourne and 25% of those in Sydney used
a language other than English (LOTEs) at home, the most widely used
being: Italian, Greek, Chinese, Arabic, Croatian/Serbian/Serbo-Croatian,
German, and Vietnamese. There were also 44,000 home users of Aboriginal languages. Of about a hundred such languages still extant, only 20–30
are used in everyday situations and acquired by children (Dixon 1989), not
including English-based Creoles (see the review by Corson on pp. 77–87).
   Australian English is based principally on the English of the London
area, with some influences from East Anglia, Ireland and elsewhere (Trudgill 1986). While there is minor variation according to region, age, gender,
and ethnicity, the main variable is social. The sociolects are on a continuum
with the variety closest to Received Pronunciation, Cultivated Australian
at the top (Mitchell & Delbridge 1965; Horvath 1983; also see reivews by
Watts in Volume 4 and by Gibbons in Volume 5).

EARLY DEVELOPMENTS

Australian sociolinguistic history can be characterized by tensions between
English monolingualism as a symbol of the British tradition, English
monolingualism as a marker of Australia's independent national identity, and multilingualism as both social reality and part of the ideology
of a multicultural and outreaching Australian society (Clyne 1991: Chap.
1). Pluralistic features in some of the six British colonies that preceded
the Australian federation (1901), including bilingual education, waned in
the late 19th century) and came to an end with the First World War. By
1917, bilingual education had been prohibited, even in non-state schools.
This set the tone for the next $5\frac{1}{2}$ decades, and post-2nd World War mass
immigration proceeded on assimilationist lines. The expectation was that
immigrants would rapidly acquire English and abandon their first language.
The language of the public domain was English only. A program of English as a Second Language was put into operation for adults in 1948 and
schoolchildren in 1970. Any (immigrant) community language maintenance efforts had to be conducted and financed by the ethnic communities
themselves.

R. Wodak and D. Corson (eds), Encyclopedia of Language and Education,
Volume 1: Language Policy and Political Issues in Education, 127–135.
© 1997 Kluwer Academic Publishers. Printed in the Netherlands.

The treatment of indigenous languages was uniformly negative and destructive until the 1970s. The white colonizers' attitudes to the indigenous people were conditioned by racism and disregarded the Aborigines as the incumbent population. Aborigines were both marginalized and forced to assimilate, linguistically and otherwise. Until 1967 they were not even citizens. Oppression, genocide and assimilation pressures, including the removal of Aboriginal children from their parents have led to the death of over one hundred languages since 1788 and the imminent death of perhaps another hundred (Dixon 1989; Schmidt 1990; and see the review by Harris & Devlin in Volume 5).

Australian English was long considered inferior in Establishment circles. The colonial tradition encouraged continuing links with England (study in England, importation of Englishmen to prestigious posts). Universities, private schools, the Anglican Church, judiciary, and Australian Broadcasting Corporation all propagated Standard British English or a variety close to it.

DEVELOPING LANGUAGE POLICY

Since the early 1970s, Australia has ceased seeing itself as a remote British outpost and has declared itself to be an independent multicultural nation in which languages and cultures from all over the world have a legitimate place. The linguistic manifestations of the new national identity have been a change in the status of both Australian English and of LOTEs used in Australia. The complementarity of these has also been recognized.

The Macquarie Dictionary (1st edition, 1981) codifies the vocabulary of Australian English, presenting British and American forms as marked. The elites in Australian society no longer regard British English as the acceptable variety. General Australian English (the more distinctively Australian variety in the middle of the continuum) is being used increasingly in most sections of society.

In the 1970s and early 80s a number of new developments brought community languages into the public domain, e.g. the lifting of restrictions on broadcasting in LOTEs and the establishment of government-funded multilingual radio and TV stations, the widening of the range of languages offered at school and university, the availability of most community languages as Matriculation subjects, public library resources in LOTEs, and a telephone interpreter service. These developments were the work of a reformist government responding to the demands of a wide alliance of interest groups at public meetings and in public statements.

All language policies remained *ad hoc* and piecemeal and it was desirable for an explicit policy to be formulated. In 1982, a bipartisan committee of parliamentarians was appointed to inquire into the need for an explicit and comprehensive national language policy encompassing *all* aspects of *all* languages in Australia. The report, delivered after 18 months of research, the hearing of 94 witnesses and 241 written submissions, was not yet a national language policy but it raised the issues that would need to be addressed in such a policy. It laid down the guiding principles of future Australian language policy: Competence in English for all; maintenance and development of languages other than English; provision of services in LOTEs; and opportunities for learning LOTEs.

The inclusion of English in the inquiry and report served to project the other languages as playing a complementary role. The section on Aboriginal languages is very sensitive to the involvement of communities in decision making and the desirability of teaching Aboriginal language in schools.

COMPREHENSIVE LANGUAGES POLICIES

The guiding principles of the report formed the basis of the National Policy on Languages (Lo Bianco 1987) which set out actual policy recommendations and implementational strategies for English and ESL teaching, LOTEs and Aboriginal education, languages in the media and in libraries, research, and curriculum development, along with budgetary allocations, most of which were accepted. It presented a rationale for maintaining and/or developing bilingualism in all Australians, based on a balance of social equity, cultural enrichment, and economic strategies. The multi-centre National Languages Institute of Australia was set up to stimulate a research base for language policy. Contrary to Eggington (1994), the National Policy on Languages is not a 'single-author policy'. The move for a national language policy, initiated by a wide coalition of interests embracing ethnic, Aboriginal, and deaf groups, academic linguists, language teachers, teacher unions and others, was described by the Australian political scientist, Donald Horne, as 'a blueprint for change stamped by the voice of ordinary citizens'. Lo Bianco had been part of this coalition; he had already chaired a representative group developing a languages-in-education policy for Victoria. His 1987 report was based on responses from states and many interest groups to the Senate report of 1984. It skilfully brought together research findings, local experience, and the aspirations of many sections of the Australian community into a coherent languages policy.

By the mid-1980s, South Australia and Victoria had already established languages-in-education policies based on the guiding principles, which recommended that LOTEs (especially those used in Australia) should be an integral part of each child's education from primary school. This actually preceded and stimulated action on the National Policy on Languages.

As economic rationalism and short-term economic objectives have dominated government policy, since about 1990, the balance has shifted towards economic strategies (rather than multiculturalism) as the motivation for the choice of languages in education, with an emphasis on Asian languages prioritized for trade, notably Japanese. The Australian Languages and Literacy Policy (= ALLP 1991) was the brainchild of the then minister, John Dawkins. While retaining (at least rhetorically) the earlier guiding principles, it emphasized English literacy and economically motivated second language learning taking precedence over socially motivated language maintenance of all but the most numerous community languages in the prioritization of 14 languages for special funding. The languages are Arabic, (Mandarin) Chinese, French, German, (Modern) Greek, Indonesian, Japanese, Italian, Korean, Russian, Spanish, Thai, Vietnamese, and Aboriginal Languages. Each state was to prioritize eight of the 14 languages and schools or education systems would receive $300 per capita for students passing the Matriculation examination in these languages. Though there is no directive against the teaching of non-prioritized languages, the teaching of such languages has decreased in some schools. Although the ALLP slightly increased funding for adult ESL programs, it was accompanied by an instrumental emphasis on survival English literacy training (intensive programs for the first 510 hours of instruction). While programs ensuing from the ALLP have probably reduced the backlog of migrants requiring ESL, its labour-market orientation has had the effect of blurring the categories of ESL learner and adult literacy learner and introduced insecurity into the adult ESL teaching profession. There were controversial recommendations on Aboriginal languages, such as an emphasis on the twenty 'healthy' languages in education to the exclusion of languages that were being revived or revitalized. Most of the funding earmarked for the catchall category 'Aboriginal languages and literacy' was intended for English literacy for Aborigines. The ALLP was preceded by a Green Paper entitled 'The language (sic) of Australia' which was so universally condemned for its insensitive monocentrism that its direction was not fully reflected in the actual policy.

Education being constitutionally a state prerogative in Australia, all states now have their own languages-in-education policy, most of which mainstream LOTEs in primary as well as secondary school and facilitate the teaching of a relatively wide range of languages. Co-operative arrangements between the states have facilitated the accreditation of 38 LOTEs (including Australian Sign Language) as Matriculation subjects. A subject, Australian Indigenous Languages for students of both indigenous and non-indigenous languages, includes options for speakers and/or learners of specific languages and an overview of indigenous languages. Several states have responded to the ALLP with very ambitious policies, such as compulsory teaching of LOTEs to all students throughout primary and secondary school by the end of the decade.

ALLP was supplemented by a reprioritization of languages based on a report (Rudd 1994) on Asian Languages and Australia's Economic Future, endorsed in 1995 by a meeting of federal and state government representatives. The Rudd Report gives special status to four priority languages, Chinese (Mandarin), Indonesian, Japanese, and Korean, recommending special funds for their development and expansion and that they be studied by 60% of students and the other languages by 40%. The report also makes recommendations on starting age, minimum time on learning task, and teaching models (a majority of more modest programs but a number of immersion programs for each language), which clearly apply to all languages. Many of the points contradict existing state policies. Victoria, for instance, has decided to continue its balance between European and Asian languages on the one hand and community and international/regional languages on the other. The Australian Advisory Council on Languages and Multicultural Education which resulted from the National Policy on Languages has been replaced by less broadly based bodies.

Although the economic drive has caused anxiety among language teachers and ethnic groups, it has also generated the policy of Productive Diversity (promulgated by the then Prime Minister Keating 1992) which emphasizes the value of cultural and linguistic resources in the workforce and workplace in trade, business and tourism. Potentially this may give self-esteem (and economic security) to bilinguals and promote language maintenance and development, for it involves relatively untapped resources for the good of the nation and the well-being of those whose skills are underutilized. Australian business has so far varied in its response to this policy.

The educational explosion fuelled by the tendency for Australians to remain at school longer has propagated fears that schools are leaving many people functionally illiterate. Various surveys have given qualified support to these anxieties. The ALLP substantially increased funding for child and adult literacy programs, including early intervention strategies, proficiency levels, ESL and literacy in the workplace. With its emphasis on English literacy, however, it leaves aside the important issue of biliteracy.

Among the positive developments for indigenous languages were the bilingual education programs started as transitional programs in 1973 in the Northern Territory, where most speakers of Aboriginal languages live. Opportunities for self-determination have led to some Aboriginal communities running their own schools, with strong Aboriginal language programs, including both bilingual and language revival programs (for revitalization, renewal and reclamation, see AILF 1993; Mc Kay 1996; see also the review by Harris & Devlin in Volume 5). Fishman (1991) sees in these the best opportunities for 'reversing language shift' in Australia. Many Aboriginal language programs stimulate the self-esteem of the community members and the status of the languages, and give the adult members a role in the school. Increasingly they ensure that the communities retain control of the language. Specially developed tertiary level courses at Batchelor College (Darwin) and various regional language centres train speakers of indigenous languages in Linguistics so that they can describe and develop materials in their own languages. The regional language centres have become foci of resources and the dissemination of research.

One of the educational consequences of economic rationalism in Australia was the recognition of the financial value of international students. This has made Australia one of the great exporters of English as a Foreign Language, especially in the Asian region.

Australian English as codified in the Macquarie Dictionary, the Australian Oxford Dictionary, and the Australian style manuals (Australia 1988; Peters 1994) now generally provides the norms for education and the media, and the models for the Australian Broadcasting Corporation and elite organizations are distinctively Australian. Peters (1994) constitutes a style manual for Australian English. Non-discriminatory (non-sexist, racist, ageist) language guidelines are to be found in the Australian Style Manual (Australia, e.g. 1988) and in Pauwels (1990).

Many public notices are given in a range of community languages. Interpreters and/or bilingual service providers are widely available in certain areas, e.g. hospitals, police, courts.

PROBLEMS AND DIFFICULTIES

As will be gleaned from the above, language policy in Australia has undergone rapid shifts due to ideological change, economic backdrop, and goals. This lack of consistency detracts from effective implementation. Rapid policy change exacerbates the trend towards top-down policy change by politicians and public servants without consultation. The location of language policy direction in the amalgamated Department of Employment, Education and Training has marginalized non-educational issues (e.g. media, interpreting/translating, language services) from explicit language policy. The problem was conspicuous during the 1996 federal election campaign, when the parties cross-listed language policies and promises under Education and Multiculturalism.

The strengths of Australian language policies bring with them problems and difficulties. The large number of languages offers great resources but limits funding to any one language. The policy of mainstreaming (bilingualism for all; making it possible for everyone to partake of multiculturalism) is being implemented but it presents some inherent problems. It means offering school language programs for children of all backgrounds. But some students may be disadvantaged, comparatively, in examinations because they do not have a home background in the language, while others may, because of their background, not benefit so much from the program. Some states are experimenting with different syllabuses and/or assessment systems but this can lead to discrimination against some, e.g. 2nd generation bilinguals with a limited home background in the language.

The federal system presents both advantages and disadvantages. During periods of federal inactivity, some states have continued to build their own language policies on the guiding principles of the emerging national policy. On the other hand, some states have been able to hold back others where united action has been necessary.

Changes in the dominant ideologies of the country have caused lapses; economic rationalism/the user pays mentality have not annihilated the principles of the language policy but have shifted the emphasis. The refunctioning of education in the interests of short-term economic goals, has disadvantaged some community languages and especially Aboriginal languages, in education.

Aboriginal languages have also suffered by sharing funding with ESL for Aborigines. Recently, economic considerations have placed an undue emphasis on the lower levels of ESL for both adults and children. Ambitious language policies without the backing of quantitatively and qualitatively adequate staffing levels (with unrealistic expectations) are leading to LOTE programs not achieving their linguistic goals.

In Australian Aboriginal cultures, there is a close link between land, language and people (the land 'owns' the people and this relationship is expressed through the language). This affects the extent to which some languages can be learned generally by 'outsiders'. It also makes the federal and state administrative units of planning inappropriate since the Aboriginal land/language units will be much smaller than a state but may be situated in more than one state.

LIKELY FUTURE DIRECTIONS

What the future holds is uncertain. Much depends on government priorities, and the direction and severity of government spending cuts. However, cultural diversity is now closely linked to the dynamic nature of Australia's national identity for the vast majority of the population. Also, Australia's commitment to globalization, participation in the Asian region, and the 2000 Olympic Games will promote multilingualism and language learning. As the language demography of Australia changes, services will be provided in more and different languages. Productive Diversity policy (whether under that name or another) needs to be implemented through government incentives but it is not clear that this will occur. It is unlikely in the present state of affairs that a full-scale open review of language policy and its implementation will be conducted, desirable though it may be. There is an overall commitment to making the experience of learning a second language part of the primary and secondary education of all Australians in a range of programs, including content-based ones. This is being implemented with less than the necessary (teacher and curriculum) resources – and if it does not succeed, second language learning and attitudes to LOTEs will not be helped. The serious threat to Aboriginal languages may be difficult to overcome though a small number of languages are expanding and will benefit from increased consciousness and activism among indigenous people. Otherwise much depends on the commitment of other Australians to reconciliation with indigenous people by the end of this century. The position of Australian English is now fully resolved. In July 1996, the Federal Government commissioned Language Australia (formerly the National Languages and Literacy Institute of Australia) to produce a National Literacy Strategy. It is to be hoped that this is seen as part of a continuing national policy on languages.

Monash University
Australia

REFERENCES

AILF: 1993, *Australian Indigenous Languages Framework. National Consultation Document*, Australian Indigenous Languages Framework Project, Adelaide.
Australia: 1988, *Style manual for authors, editors and printers*, 4th edition, Australian Government Publishing Service, Canberra.
Clyne, M.G.: 1991, *Community Languages The Australian Experience*, Cambridge University Press, Cambridge.
Dawkins, J.: 1991, *Australian Languages and Literacy Policy*, Australian Government Publishing Service, Canberra.
Delbridge, A. et al. (eds.): 1981, *The Macquarie Dictionary*, Macquarie Library, St. Leonards.
Dixon, R.M.W.: 1989, *Australian Languages*, Department of Aboriginal Affairs, Canberra.
Djité, P.G.: 1994, *From Language Policy to Language Planning*, National Languages and Literacy Institute of Australia, Canberra.
Eggington, W.G.: 1994, 'Language policy and planning in Australia', *Annual Review of Applied Linguistics* 14, 137–55.
Fishman, J.A.: 1991, *Reversing language shift*, Multilingual Matters, Clevedon.
Horvath, B.: 1983, *Variation in Australian English*, Cambridge University Press, Cambridge.
Kaldor, S. & Malcolm, I.: 1991, 'Aboriginal English – An overview', in S. Romaine (ed.), *Language in Australia*, Cambridge University Press, Cambridge, 67–83.
Lo Bianco, J.: 1987, *National Policy on Languages*, Australian Government Publishing Service, Canberra.
McKay, G.: 1996, *The Land Still Speaks* (= Commissioned Report No. 44, National Board of Employment, Education and Training), Australian Government Publishing Service, Canberra.
Mitchell, A.G. & Delbridge, A.: 1965, *The Speech of Australian Adolescents*, Angus and Robertson, Sydney.

Ozolins, U.: 1991, 'National languages policy and planning: migrant languages', in S. Romaine (ed.), *Language in Australia*, Cambridge University Press, Cambridge, 329–48.

Ozolins, U.: 1993, *The Politics of Language in Australia*, Cambridge University Press, Canberra.

Pauwels, A.F.: 1990, *Non-discriminatory Language*, Australian Government Publishing Service, Canberra.

Peters, P.: 1994, *Cambridge Australian English Style Guide*, Cambridge University Press, Cambridge.

Rudd, K.M.: 1994, *Asian Languages and Australia's Economic Future*, Australian Government Publishing Service, Canberra.

Schmidt, A.: 1990, *The Loss of Australia's Aboriginal Language Heritage*, Aboriginal Studies Press, Canberra.

Senate: 1984 *National Language Policy*, (= Report of the Senate Committee on Education and the Arts.) Australian Government Publishing Service, Canberra.

Trudgill, P.: 1986, *Dialects in Contact*, Blackwell, Oxford.

Walsh, M.: 1991, 'Overview of indigenous languages of Australia', in S. Romaine (ed.), *Language in Australia*, Cambridge University Press, Cambridge, 27–48.

THOMAS K. RICENTO

LANGUAGE POLICY AND EDUCATION IN THE UNITED STATES

The purpose of this review is to provide a balanced description of important aspects of language policy in the U.S. as they relate, either directly or indirectly, to educational practices in the United States. Language policies derive from the following sources: official enactments of governing bodies or authorities, such as legislation, executive directives, judicial orders or decrees, or policy statements; and non-official institutional or individual practices or customs. Policies may also evolve as a consequence of actions governments do *not* take, for example, by not providing support for the teaching or learning of a particular language, or language variety, or by designating and promoting an official language and ignoring other languages, or by failing to provide adequate resources to ensure all groups have equal opportunities to acquire the official language in educational settings. Policies may also evolve from grass roots movements and become formalized through laws, practices, or some combination of both. In this review, theoretical perspectives on language policy and education will be addressed only briefly (for background information, see Wiley 1996a; also see reviews by Christian & Rhodes in Volume 4; and by McCarty and by Faltis in Volume 5).

EARLY DEVELOPMENTS

The focus of much of the earliest work in language policy in the U.S. was on the status of English vs. non-English languages from the colonial period through the mid-nineteenth century. Conklin and Lourie (1983) describe the history of languages in North America, beginning with the arrival of the first Europeans in the 16th century; Heath and Mandabach (1983) describe the British legacy of tolerance toward the use of non-English languages coupled with an aversion to rigid standardization of English prevalent in the United States until the mid-nineteenth century. However, tolerance was limited to speakers of European languages; Native American languages and cultures were stigmatized, and government policy, beginning in 1802, was to separate Indians from their cultures (Leibowitz 1971). Colonies, such as Virginia and South Carolina (and later, many states) passed 'compulsory ignorance laws' which made it a crime to teach slaves, and sometimes free-blacks, to read or write (Crawford 1992). Beginning in the 1850s, the development of a common public school system, coupled with a nativist

R. Wodak and D. Corson (eds), Encyclopedia of Language and Education,
Volume 1: Language Policy and Political Issues in Education, 137–148.
© *1997 Kluwer Academic Publishers. Printed in the Netherlands.*

movement beginning in the 1880s, led to the imposition of English as the sole language of instruction in public and most parochial schools by the 1920s (Heath 1981). Prior to 1889, only three states had laws prescribing English as the language of instruction in private schools, while by 1923, thirty-four states required English (Leibowitz 1971: p. 7). In California (1921) and Hawaii (1920), a series of laws were passed aimed at abolishing Japanese language schools; by 1923, twenty-two states had laws prohibiting the teaching of foreign languages in primary schools. In *Meyer v. Nebraska* (1923), the U.S. Supreme Court found a 1919 Nebraska statute that forbade teaching in any language other than English to be unconstitutional, and in 1927, the Court upheld a ruling by the Ninth Circuit Court of Appeals (1926) which had found laws prohibiting the teaching of non-English languages in twenty-two states to be unconstitutional (Tamura 1993).

The period 1930 to 1965 was relatively uneventful with regard to federal intervention in language policy issues, with several notable exceptions, such as the continued intrusion of U.S. influence in language-in-education policy in Puerto Rico (Resnick 1993), and restrictive policies towards the use of Japanese and German in public domains from the 1930s through World War II. However, the failure of the federal and state governments to address the educational needs of language minority students and other historically marginalized groups is an example of policy-making through inaction.

MAJOR CONTRIBUTIONS

Beginning in the 1960s, the federal government took a more active role in accommodating and, in some cases, promoting non-English languages in education. The federal role increased in two ways: increased expenditures under Titles I, IV, and VII of the Elementary and Secondary Education Act (now called the Improve America's Schools Act, or IASA), and an increased role in the enforcement of civil rights laws in education (Macias 1982). The first major federal involvement in the area of status planning was the Bilingual Education Act (BEA) of 1968 which authorized the use of non-English languages in the education of low-income language minority students who had been segregated in inferior schools, or had been placed in English-only (submersion) classes (Lyons 1992: p. 365). Other federally supported programs which deal with language and education include the Native American Language Act of 1990, which endorses the preservation of indigenous languages, and requires government agencies to ensure that their activities promote this goal, and the National Literacy Act of 1991, which authorized literacy programs and established the National Institute for Literacy.

Title VI of the 1964 Civil Rights Act and the Equal Educational Opportunities Act of 1974 have provided the statutory bases, while the equal protection clause of the Fourteenth Amendment of the U.S. Constitution has provided the constitutional rationale for expanding educational opportunities for language minority students in a number of important court cases (see Fernandez 1987). Among the most significant of these was the *Lau v. Nichols* (1974) decision, in which the United States Supreme Court, relying on sections 601 and 602 of Title VI of the 1964 Civil Rights Act, found that the San Francisco School District had failed to provide a meaningful educational opportunity to Chinese ancestry students due to their lack of basic English skills. The Court did not specify an appropriate remedy; however, the Office for Civil Rights of the Department of Education wrote guidelines (the Lau Remedies) which instructed school districts how to identify and evaluate limited and non-English-speaking children, instructional "treatments" to use, including bilingual education, exit criteria and professional teacher standards. Political opposition to one remedy, so-called maintenance bilingual education programs, has led to increased federal support for transitional bilingual education programs, in which students are exited to English-only classrooms after three years in bilingual classrooms, as well as for alternative instructional models, such as English as a second language (ESL) programs.

Before 1978, children of native American backgrounds were not eligible for admission to federally funded bilingual programs because English was reported as their dominant language. However, linguists and educators concluded that the variety of English used ('Indian English' code) creates difficulties in the English-only classroom. By 1986–87, only about 11% of Title VII bilingual education grants were designated for Indian children (about $10 million). In 1992, the Indian Nations at Risk Task Force reported to the Secretary of Education on its goals for the year 2000 for American Indian and Alaska Native students. They recommended that: (1) all schools serving Native students provide opportunities for students to maintain and develop their tribal languages; (2) all Native children have early childhood education providing the needed "language, social, physical, spiritual, and cultural foundations" for school and later success; (3) state governments develop curricula that are "culturally and linguistically appropriate", and implement the provisions of the Native American Language Act of 1990 in the public schools (Waggoner 1992a: p. 3). A number of factors have prevented successful implementation of the Task Force recommendations (Crawford 1989: p. 247). In an effort to fortify the status of their ancestral languages, however, a number of tribes adopted official language policies in the 1980s, including the Navajo, Red Lake Band of Chippewa, Northern Ute, Arapahoe, Pasqua Yaqui, and Tohono O'odlam (Papago) (Crawford 1989: p. 246).

Policy for English as a second language education has been subsumed under a variety of federal and state programs, including Chapters I and

VII of the Elementary and Secondary Education Act (ESEA, now called the Improve America's Schools Act, IASA), the Head Start Program, the National Literacy Act of 1991, the Immigration Reform and Control Act (IRCA) of 1986, the Adult Education Act (AEA) and the Carl D. Perkins Vocational and Applied Technology Education Act (Perkins Act). According to the 1990 census, nearly 32 million persons 5+ years of age speak a language other than English at home, and of those, 14 million report they did not speak English well. Data from other surveys, such as the National Adult Literacy Survey, confirm that the number of adults requiring ESL services is somewhere between 12 and 14 million (Chisman, Wrigley & Ewen 1993). Despite the demonstrated need for English language programs for adults, there has been little coordination among the various federal, state or private funding sources, and no overarching policy approach to meet this population's educational needs (Wrigley & Ewen 1995). With regard to the public schools, in the 1990–91 school year, only about 15 per cent of the roughly 3 million school-age LM children requiring specialized instruction were enrolled in Bilingual Education Act-funded programs, and more than 500,000 children needing English language instruction did not receive any.

According to the results of a survey of public schools in the United States conducted by the American Council on the Teaching of Foreign Languages (ACTFL), more than six million students were enrolled in foreign language courses in grades 7–12 Fall, 1994. This represents a 3.9% increase in enrollments since 1990. Among high school students (grades 9 through 12), slightly more than 5 million students (42.2% of all public high school enrollees) were studying a foreign language in 1994, the highest enrollment rate since 1928, and an increase of 3.8% over 1990 (Draper & Hicks 1996: p. 303). Among elementary schools (based on data from 24 states), 5% of students in grades Kindergarten through six were enrolled in non-exploratory foreign language courses in 1994, compared to 4.24% (22 states reporting) in 1990 (Draper & Hicks 1996: p. 303). Spanish continues to attract the greatest number of students, accounting for 64.5% of all language enrollments, K–12th grade; French accounts for 22.3% and German for 6.1% of foreign language enrollments. The fastest growing language is Japanese, which increased from 0.23% to 0.36% of total secondary school enrollments between 1990 and 1994. Data on foreign language enrollments in postsecondary institutions for the 1995 school year have been compiled by the Modern Language Association (Brod & Huber, in press). The data are based on results of a questionnaire sent to the registrars of 2,772 institutions, with 97.7% of the institutions responding. The twelve most studied languages, followed by total number of enrollments and percentage of total foreign language enrollments, are: Spanish (606,286) (53.2%); French (205,351) (18%); German (96,262) (8.5%); Japanese (44,723) (3.9%); Italian (43,760) (3.8%); Chinese (26,471) (2.3%); Latin (25,897) (2.3%); Russian (24,729) (2.2%); Ancient Greek (16,272) (1.4%); Hebrew (Biblical and Modern) (13,127) (1.2%); Portuguese (6,531) (0.6%); and Arabic (4,444) (0.4%). Enrollments in Arabic and Chinese increased significantly since 1990 (28% and 36%, respectively), while enrollments in French, German and Russian declined an average of 32% during the same period. Although study of a number of languages has grown in the past decade, increases in the number of students attending college, along with fluctuations in enrollments among various languages, has resulted in fairly steady registrations in modern foreign languages per one hundred college students since 1977, ranging from 7.3 to 8.2.

Among the nearly 32 million people in the U.S. aged 5+ who speak a language other than English at home – an increase of 38% from 1980 (Waggoner 1992b) – about 17 million (56%) speak Spanish. Nearly 2 million persons speak French at home, while 1.5 million speak German and 1.3 million each speak Chinese languages or Italian. Polish, Korean, and Vietnamese are spoken by at least half a million people each (Waggoner 1992b).

WORK IN PROGRESS

Issues which have received attention in the literature in recent years include the education of speakers of minority (non-English) languages and non-standard varieties of English, education for the deaf, literacy, and preparation of teachers for the increasingly diverse school age population in the United States.

Despite significant within group gains in educational achievement, many language minority (LM) students perform less well scholastically than their majority peers (see Genesee 1994). Although the population of LM students is greatest in selected states (California, Texas, New York, Florida, Illinois, New Jersey, Arizona, and Pennsylvania), LM students reside in all fifty states. Current federal law requires that LM students be identified and, where numbers warrant it, appropriate instructional programs be implemented to ensure LM students have access to the core curriculum. Given the decentralized structure of the U.S. educational system, local educational agencies (LEAs), such as school boards and districts, must implement state-mandated programs designed to meet the special educational needs of LM students. Although an ambitious set of national educational goals was identified in Goals 2000 (with minimal reference to LM populations) during the administration of President George Bush, states are offered no guidance in how they might best achieve the goals. The lack of a coherent national language policy reflects, in part, broader social divisions about the role of education, and especially language(s), in society (see Arias & Casanova 1993). For example, pluralists favor maintaining immigrant and indigenous non-English languages and argue that all students – majority and minority – benefit cognitively, as well as socially, by educational programs which develop two languages; assimilationists, on the other hand, believe maintenance of non-English languages is a private matter, and that the most important measure of success for bilingual programs is how fast children acquire English, not the long-term academic achievement of students. Ramirez et al. (1991) provide the best evidence to date that late-exit transitional bilingual education programs are superior to most early-exit or so-called English immersion (submersion) programs in terms of students' long term academic achievement in English-mediated instruction. However, explaining underlying causes of student success (and failure) is extremely complex, and cannot be undertaken without reference to issues of language and identity, and socioeconomic status, among many other variables. For example, members of some LM groups are able to acculturate to the mainstream (English-speaking) society very rapidly, regardless of whether their non-English native language is included in the curriculum, and without losing their cultural (even linguistic) identity; on the other hand, members of other groups, with different histories in the United States, often including segregated and inferior public schooling, have come to believe that full socioeconomic access to the dominant (English-speaking) culture is not a viable option, and as a result are more at risk for school failure, regardless of the curriculum they are exposed to in school. Groups also vary in group adhesion, often displaying wide intra-group variation in members' attitudes toward language maintenance and cultural assimilation (Paulston 1994: p. 16).

The publication of *A Nation at Risk* in 1984 rekindled a national debate on the 'literacy crisis'. The 1992 National Adult Literacy Survey (NALS), a comprehensive survey of English literacy in the United States, found, among other things, that 40 to 44 million adults (21 to 23 per cent of the adult population) performed at the lowest levels in tasks involving prose literacy. The fact that twenty-one per cent of the respondents were immigrants still acquiring English who were unfamiliar with U.S. culture complicates the findings. Also, the findings do not indicate how well respondents, both native English and non-native English speakers, are able to cope with literacy challenges on a daily basis. These reports and concerns about American competitiveness in the global economy have led, in recent years, to the creation of programs for workplace and family literacy. In school settings, policy and curricula have tended to focus on the acquisition of literacy in Standard English, with little attention paid, until recently, to the acquisition and maintenance of non-English literacies, or to the effects of Standard English policies on speakers of so-called non-standard varieties of English, such as African American Language (AAL) (Wiley 1996b).

In recent years, a movement has emerged within the Deaf community in the U.S. to promote the teaching of American Sign Language, rather than English, as the first language of deaf persons, preferably in bilingual

(ASL/English)-bicultural programs. This recommendation is based on research which shows that the acquisition of English literacy by deaf students instructed in sign systems, such as Manually Coded English (MCE), is less successful than it is for students who have had access to ASL during their formative language acquiring years. Critics, who oppose removing deaf children from their hearing parents to learn ASL and become acculturated into the Deaf community, argue this will result in permanent separation and rejection of English. Proponents of ASL as a first language view this as a language rights issue, since policies promoting oralism and restricting the use of sign language, usually developed by hearing persons, have historically oppressed the Deaf community and limited their social and economic advancement (see the review by Branson & Miller).

An important policy issue, given the increasing diversity of the school age and adult population in the U.S., concerns the preparation of teachers. State credentialing authorities have, in recent years, modified requirements for teacher certification to include courses in second language acquisition, culture, and methods and materials appropriate for linguistically and culturally diverse populations. Professional teacher organizations have lobbied state and federal agencies for greater funding and recognition of the specialized training required for teaching in multilingual and multicultural classrooms and schools. Many states now offer a certificate or endorsement in English as a Second Language (ESL) and Bilingual Education (in various non-English languages). Publications integrating theory and practice in the education of LM students include Garcia and Baker (1995), Genesee (1994), and Milk, Mercado and Sapiens (1992).

PROBLEMS AND DIFFICULTIES

The federal government's role in expanding educational opportunities for minorities, including language minorities, has been challenged in recent years on a number of fronts. Opposition to bilingual education – especially developmental bilingual education – began in the earliest years of federal involvement (see Ricento, forthcoming, for a discussion); changes in the types of programs – and funding levels – authorized by Congress began with the 1974 reauthorization of the Bilingual Education Act (BEA); in that document, the nature of bilingual education was more narrowly defined than in earlier policy documents, reflecting a popular backlash against so-called "affirmative ethnicity"; a bilingual education program was defined as one in which "there is instruction given in, and study of, English and, to the extent necessary to allow a child to progress effectively through the educational system, the native language of the children of limited English-speaking ability" (cited in Lyons 1990: p. 69). In the 1980s, funding for alternative programs, such as ESL and structured immersion, was increased. By the Fiscal Year 1993 appropriation for the BEA, programs that did not require the use of the limited English proficient's native language increased from 6% (FY 1988) to 23% (FY 1992); funding levels for personnel training, multifunctional resource centers, data collection, evaluation assistance centers, and a fellowship program to support doctoral students in bilingual education were decreased from between 12% and 20% over 1988 levels, after adjusting for inflation (Ricento 1996: p. 143).

Groups that oppose bilingual education, such as U.S. English, also tend to oppose other types of federal accommodations to non-English speakers, such as bilingual ballots and the publication of government documents, forms and brochures in non-English languages (although a recent study by the U.S. General Accounting Office found that 99.4% of the documents produced by the federal government are in English, excluding documents from the State and Defense departments). Such provisions and programs are often cited by opponents as examples of "ethnic-based" entitlements (for example, see Imhoff 1990). These groups also tend to strongly advocate the establishment of English as the official language of the United States, or of governmental entities at all levels. This movement began in the early 1980s under the leadership of the late U.S. Senator S.I. Hayakawa who introduced a constitutional amendment (S.J. Res. 72) in 1981 declaring English the official language of the United States. Although the bill was never reported out of committee, by 1990, seventeen states had adopted laws or amended their constitutions declaring English the official state language (Crawford 1992: p. 16). On August 1, 1996, the U.S. House of Representatives, under Republican leadership, passed for the first time in U.S. history a bill declaring English the official language of the U.S. government (H.R. 123, The English Language Empowerment Act). Provisions of the bill include repeal of federal bilingual ballots and a prohibition against federal employees communicating in writing in non-English languages, although they may communicate orally in languages other than English. The Senate failed to act on a similar bill in the 104th Congress, thereby preventing the 104th Congress from enacting an official English law. The issue, however, is likely to return in subsequent sessions of Congress.

Although research in second language acquisition has provided clear evidence of the benefits of late-exit bilingual education programs (Ramirez et al. 1991) , of the effectiveness of second language immersion programs for monolingual English speakers (Lambert & Tucker 1972), of the transferability of conceptual knowledge learned in one language to another language (Cummins 1979), and of the social and affective benefits of programs and curricula which value the culture and language of so-called non-mainstream students (Baker 1993), these findings have been distorted and politicized by opponents. Professional education organizations, such as Teachers of English to Speakers of Other Languages (TESOL), the National Association for Bilingual Education (NABE), the Modern Language Association (MLA), and the National Council of Teachers of English (NCTE), among many others, have offered their expertise on language education matters to policy makers at the state and federal level. However, the issues surrounding language in education policy – the use of non-English languages as the medium of instruction, the teaching of foreign languages from kindergarten through college, the maintenance of non-English languages through education, the valuing of non-English – as well as English – literacy among immigrant populations, the development of bilingual-bicultural language programs for the Deaf – have histories which extend back to the mid-nineteenth century. For example, the effects of the Americanization campaign (roughly 1914–1924) (McClymer 1982), which saw severe restriction of non-English languages in public and private domains at the same time the teaching of English to adults through civics classes was promoted by the states and the federal government, continue to influence and shape attitudes, and hence policy, with regard to the learning and teaching of languages.

LIKELY FUTURE DIRECTIONS IN RESEARCH AND PRACTICE

Research in language policy and planning is subsumed under three general headings: processes, agents and goals. Under processes, researchers investigate the mechanisms by which and through which language policies are developed, implemented, and evaluated. Examples of possible research topics in the coming decade include: the implementation of federal language policies at the state and local level; the role played by grassroots organizations in articulating policy and influencing legislative processes; the evaluation of policies by different constituencies; the implementation and evaluation of specific program types in specific educational settings; the interplay of the various components which collectively, and individually, determine language policies. Agents refers to the public and private individuals and collectivities which promote various policies. Examples of areas likely to be researched include: who controls language policy agendas, and by what means; what are the sources of authority for those agents who argue for particular policies; what are the characteristics of various interest groups that promote particular policies; what role do the media play in promoting particular policy views? Goals refers to sociopolitical and/or economic objectives sought by particular language policies. Examples of research topics in this area include: assessing the differences between stated and unstated goals; investigation of language in education policies from sociohistorical perspectives; articulation of alternative societal goals and the development of specific policies to achieve those goals; comparative analysis of language policy goals among polities.

A good sampling of new directions in language policy research is found in Hornberger and Ricento (1996).

Regarding changes in practice, as federal involvement in the policy arena has decreased in recent years (at least in certain areas), the states are likely to play a greater role in policy development and implementation. Secondly, despite significant opposition to specialized language programs for LM and mainstream school-age children, a number of states and localities have created innovative programs involving two-way bilingual programs in languages as diverse as Cantonese and Portuguese. A growing number of states has increased foreign language requirements in elementary and secondary schools. Professional language and education organizations have, in many cases, been successful in influencing the legislative process at the state and federal levels. As more research in language policy becomes available to decision-makers, and as more trained scholars enter the field, the impact on language policy development, implementation and evaluation could be significant.

The University of Texas at San Antonio
USA

REFERENCES

Arias, M.B. & Casanova, U. (eds.): 1993, *Bilingual Education: Politics, Practice, Research,* University of Chicago Press, Chicago.

Baker, C.: 1993, *Foundations of Bilingual Education and Bilingualism,* Multilingual Matters, Clevedon.

Brod, R. & Huber, B.: in press, 'Foreign language enrollments in United States institutions of higher education, Fall 1995', *ADFL Bulletin* 28(2), Winter, 1997.

Chisman, F.P., Wrigley, H.S., & Ewen, D.T.: 1993, *ESL and the American Dream,* Southport Institute for Policy Analysis, Washington, D.C.

Conklin, N.F. & Lourie, M.A.: 1983, *Host of Tongues: Language Communities in the United States,* The Free Press, New York.

Crawford, J.: 1989, *Bilingual Education: History, Politics, Theory and Practice,* Crane Publishing Co., Trenton, NJ.

Crawford, J.: 1992, *Hold Your Tongue: Bilingualism and the Politics of "English Only",* Addison-Wesley, Reading, MA.

Cummins, J.: 1979, 'Linguistic interdependence and the educational development of bilingual children', *Review of Educational Research* 49, 222–251.

Draper, J.B. & Hicks, J.H.: 1996, 'Foreign language enrollments in public secondary schools, Fall, 1994: Summary report', *Foreign Language Annals* 29(3), 303–306.

Fernandez, R.R.: 1987, 'Legislation, regulation, and litigation: The origins and evolution of public policy on bilingual education in the United States', in W.A. Van Horne (ed.), *Ethnicity and Language,* The University of Wisconsin System, Institute on Race and Ethnicity, Milwaukee, 90–123.

Garcia, O. & Baker, C. (eds.): 1995, *Policy and Practice in Bilingual Education: Extending the Foundations,* Multilingual Matters, Clevedon.

Genesee, F.: 1994, *Educating Second Language Children,* Cambridge University Press, Cambridge.

Heath, S.B.: 1981, 'English in our language heritage', in C.A. Ferguson & S.B. Heath (eds.), *Language in the USA*, Cambridge University Press, Cambridge, 6–20.

Heath, S.B. & Mandabach, F.: 1983, 'Language status decisions and the law in the United States', in J. Cobarrubias & J.A. Fishman (eds.), *Progress in Language Planning: International Perspectives*, Mouton, Berlin, 87–105.

Hornberger, N.H. & Ricento, T.K.(eds.): 1996, *Language Planning and Policy and the ELT Profession*, Special Topic Issue, *TESOL Quarterly* 30(3).

Imhoff, G.: 1990, 'The position of U.S. English on bilingual education', in C.B. Cazden & C.E. Snow (eds.), *The Annals of the American Academy of Political and Social Science*, 48–61.

Lambert, W.E. & Tucker, R.: 1972, *Bilingual Education of Children. The St. Lambert Experiment*, Newbury House, Rowley, MA.

Leibowitz, A.H.: 1971, 'Educational policy and political acceptance: The imposition of English as the language of instruction in American schools', Eric No. ED 047 321.

Lyons, J.J.: 1992, 'Secretary Bennett versus equal educational opportunity', in J. Crawford (ed.), *Language Loyalties: A Source Book on the Official English Controversy*, University of Chicago Press, Chicago, 363–366.

Lyons, J.J.: 1990, 'The past and future directions of federal bilingual-education policy', in C.B. Cazden & C.E. Snow (eds.), *The Annals of the American Academy of Political and Social Science*, 66–80.

Macias, R.: 1982, 'U.S. language-in-education policy: Issues in the schooling of langauge minorities', in R.B. Kaplan (ed.), *Annual Review of Applied Linguistics*, Newbury House, Rowley, MA, 144–160.

McClymer, J.F.: 1982, 'The Americanization movement and the education of the foreign-born adult, 1914–25', in B.J. Weiss (ed.), *American Education and the European Immigrant: 1840–1940*, University of Illinois Press, Urbana, 96–116.

Milk, R., Mercado, C. & Sapiens, A.: 1992, 'Re-thinking the education of teachers of language minority children: Developing reflective teachers for changing schools', *Occasional Papers in Bilingual Education*, National Clearinghouse for Bilingual Education, Washington, D.C., 6, Summer 1992.

Paulston, C.B.: 1994, *Linguistic Minorities in Multilingual Settings: Implications for Language Policies*, John Benjamins, Amsterdam.

Ramirez, J.D., et. al.: 1991, *Final Report: Longitudinal Study of Structured Immersion Strategy, Early-Exit, and Late-Exit Transitional Bilingual Education Programs for Language-Minority Children*, Aguirre International, San Mateo, CA.

Resnick, M.C.: 1993, 'ESL and language planning in Puerto Rican education', *TESOL Quarterly* 27(2), 259–273.

Ricento, T.K.: (forthcoming), 'National language policy in the United States', in T.K. Ricento & B. Burnaby (eds.), *Language and Politics in the United States and Canada: Myths and Realities*, Mahwah, NJ, Lawrence Erlbaum.

Ricento, T.K.: 1996, 'Language policy in the United States', in M. Herriman & B. Burnaby (eds.), *Language Policies in English-dominant Countries*, Multilingual Matters, Clevedon, 122–158.

Tamura, E.H.: 1993, 'The English-only effort, the anti-Japanese campaign, and language acquisition in the education of Japanese Americans in Hawaii', *History of Education Quarterly* 33(1), 37–58.

Waggoner, D.: 1992a, 'Indian nations task force calls for maintenance of languages and cultures', in D. Waggoner (ed.), *Numbers and Needs: Ethnic and Linguistic Minorities in the United States*, Washington, D.C. 3,5, 2.

Waggoner, D.: 1992b, 'Four in five home speakers of non-English languages in the US speak one of eight languages', in D. Waggoner (ed.), *Numbers and Needs: Ethnic and Linguistic Minorities in the United States,* Washington, D.C. 2,5,1.

Wiley, T.G.: 1996a, 'Language planning and language policy', in S.L. McKay & N.H.

Hornberger (eds.), *Sociolinguistics and Language Teaching*, Cambridge University Press, Cambridge, 103–147.

Wiley, T.G.: 1996b, *Literacy and Language Diversity in the United States*, Center for Applied Linguistics and Delta Systems, Washington, D.C. & McHenry, IL.

Wrigley, H.S. & Ewen, D.T.: 1995, *A National Language Policy for ESL*, Center for Applied Linguistics, National Clearinghouse for ESL Literacy Education, Washington, D.C.

BARBARA BURNABY

LANGUAGE POLICY AND EDUCATION IN CANADA

This sketch of Canadian language legislation and policies touches on background information, French and English as official languages, official and minority language policies for immigrants, and policies on Aboriginal languages (also see reviews by Heller in Volume 3; by Christian & Rhodes in Volume 4; and by McCarty and by Faltis in Volume 5).

Canada, a large country with a relatively small population (28 million), has a parliamentary democracy. Created legally in 1867, it now has ten provinces and two territories. Constitutionally, the federal government has jurisdiction over Aboriginal matters and the territories, the provinces over education; responsibility for immigration is shared.

In about 1500, Aboriginal people lived across what is now Canada, speaking about 450 languages and dialects from 11 language families. Immigration, starting with colonization by Britain and France, has since increased the population and changed its ethnic/racial mixture. Although immigration from northern and western Europe predominated earlier, the proportion of immigrants from other continents has increased, particularly since the 1960s. In 1991, 63% of the population reported English as mother tongue, 25% French, less than 1% Aboriginal languages, and 13% other languages (Statistics Canada 1992: p. 1).

FRENCH AND ENGLISH AS OFFICIAL LANGUAGES

Struggles between France and Britain, then Francophones and Anglophones dominate Canada's recorded history. In the 19th century, Canadian legal rights for the 'English' and 'French' populations focussed on religion rather than language (Neatby in Commissioner of Official Languages 1992: pp. v–ix). Legislation specifically on language was rare. However, in the early 20th century, increased secularism, industrialization, national attention on Canada's role in the British Empire, and massive immigration encouraged a movement to 'Anglo-conformity', especially through legislated use of English as the language in schools in most provinces. Francophones in Quebec were isolated in a French-language, church-run school system and in the social and political use of French in some areas of Quebec. Only superficially did the federal government recognize the constitutionally equal status of French with English in Parliament, in federal courts, and in the legislature and courts of Quebec.

R. Wodak and D. Corson (eds), Encyclopedia of Language and Education,
Volume 1: Language Policy and Political Issues in Education, 149–158.
© *1997 Kluwer Academic Publishers. Printed in the Netherlands.*

After 1945, industrialization, immigration, and a low birth-rate among Francophones threatened the critical mass of French even in Quebec (Neatby in Commissioner of Official Languages 1992: p. vii). Most non-French immigrants to Quebec chose English as their second language, English being the dominant language of large business in Quebec, centred in Montreal. Being ethnically Quebecois and unilingually Francophone was a severe economic disadvantage in the early 1960s (Wardhaugh 1983: pp. 74–80). In the 1960s, Francophones in Quebec, through the "Quiet Revolution" movement, acted to gain more control. In 1963, the Quebec government created a ministry of education, replacing the parochial education system.

Such pressures moved the federal government to take the constitutionally 'equal' status of the French language seriously. It established the Royal Commission on Bilingualism and Biculturalism (1963–1971) which made an elaborate study of political, cultural, and economic use of all languages in Canada except the Aboriginal languages. The impact of its research began in 1964 with language training for public servants, leading, in 1973, to measures to make English and French equitably the languages of work in the federal civil service (Commissioner of Official Languages 1992: pp. 14–17; Beaty 1989: p. 186).

From 1967 on, some provinces, anticipating the commission's impact, changed their education acts towards more use of French as language of instruction (Commissioner of Official Languages 1992: pp. 14–15). In a Montreal suburb, a group of Anglophone parents in 1965 persuaded a school board to teach their children through the medium of French so that the children would learn it as a second language faster and more effectively (Lambert & Tucker 1972). This launched the now popular 'French immersion' programs across the country. In virtually every part of the country, various versions of these programs are now a significant part of Canadian public education (Swain, this encyclopedia Volume V; Swain & Lapkin 1982).

The main outcome of the Royal Commission's Report was the *Official Languages Act* of 1969, making English and French Canada's official languages.

> In addition to declaring that English and French are to have 'equality of status and equal rights and privileges' for all the purposes of the Parliament and Government of Canada, the Act specifically imposes duties on all federal institutions to provide their services in either English or French: in the National Capital Region and in such 'bilingual districts' as might be subsequently designated, at their head offices, and in any other locations where there was 'significant demand' for such services. The Act also created the position of Commissioner of Official Languages to

oversee its implementation and generally act as official languages ombudsman. (Beaty 1989: pp. 185–186)

Beaty summarizes the main programs supporting the *Official Languages Act* as encouraging 'a more general climate of respect and support for Canada's official languages in other jurisdictions and in Canadian society as a whole':

- by supporting minority groups [English in Quebec and French elsewhere] in their attempts to achieve provincial recognition of their legal rights and their special linguistic needs;
- by fostering and helping to finance minority language education . . . ;
- by giving similar financial encouragement to the effective learning of English and French as a second language country-wide; and
- by supporting the efforts of national, private and voluntary organizations to develop their own capacity to do business in both official languages. (Beaty 1989: p. 190–191)

In 1970–1971, the federal government began its Official Languages in Education (OLE) Program. Education being a provincial responsibility, the federal government could not legislate on it directly but could encourage compliance by offering funding. Following the Royal Commission's recommendation that the federal government support the provinces in providing English education for Anglophones in Quebec and French education for Francophones in the other provinces, and in improving second official language instruction, the OLE has made transfer payments to provinces, monitored by the Commissioner of Official Languages. Although the enrolment in English schooling in Quebec and French schooling elsewhere has not changed substantially since 1971, numbers of children in second official language programs have (Peat Marwick & Churchill 1987: section III), especially French immersion programs (Canadian Education Association 1992: p. 3).

The province of New Brunswick declared itself bilingual in 1969, and most provinces legislated more status for French in the next few years. A series of actions in Quebec, especially relating to parents' rights to have their children educated in languages other than French, provoked controversy. Separatism became a driving force in the province, but the Quebec government in 1980 lost a referendum for a mandate to negotiate 'sovereignty association' (Quebec nationalism within the Canadian state) with the federal government (Commissioner of Official Languages 1992: pp. 9–22; Labrie 1992: pp. 30–32). In this climate, the nation made a number of efforts in the 1970s to prevent a total rift with Quebec.

In 1980, the federal government 'patriated' the constitution, providing a major opportunity for constitutional changes. Canada's constitution was an act of the British Parliament; patriation meant enacting some form of it through the Canadian Parliament. The 1982 *Constitution Act* left the major structure, such as the responsibilities of the federal and provincial governments, the same. It added an amending formula, as well as the *Canadian Charter of Rights and Freedoms*, which included central developments on language since the early 1960s, such as the official language status of English and French for the governments of Canada and New Brunswick. The *Charter* cannot be amended by the federal government alone, but through a formula requiring provincial support. Also, citizens can now challenge all legislation and policies in court against the *Charter* provisions.

Crucially, Quebec did not agree to the *Constitution Act* because of concerns about its amending formula. Despite attempts at resolution, 1996 finds federal relationships uneasy, with the inclusion of Quebec in the constitution unresolved. As for language in education, the *Act* precipitated many legal actions to bring mother-tongue education provisions for Francophone children in English Canada and Anglophone children in Quebec into line with the *Charter* (Foucher 1985; Martel 1991). However, official second language programs for Anglophones and Francophones have been relatively uncontroversial.

The evolution of English and French as official languages and languages of education, work, commerce, and so forth during the past thirty years certainly provides no perfect model for language relations, especially since it has not yet satisfied either party. However, it has set a certain standard for some other language minorities in the country. The intense negotiations between Quebec and the rest of Canada still dominate discussion at the national and provincial levels.

LANGUAGE ISSUES FOR SPEAKERS OF NON-OFFICIAL LANGUAGES

Reading official statements, one would scarcely believe that Canadians speak languages other than English and French. Federal statements carefully refer to speakers of non-official languages as other *cultural* groups. However, given the important role of immigration in Canada, to say nothing of the special position of the Aboriginal peoples, non-official languages are very much in evidence. This section discusses language issues for speakers of non-official languages other than Aboriginal ones (see also Corson & Lemay 1996: ch. 5; and see the review by Corson on pp. 77–87). It refers to 'immigrants' even though non-official language issues often continue well into the second and third generations after immigration.

Official Language Training for Those Who Speak Neither Official Language

Federal legislation covers official languages for those who speak an official language already; no federal legislation even suggests that speakers of neither English nor French have the *right* to support in learning one of those languages. However, some programs relate to issues of language for residents of Canada who do not speak either official language. Federal policy on official languages in education for Anglophones or Francophones refers almost entirely to children's education, but official language training for non-official language groups mainly targets adults, largely because the federal government strongly links immigration to the labourforce.

The *Official Languages Act* (1969) makes no provisions for the learning of official languages by residents of Canada who do not speak either language (well). However, in 1971, the federal government declared itself by policy multicultural. Clearly aimed at calming backlash among non-English/French groups over the declaration of official languages, the multiculturalism policy pledged to promote respect and support for all of Canada's languages and cultures. The original policy stated that 'the government will continue to assist immigrants to acquire at least one of Canada's official languages in order to become full participants in Canadian society' (Saouab 1993: p. 4). The policy passed through various stages, none including direct support for official language training for immigrants, and evolved into the present *Multiculturalism Act* (1988), which mainly fosters non-English and French cultures, anti-racism, and affirmative action in support of visible minorities.

Since about 1970, the *Immigration Act* has made knowing one official language an advantage in admissibility for certain classes of immigrants, but only a minority of applicants are assessed this way. To become a Canadian citizen applicants must demonstrate a 'reasonable' knowledge (undefined) of either official language. From the early 1970s to the late 1980s, the federal department responsible for the *Citizenship Act* made agreements with most provinces for partial funding of provincial language and citizenship training for adults.

However, the federal government emphasized more the economic impact of immigration. The federal agency responsible for employment included language training for immigrants 'bound for the labourforce' under its large program of employment (re)training from the late 1960s to about 1990. The provinces' community colleges did the training (to accommodate education as a provincial responsibility) but federal officials chose the students. This program provided about 24 weeks of full-time training with a training allowance. Controversy surrounded this program, especially concerning decisions on who was destined for the labourforce. Meanwhile, since the 1960s, provinces, local authorities, and non-governmental organizations (NGOs) have provided a variety of language training to immigrants.

Since 1991, the employment-related federal program has been replaced by one serving immigrants who do not yet have Canadian citizenship, regardless of their labour market intentions, and a smaller, occupation-specific one for immigrants with more English/French. They include individual assessment against nation-wide language standards, counselling, and recommendations on local programs. Private and public institutions bid annually for contracts to provide training, either generic or targeted (e.g. for immigrants with low levels of education). Childminding and transportation may be provided, but no training allowances. Criticisms of this program include: that newcomers who have obtained Canadian citizenship are not eligible; that federal authorities have left provinces and NGOs with the burden of most language training; and that the one-year contract bids stress the bidding agencies (Burnaby 1992, 1996).

ESL for schoolchildren is simpler than adult programs only in being delivered almost exclusively by school boards. In areas where there is little immigration (e.g. the Atlantic provinces), immigrant children may be unevenly served if at all; however, in high-immigration regions, they usually get at least minimal attention, such as special classes, withdrawal from regular classes for part of the day, or sensitization of regular teachers to their needs (Ashworth 1992: pp. 36–40). There are no bilingual programs to help orient children to Canadian schooling. Some part-time classes for immigrant women have been funded as 'parents and preschoolers' programs so that the children get some language training too.

Teaching of Non-Official Languages as Ancestral Languages

Clearly Canada greatly values its official languages. But what of the value of other languages that immigrants bring to Canada? In the era of total Anglophone power, the system viewed languages other than English with suspicion, and encouraged immigrants, especially children, to forget their mother tongues. From the 19th century, some immigrant communities organized and funded non-official language classes for their children. Until the early 20th century, when provincial education acts were changed to prevent them, there were some publically-supported bilingual schools. Some religious groups struggled long into this century against compulsory English schooling (Ashworth 1992: p. 40). Some immigrant groups have continued to fund private multilingual schools or classes in non-official languages.

The *Official Languages Act* of 1969 provoked a climate of linguistic uncertainty for non-official languages; the 1971 policy of multiculturalism hinted at some recognition of them. In 1977, under that policy, the federal government created the Cultural Enrichment Program. It included support for the teaching of non-official languages, primarily to children of communities where the target language was a 'heritage language' (the mother tongue or ancestral language of the children). Extensive and vitriolic resistance to the establishment of heritage language classes at public expense developed (Cummins & Danesi 1990: ch. 3; d'Anglejan & de Koninck 1992: pp. 100–101; Fleras & Elliott 1992: pp. 155–159). Since 1977, some programs have been associated with the schools and at least partially publically funded, and new ones have been created in the schools, but most remain non-academically-recognized add-ons (Ashworth 1992; Canadian Education Association 1991; d'Anglejan & de Koninck 1992; Toohey 1992). Although the multiculturalism policy and *Act* encouraged the learning of the official languages, heritage language programs were never associated with *fiscal* support for official language training programs (i.e. linked to issues of children at risk concerning the learning of English or French).

LANGUAGE POLICIES FOR ABORIGINAL PEOPLES

Official policy has largely considered Aboriginal peoples and their languages as outside the debates outlined above. Since Confederation in 1867, Aboriginal people – 'Indians' in the *British North America Act* of 1867 and 'Eskimos' by a court ruling in 1939 – were constitutionally the federal government's responsibility for all services. The Royal Commission on Bilingualism and Biculturalism excluded them on the grounds that their issues were more properly dealt with elsewhere. They have not been included, largely by their own choice, in subsequent definitions of cultural minorities. Administrations kept them isolated from the rest of the population. Such separate treatment did leave open opportunities for special policies suited to their unique needs; unfortunately, most of these opportunities have been wasted in racist and assimilative ways (Corson & Lemay 1996: ch. 2).

Comparison of the proportions of mother tongue speakers of Aboriginal languages among the Aboriginal population from the censuses of 1951 to 1981 dramatically illustrates a decline of Aboriginal languages. In 1951, 87.4% of the Aboriginal population had an Aboriginal language as a mother tongue whereas in 1981 it was 29.3% (Burnaby & Beaujot 1986: p. 36). Clearly, Aboriginal languages in Canada are at great risk (some much more than others).

Although Aboriginal languages were sometimes used in Aboriginal education in the 19th and early 20th centuries, more often draconian Aboriginal education policies forced Aboriginal children to speak English or French in school, even to the extent of severe physical punishment for speaking an Aboriginal language. Until about the 1950s, schooling for Aboriginal children was mostly contracted to Christian groups; a later policy moved to integrate all Aboriginal children into provincial schools or, in remote areas, to establish federally-run schools. Today, those federal schools are largely run by local Aboriginal authorities. Since the 1960s, Aboriginal languages have increasingly been taught in Aboriginal and provincial schools as subjects of instruction (Assembly of First Nations 1990; Kirkness & Bowman 1992). In addition, Aboriginal languages have been introduced recently as medium of instruction up to the third grade in some schools in the territories and Quebec, where the children begin school speaking only or mainly their Aboriginal language. Aboriginal language immersion programs have begun in several southern communities, where the children start school speaking only or mainly an official language. For complex reasons relating to the *Official Languages Act*, nine Aboriginal languages have been made official languages in the Northwest Territories together with English and French.

Despite improvements in Aboriginal language programming in schools, Churchill's (1986) findings that policies for indigenous groups cluster at the lower levels of his scale of policy development – in that most programs are for the youngest children, only for a few years, inadequately funded, and seen to be transitional to fluency in an official language – still stands. Although there are many more programs in the mid-1990s, current survey data give the same impression Clarke and MacKenzie (1980) got in their study of Aboriginal language programs – namely, that Aboriginal language programs give only lip service to pluralism and are actually assimilationist in intent.

CONCLUSIONS

Canada's largest minority, Francophones, have challenged Canadian Anglo-dominance to the point of constitutional crisis. Smaller linguistic groups unfavourably compare the resources supporting official language services for English and French speakers with those available to them even to learn a first official language, much less enhance their own languages. Aboriginal groups, many of whose languages face extinction, struggle particularly about priorities between language efforts and political and economic recognition. A needs assessment of language resources in the new global order might recommend a reorganization of Canada's language emphases.

Ontario Institute for Studies in Education
University of Toronto
Canada

REFERENCES

Ashworth, M.: 1992, 'Views and visions', in B. Burnaby & A. Cumming (eds.), *Socio-political Aspects of ESL in Canada*, OISE Press, Toronto, 35–49.

Assembly of First Nations: 1990, *Towards Linguistic Justice for First Nations*, Education Secretariat, Assembly of First Nations, Ottawa.

Beaty, S.: 1989, 'A new official languages act for Canada – Its scope and implications', in P. Pupier & J. Woehrling (eds.), *Language and Law: Proceedings of the First Conference of the International Institute of Comparative Linguistic Law*, Wilson and Lafleur, Montreal, 185–193.

Burnaby, B. & Beaujot, R.: 1986, *The Use of Aboriginal Languages in Canada: An Analysis of 1981 Census Data*, Social Trends Analysis Directorate and Native Citizens Directorate, Department of the Secretary of State, Ottawa.

Burnaby, B.: 1992, 'Official language training for adult immigrants in Canada: Features and issues', in B. Burnaby & A. Cumming (eds.), *Socio-political Aspects of ESL in Canada*, OISE Press, Toronto, 3–34.

Burnaby, B.: 1996, 'Language policies in Canada: An overview', in M. Herriman & B. Burnaby (eds.), *Language Policy in English-Dominant Countries: Six Case Studies*, Multilingual Matters, Clevedon, England.

Canadian Education Association: 1991, *Heritage Language Programs in Canadian School Boards*, Canadian Education Association, Toronto.

Canadian Education Association: 1992, *French Immersion Today* (CEA Information Note), Canadian Education Association, Toronto.

Churchill, S.: 1986, *The Education of Linguistic and Cultural Minorities in the OECD Countries*, Multilingual Matters, Clevedon, England.

Clarke, S. & MacKenzie, M.: 1980, 'Education in the mother tongue: Tokenism versus cultural autonomy in Canadian Indian schools', *Canadian Journal of Anthropology* 1(2), 205–217.

Commissioner of Official Languages: 1992, *Our Two Official Languages Over Time* (revised edition), Office of the Commissioner of Official Languages, Ottawa.

Corson, D. & Lemay, S.: 1996, *Social Justice and Language Policy in Education: The Canadian Research*, OISE Press, Toronto.

Cummins, J. & Danesi, M.: 1990, *Heritage Languages: The Development and Denial of Canada's Linguistic Resources*, Our Schools/Our Selves Education Foundation and Garamond Press, Toronto.

d'Anglejan, A. & De Koninck, Z.: 1992, 'Educational policy for a culturally plural Quebec: An Update', in B. Burnaby & A. Cumming (eds.), *Socio-political Aspects of ESL in Canada*, OISE Press, Toronto, 97–109.

Fleras, A. & Elliott, J.L.: 1992, *The Challenge of Diversity: Multiculturalism in Canada*, Nelson Canada, Scarborough, Ontario.

Foucher, P.: 1985, *Constitutional Language Rights of Official-Language Minorities in Canada: A Study of the Legislation of the Provinces and Territories Respecting Education Rights of Official-Language Minorities and Compliance with Section 23 of the Canadian Charter of Rights and Freedoms*, Supply and Services Canada, Ottawa.

Kirkness, V. & Bowman, S.: 1992, *First Nations and Schools: Triumphs and Struggles*, Canadian Education Association/ Association canadienne d'éducation, Toronto.

Labrie, N.: 1992, 'The role of pressure groups in the change of the status of French in Québec since 1960', in U. Ammon & M. Hellinger (eds.), *Status Change of Languages*, De Gruyter Verlag, Berlin and New York, 17–43.

Lambert, W.E. & Tucker, G.R.: 1972, *Bilingual Education of Children: The St. Lambert Experiment*, Newbury House, Rowley, Massachusetts.

Martel, A.: 1991, *Official Language Minority Education Rights in Canada: From Instruction to Management*, Office of the Commissioner of Official Languages, Ottawa.

Peat, Marwick and Partners & S. Churchill: 1987, *Evaluation of the Official Languages in Education Program: Final Report*, Peat, Marwick and Partners, Ottawa.

Royal Commission on Bilingualism and Biculturalism: 1967, *Report of the Royal Commission on Bilingualism and Biculturalism: General Introduction and Book I, The Official Languages*, The Queen's Printer, Ottawa.

Saouab, A.: 1993, *Canadian Multiculturalism*, Library of Parliament, Research Branch, Supply and Services Canada, Ottawa.

Statistics Canada: 1992, *Mother Tongue: The Nation* (catalogue number 93-313), Statistics Canada, Ottawa.

Swain, M. & Lapkin, S.: 1982, *Evaluating Bilingual Education: A Canadian Case Study*, Multilingual Matters, Clevedon, England.

Toohey, K.: 1992, 'We teach English as a second language to bilingual students', in B. Burnaby & A. Cumming (eds.), *Socio-political Aspects of ESL in Canada*, OISE Press, Toronto, 87–96.

Wardhaugh, R.: 1983, *Language and Nationhood: The Canadian Experience*, New Star Books, Vancouver.

SOPHIE BABAULT AND CLAUDE CAITUCOLI

LINGUISTIC POLICY AND EDUCATION IN FRANCOPHONE COUNTRIES

The concept of francophone countries can be related to various realities depending on whether one puts them on a strict linguistic plan (for which the criteria, moreover, is often hard to define) or on the basis of that political-cultural institution itself: 'la Francophonie'. If the people of the 49 states grouped together under the banner of the francophone countries total more than 300 million, the actual number of French speakers does not, in fact, seem to pass 120 million.

Three major categories are therefore apparent within the francophone community: apart from the areas where French is the mother-tongue for the majority of the population (French Belgium, French Switzerland ...), are to be found countries where French is not generally the mother-tongue, although it retains a privileged position by virtue of its political or social status, and finally countries belonging to the francophone organisations in spite of a limited use of the French language (Vietnam, Egypt ...).

This article will focus mainly on the second category outlined, which by and large corresponds to the old Belgian or French colonies in Africa and the Indian Ocean, for which the problem of languages and teaching constitutes a major theme, hotly debated, although extremely complex (also see reviews by Sprenger-Charolles & Behennec in Volume 2; by Kettemann in Volume 4; and by Gerin Lajoie in Volume 5).

EARLY HISTORY

The French colonial policies on the subject of language and education followed, since the first arrival of the French on african soil, a clearly stated principle that allowed no exception: that the one and only language of teaching was to be French. This principle was the logical outcome of theories which owed much to the cultural supremacy of Europe in relation to the colonies and reduced local languages to dialects of a rudimentary nature, 'suitable for the primitive but hardly satisfactory for the semi-civilised' (C. Renel, Head of teaching at Madagascar from 1906 to 1926, as quoted by Esoavelomandroso 1976: p. 124).

The approach adopted by Belgium was, at the root, markedly different to that of France, since teaching in the first three years of primary school was in both French and the local languages (Kinyarwanda in Rwanda, Swahili, Lingala, Ciluba and Kikongo in Zaire ...). However, these two models

R. Wodak and D. Corson (eds), Encyclopedia of Language and Education,
Volume 1: Language Policy and Political Issues in Education, 159–167.
© *1997 Kluwer Academic Publishers. Printed in the Netherlands.*

of linguistic policy rapidly merged: a knowledge of French in the Belgian colonies was often the sole criteria for admission to secondary education.

It is important to note that, for Belgium and France alike, the philosophy of teaching in the colonies was less a response to a humanistic ideal than a 'utilitarian cynicism' (Mialaret & Vial 1981: p. 89): it was in fact, above all, necessary for the colonial power to train native auxiliaries. Teaching French to the whole population was not envisaged as this thought from Faidherbe in *Le Moniteur du Sénégal* (7th April, 1857) shows: 'The trade of the river will always be carried out by the natives ... But in a few years, positions in government, as with promotion in the navy and the army, will only go to those who speak fluent French' (as quoted in Olivieri and Voisin 1984: p. 219).

So, with the extremely low rate of scholarisation, only a handful of privileged people had the possibility of developing a fluency in the French language and thus attaining administrative posts. The rest were only allowed to develop the rudiments of French and were therefore confined to menial employment.

POST-COLONIAL POLICIES

The attainment of independence in the majority of the French African countries from 1960 gave an enormous boost to movements for the development of national cultures and languages. African linguistic policies developed, research centers multiplied. It was not, however, easy to free the institutional system from the grip of the French language, which, as we have seen, occupied a central position in the running of the colonised countries. Let us not forget, moreover, besides countries like Burundi, Madagascar or the countries of Maghreb, where a single national language is understood and spoken by near total of the population, the number of recorded languages elsewhere ranges from three to hundreds (about 300 in Zaire). Two different kinds of debates, therefore, developed progressively and continue to be sustained (Ouane 1995).

National Language versus National Languages

If one admits that it is better to be taught in the maternal language not only due to the fact that it greatly eases learning, but further still because it is about a right, that of having available ones own means of expression, it seems particularly difficult to guarantee this right in a multi-lingual context. Is it necessary, then, to favour a single national language, or instead choose several, and, if so, according to which criteria? This debate concerns at the same time both the educational institution itself and the programmes for adult literacy set up in the majority of the countries.

National Language(s) versus International Language(s)

The pedagogical and cultural evidence in favour of teaching in the mother-tongue are undeniable. However, the temptation is great, in a multi-lingual context, to prefer 'exoglossia' to a difficult choice between languages culturally and politically marked. In support of this argument (international languages as instruments of national unity), can be added the following points:

- a generalised use of maternal languages carries with it risks of isolation in limiting the practice and development of international languages;
- the introduction of maternal languages as the means of instruction is difficult to realise in the economic plan (problems of translation, producing and publishing in these languages);
- the parents themselves often reject the idea of teaching in the mother-tongue, considering it as 'teaching on the cheap' in a society where the former colonial language still holds a position of great prestige (most notably as a condition of upward social mobility).

The controversy sustained by the lively contributions to the two debates has given rise to different interpretations according to the country. Three major trends, therefore, stand out in the area studied: one can distinguish the states which have exclusively kept French as the medium of instruction since their independence, those which have tried to replace French with national languages without, however, leaving the experimental stage, and finally those which have a generalised usage of one or more national languages.

The first group includes countries such as Comoros (where studies are however underway on the introduction of Comoran in the primary education sector), Djibouti, Cameroon (which is distinguished by the choice of a bilingual education in French and English), the Ivory Coast and Gabon.

The second example merits attention for several reasons. It denotes first of all an active attitude, linked to a will to change on the part of governments. One notes, furthermore, how frequently this occurs: according to Poth (1988), 32 to 39 African states have in the course of the past 30 years embarked on a programme of education in the maternal languages.

The third profile includes Algeria, Morocco, Tunisia, Burundi, Rwanda, Zaire, Madagascar and Guinea. In the three former Belgian colonies, as well as in the countries of the Maghreb, the usage of the mother tongue(s) now seems irreversible. The case of Zaire is moreover exemplary, since four languages are jointly used. The reforms put in place by Madagascar and Guinea, on the other hand, ended in failure, and the authorities have now reestablished teaching in French.

MAJOR CONTRIBUTIONS AND
WORK IN PROGRESS

The 1980s saw the development of a clear-cut policy in relation to the situation of the French language in French Africa: it had in fact become evident that the concept of French as the maternal language, inherited from the colonial period, was not only totally unsuitable for the reality, but also that the French language had neither the same status nor the same functions as the other foreign languages, that it was in some way a favoured foreign language or even, according to the terminology used by the majority of researchers, 'a second language'. The recognition of this particular status involved the necessity of studying the consequences of this on the standards of teaching (French or in French). Thus, in 1987 the first issue of the teaching periodical *Diagonales* was published, devoted to the problems of French as a second language, as Pêcheur (April 1987: p. 4) stated in the first editorial, 'the time has come to define a genuine methodology of French as a second language which will focus on dealing with the specific problems linked with such a limited context'. Vigner (1987) was one of the first to prepare the way for a structured debate on the question of French as a second language ('a specific subject'). This argument was developed by Cuq (1991), who, after having clarified the positions of French as a second language, attempted to formulate a definition, and Besse, Ngalasso and Vigner (1992), who edited an issue of *Etudes de Linguistique Appliquée* centred on this theme and its implications.

A lot of studies have moved towards an adaptation of the teaching of French in this particular socio-linguistic context. It is worth noting the studies carried out by the two francophone organisations: A.C.C.T. (*Agence de Coopération culturelle et Technique*), which presented in 1988 some examples of French-speaking education systems taking into account national languages; C.O.N.F.E.M.E.N. (*Conférence des Ministres de l'Ed-ucation Nationale ayant en commun l'usage du français*), which published in 1986 an assessment on the integration of national languages in the education system (including the programmes of literacy) and carried out from 1985 to 1991 an extensive study of nine French-speaking African countries, with the aim of developing a greater understanding of the language needs and the major factors involved in both French and national languages for primary school pupils, with the aim of leading a debate on the subject of teaching programmes in French (C.O.N.F.E.M.E.N. 1991). Dumont (1986) provides a critique on the methodology of the teaching of French in Black Africa and puts forward a genuine assessment of the situation with regard to communication, and an in depth examination of the African reality (the emergence of an African French and the entry of African languages into the educational system). Finally, Elamin (1990) reflects on the status of the teaching of French in Africa and advocates new linguistic-educational policies for a better usage of the French language.

The fact that almost all of the countries in the areas studied may be classed as 'Developing Countries', plus the frequently noted difference between intentions at the outset and the later reality in relation to linguistic policy and education, led some researchers to question the link between language and economic development. Although linguistic problems play a major role in the process of development, especially through the medium of the school, which is an essential element in any developmental policy, it is also important, on the other hand, that economic aspects are not neglected in favour of the implementation of proposals for linguistic planing. The study led by Chaudenson and Robillard (1991) thus put forward an analysis of linguistic features in correlation with the economy and development: a study of the links between language and the economy, the situation with regard to interdiscipliniary research, a cost-benefit analysis of possible models for African education, an approach of multi-lingualism as a factor of development, etc.

A great many studies over the past years have been devoted to an overview of the French-speaking world. One such study, by Chaudenson (1991), put forward an interesting approach with its analytical framework of the linguistic situation in the French-speaking world aimed at establishing a typology and determining strategies for linguistic planning. The difficulty being naturally of finding objective criteria for evaluation, the author chose to group the various characteristics relating to the linguistic situations found in the relevant countries according to two particular variables – 'status' ('all the factors which arise from the legal, political and economic system') and 'corpus' (that which concerns, in the broadest sense, language production') – for which precise definitions have been given. In spite of some artificiality, this framework has the merit of allowing for a comparison of a variety of situations with the help of well-defined criteria. The first attempts at evaluation using this model, which covers a great many of the French-speaking African countries, are presented in the same volume. Note also the work carried out by Robillard and Beniamino (1993 and 1996) which presents a panorama of the status of French in the French-speaking world. The studies delving into this question for a particular country are very numerous and cannot all be quoted here.

The observation of developments within the French language (Lafage 1976; I.F.A. group 1988) has led researchers such as Manessy (1984) or Dumont (1990) to record and explore the emergence of a genuine 'African French'; the direct result of the taking of the French language by the African population, where its specific usage, as far as phonological, lexical, semantic and grammatical factors are concerned, is to be considered as regional variants. This approach rejects hierarchical conceptions of the language, based on the 'French of France', which would in this case represent the norm against which deviance could be measured, and calls for a 'global vision of the French language, highlighting particular African, Belgian, Canadian or French etc. expression' (Dumont 1990: p. 160). Francard (1994) explores the concept of linguistic insecurity, Chaudenson (1995) confronts the problem of evaluating linguistic competences within the francophone countries. These problematics directly relate to the education system, whilst highlighting the major question: 'Which French do we need to teach ?'

PROBLEMS AND DIFFICULTIES

Generally, the linguistic policies of the former French colonies have produced disappointing results. Policies for the promotion and integration of national languages within the education systems have had varying degrees of success. Senegal, Congo and Burkina Faso quickly halted their programmes already underway. Other countries, such as the Central African Republic, Mali and Niger, continued their programmes for ten to twenty years, without, however, showing much enthusiasm for expansion, in spite of sometimes some very positive results. The case of Guinea is particularly notable: in 1968 a radical reform progressively introduced teaching in eight national languages in primary and secondary education; this reform, poorly prepared, produced disastrous results, and in 1984 with the death of Sékou Touré, French once again took its place as the language of instruction. Regarding policies for literacy in national languages, the results have been difficult to evaluate.

Faced with these hardly encouraging results, one is justified in wondering why so few of the linguistic policies in Africa work. It is necessary of course to take into account the economic difficulties of countries in the process of development: in Burkina Faso, where the level of scholarisation in 1990 was 28.8% in the primary sector, and 6% in the secondary, the education budget represents a quarter of the national budget, which does not, however, prevent the situation from deteriorating from year to year (insufficiently trained teachers, low in number and poorly paid, without premises and teaching materials ...).

However, beyond the economical constraints, one can wonder why people are afraid of using African languages as a vehicle for teaching. Aren't they rather afraid of populations speaking these languages? What is it concerned with, in fact, if not, by the intermediary of language, a disguised struggle for the possession and maintenance of power? One thus notices in the attitudes and stands of the different actors numerous contradictions, due in part to the political reasons which have motivated them. Why, for example, do certain elites express themselves in favour of teaching in the mother-tongue, whilst at the same time sending their own children to private establishments guaranteeing an education in French? It would seem that a key element in the language of teaching is to be found in its interdependence with a number of factors in different domains and its relationship with the struggle for power.

FUTURE DIRECTIONS

It is therefore necessary to continue the study and lexical development of national languages, programmes of literacy and the introduction of national languages into the education system. It is equally important to better understand the specific problems of French outside the hexagon, to take into account the emergence of endogenous norms and to put forward methodologies and materials adapted to the needs and demands of development. In this area, one can cite the major studies currently under the aegis of the AUPELF-UREF, most notably by the networks *Le français en francophonie* and *Sociolinguistique et dynamique des langues*. The first network enabled a team led by Lafage and Queffelec to update the *Inventaire des particularités lexicales du français en Afrique noire* and to continue research on regional variations of French. In the second one, Dumont and Maurer attempted to construct a sociolinguistic analysis of the teaching relationship while Chaudenson embarks an evaluation of the linguistic competencies of 'recognized' French speakers.

Beyond these economical and technical questions, one has to consider the possibility of establishing coherent and effective linguistic policies. Guespin and Marcellesi (1986: p. 5) developed the concept of 'glotto-politique' which covers 'all the language phenomena where societal actions take the form of policy'. Within this perspective, it is easier not only to understand the representation and actions of the different institutions (media, educators ...) but also the linguistic ideology of the users, as demonstrated by their linguistic behaviour and 'epilinguistic' speech. This leads equally, to the consideration of the 'glottopolitical' role of the linguist. In analysing a situation, for example by revealing implicit norms which govern language behaviour within a community, the expert does more than merely respond to social demand with a linguistic technique: he by necessity intervenes in the process which he is studying.

Finally, all will depend in the future on the choice made by the francophone institutions and the relationships they maintain with the states concerned. 'The realities of the failure of "all French" in the educational policies, or the (discreet) speaking out of the French linguists who are interested in the francophone countries, in order to highlight the extreme diversity of situations and the reality of plurilinguistics – have these in fact had any effect (D. Baggioni 1996: p. 801)?'

University of Rouen
France

REFERENCES

A.C.C.T.: 1981, *Etudes africaines en Europe. Bilan et inventaire*, ACCT-Karthala, Paris.
A.C.C.T.: 1988, *Langues africaines et enseignement du français. Innovations et expéri-ences*, A.C.C.T., Paris.
Baggioni, D.: 1996, 'Eléments pour une histoire de la francophonie (idéologie, mou-vements, institutions)' in D. de Robillard & M. Beniamino (eds.), *Le français dans l'espace francophone*, tome 2, Champion, Paris, 789–806.
Besse, H., Ngalasso, M.M. & Vigner, G. (ed.): 1992, *Etudes de Linguistique Appliquée* 88, Paris.
C.O.N.F.E.M.E.N.: 1986, *Promotion et intégration des langues nationales dans les systèmes éducatifs bilan et inventaire*, Champion, Paris.
C.O.N.F.E.M.E.N.: 1991, *Etude comparative des besoins langagiers et des centres d'intérêt en français et en langues nationales chez les élèves de l'école primaire. Rapport final*, CONFEMEN-ACCT, Dakar.
Calvet, L.J.: 1974, *Linguistique et colonialisme. Petit traité de glottophagie*, Payot, Paris.
Chaudenson, R. (ed.): 1991, *La francophonie: représentations, réalités, perspectives*, Didier Erudition, Paris.
Chaudenson, R. (ed.): 1995, *Vers un outil d'évaluation des compétences linguistiques en français dans l'espace francophone*, Didier Erudition, Paris.
Chaudenson, R. & Robillard, D. de: 1989, *Langue, économie et développement*, Didier Erudition, Paris.
Cuq, J.P.: 1991, *Le français langue seconde*, Hachette, Paris.
Dumont, P.: 1986, *L'Afrique noire peut-elle encore parler français?*, L'Harmattan, Paris.
Dumont, P.: 1990, *Le français langue africaine*, L'Harmattan, Paris.
Elamin, Y.: 1990, *Le statut de l'enseignement du français en Afrique. Aspects constitution-nels, sociolinguistiques et pédagogiques*, thèse de doctorat, université Paris III.
Esoavelomandroso: 1976, 'Langue, culture et civilisation à Madagascar: malgache et français dans l'enseignement officiel (1916–1940)', *Omaly sy anio* 3–4, 105–155, Antananarivo.
Francard M. (ed.): 1994, *Cahiers de l'Institut de linguistique de Louvain-la-Neuve* 1994 vol. 1.
Guespin, L. & Marcellesi, J.B.: 1986, 'Pour la glottopolitique', *Langages* 83, 5–34.
I.F.A. group of A.E.L.I.A.: 1988, *Inventaire des particularités lexicales du français en Arique noire*, E.D.I.C.E.F. (U.R.E.F.), Paris (first ed., 1983, A.U.P.E.L.F.-A.C.C.T., Montréal).
Kühnel, R.: 1994, *Die sprachliche Situation an Hochschulen des Maghreb und die offizielle Sprachpolitik -eine soziolinguistische Untersuchung*, thèse de doctorat, Universität Leipzig.
Lafage, S.: 1976, *Français parlé et écrit en pays éwé (Sud-Togo)*, thèse de doctorat, université de Nice.
Manessy, G. & Wald, P.: 1984, *Le français en Afrique noire tel qu'on le parle tel qu'on le dit*, L'Harmattan, Paris.
Mialaret, G. & Vial, J.: 1981, *Histoire mondiale de l'éducation*, Presses Universitaires de France, Paris.
Olivieri, C. & Voisin, J.P.: 1984, 'Le français dans les pays francophones et de l'Océan Indien', in D. Coste (ed.), *Aspects d'une politique de diffusion du français langue étrangère depuis 1945*, Hatier, Paris, 219–225.
Ouane, A. (ed.): 1995, *Vers une culture multilingue de l'éducation*, Institut de l'UNESCO pour l'Education, Hamburg.
Pêcheur, J.: 1987: 'Editorial', *Diagonales* 1, 4.
Porges, L.: 1988, *Sources d'information sur l'Afrique noire francophone et Madagascar*, La Documentation Française, Paris.

Poth, J.: 1988, *L'enseignement des langues maternelles africaines à l'école . . . Comment?*, UNESCO-BREDA, Dakar.

Robillard, D. de & Beniamino, M. (ed.): 1993, *Le français dans l'espace francophone*, tome 1, Champion, Paris.

Robillard, D. de & Beniamino, M. (ed.): 1996, *Le français dans l'espace francophone*, tome 2, Champion, Paris.

Vigner, G.: 1987, 'Français langue seconde, une discipline spécifique', *Diagonales* 4, 42–45.

UTE SMIT

LANGUAGE POLICY AND EDUCATION IN SOUTH AFRICA

After 30 years of seemingly immutable, top-down language policy in education in South Africa, the early 1990's and the dismantling of apartheid
have brought considerable momentum into the language discussion. Since
the first democratic and general elections in 1994, this has led to radically
new suggestions and policy formulations for the ca. 40 million inhabitants
of this multilingual country. The new Constitution of South Africa (Act
No 200 of 1993) has given official status, formerly granted to English and
Afrikaans only, to the 11 major languages (estimates of percentages of L1
speakers of the population given in brackets, cf. Webb ed. 1995: p. 16):
isiZulu (22%), isiXhosa (17%), Afrikaans (15%), Sepedi (10%), English
(9%), Setswana (8%), Sesotho (7%), Xitsonga (4%), siSwati (3%), Tshiv-
enda (2%), and isiNdebele (1.5%). Concerning the language-in-education
policy, the new developments have sparked off wide-spread interest, responses and involvement in South Africa, not only with the small group
of expert policy makers, but also with a wide range of socio-linguistic,
educational, and political interest groups. In accordance with the present
government's credo of grassroots' involvement and consultancy, all of
these interested parties have been asked for their input to the central governmental documents on language policy in education for the future. At the
time of writing, this consultation process has not been concluded and official statements of the Ministers of Education and of Arts, Culture, Science
and Technology, as well as concurrent amendments to the language-in-
education policy, are still outstanding (also see reviews by Janks in this
volume; and by Rodseth in Volume 4).

EARLY DEVELOPMENTS UP TO 1948

The language-in-education situation prior to 1948, when legally enforced
apartheid was introduced, can be described as an ongoing rivalry and
competition between the two white – originally European – population
groups, the Dutch/Afrikaans L1 speakers ('Afrikaners') and the English
L1 speakers. Up to the 20th century, institutionalised education was characterised by either monolingualism or transitional bilingualism. With the
English take-over of the Cape from the Dutch in 1806, the main medium of
instruction changed from Dutch to English, as it also did in the other British
province, Natal. In the newly-founded Dutch republics, the Transvaal and
the Orange Free State, on the other hand, education was provided in Dutch

R. Wodak and D. Corson (eds), Encyclopedia of Language and Education,
Volume 1: Language Policy and Political Issues in Education, 169–178.
© *1997 Kluwer Academic Publishers. Printed in the Netherlands.*

at first, but then in English, after Britain had taken over power in the late 19th century (Davenport 1991; Gough 1991).

In accordance with more general social planning, decisions were taken by whites for whites. Education for other groups was largely left in the hand of missionaries. Due to their belief that the Bible should be accessible to everyone in their mother tongue, they provided basic education in the respective L1, and retained English for further education. Missionary education thus meant transitional bilingualism: basic literacy in the mother tongue and total immersion in English in secondary and tertiary education (Alexander 1989).

In 1910, with the founding of the Union of South Africa, the first official bilingual language policy in education was passed. In order to unite the rivalling white groups, English and Dutch (replaced by Afrikaans, the newly-established identity marker of the Afrikaners, in 1925) were given equal rights (Steyn 1989). While this led to dual medium and bilingual schools for white pupils (Malherbe 1977), the language-in-education situation for the other population groups remained unchanged (Hartshorne 1987).

MAJOR CONTRIBUTIONS SINCE 1948

In the 1950s the ideology of apartheid brought considerable changes to the South African linguistic landscape. For the first time, language planning in education was done centrally and stood directly under governmental control. Language planning was of a top-down nature, enforced by a few on all. Differentiation between the various racially defined population groups was introduced to enhance their separate development and, at the same time, to secure the hegemony of the whites. The general aim was Afrikaner domination, to be reached on two levels. On the level of the individual population groups, the respective indigenous languages were crucial in characterising these groups along apartheid lines and were thus set in as obligatory mediums of instruction in primary education. On the national level, the long-term objective was to establish Afrikaans as main medium of intranational communication. For historical and socioeconomic reasons, however, the national aim could not be implemented, mainly because English had by that time already been widely established as main language of public discourse and higher education, nationally as well as internationally. Thus both languages had to be accredited as official languages and also languages of higher education.

The apartheid ideology obviously required very detailed language-in-education policies for each population group. These can be summarised as follows (Gough 1991a; Hartshorne 1987; Hartshorne 1995; Heugh 1995b; NEPI 1992): Every black South African, classified from birth as belonging to a specific racial group, was allowed to attend schools designated for that group only. Primary education was undertaken in the relevant mother tongue, and the two official languages, English and Afrikaans, were introduced as subjects in the first year of schooling. In the fifth year an immediate language transition to the so-called 50:50 policy was envisaged, i.e. English should be the medium of instruction for half of the school subjects and the other half should be taught in Afrikaans. When, in 1976, an attempt was made to strictly enforce this policy, pupils revolted in what became known as the 'Soweto uprising'. Because of the resulting turmoil this policy was finally abandoned and parents were officially allowed to decide on the desired medium of instruction of their children. For the other three 'racial' groups, i.e. whites, Indians (i.e. South Africans of Indian descent), and so-called coloureds (i.e. South Africans of racially-mixed descent), the language-in-education situation was simpler insofar as only the two official languages needed to be considered. For all three groups, either English or Afrikaans was dictated as medium of instruction. The other language was, as L2, compulsory as subject from the third school year onwards. Differences were made between the groups with regard to which language was to be used as medium. While white pupils were offered education in their home language, the major language of the area in which the school was situated was medium of instruction for Indian and initially also coloured pupils. In 1968 this regulation changed for coloured pupils who then had to attend classes taught in their home language.

These apartheid regulations had such an impact on education in South Africa that, since they started to be amended in 1991, it has taken some years of research, collecting of new suggestions and nation-wide discussions in order to change the old system, built on segregation, into a new one that is aimed at a more integrated society. Suggestions for the content, form and implementation of a new language policy in education were gathered from the various stakeholders in the South African society. Thus input from the whole spectrum of socio-political ideologies and beliefs has been invited and considered (Reagan 1995). The resulting language-in-education policy suggestions reflect three main lines of argumentation, differing with regard to their views on the more general societal role of language planning and on the position of mono- versus multilingualism (Alexander 1995; Heugh 1995a; Heugh 1995b). The role allotted to language planning can be placed on a continuum with eventual assimilation into monolingualism at the one end and acceptance and development of multilingualism at the other.

The first of these three main lines of argumentation interprets the multiplicity of languages as a problem and supports the assimilatory policy of implementing English as main language of intranational communication, set off against the other languages to be used regionally. Representatives of this option thus suggest transitional bilingualism from the regional or local L1s to the national language, i.e. English. With reference to the non-diminution of existing language rights and the practical language situation in the country, a similar suggestion proposes the joint use of Afrikaans and English as languages of intranational communications, and therefore expands the line of argumentation to one of transitional trilingualism (Schuring 1993).

The second line of argumentation recognises the present hierarchical difference between English and the other languages, and tries to combine the aim of assimilation with the aim of acknowledging individual languages as well as regional multilingualism. This approach, as supported by the African National Congress (ANC) and the National Education Policy Investigation (NEPI) in their basic research, undertaken between 1990 and 1992, has been described as one suggesting a 'laissez-faire' policy (Heugh 1995a: p. 340). While the ANC (1992, 1994) recognises the equality of the 11 languages and proposes special support for each of them, it is also bound to its general principle of individual choice. At the moment this means that the general preference for English as language of education must be accepted. This tension between present preferences for English (de Klerk 1996) and the awareness of the sociolinguistic plurality of the country also becomes visible in the NEPI research, undertaken to identify and evaluate policy options for education according to the principles of democracy, and of redressing historical imbalances. Concerning the future language-in-education policy (Luckett 1993; NEPI 1992), the team suggests that English should not replace L1 instruction and, more generally, that the language policy should facilitate additive rather than subtractive bi- or multilingualism. Since this asks for school-specific decision taking, NEPI recommends flexible policies that would allow spontaneous reactions to the actual situations of communication and the students' needs. In view of the generally accepted language status and attitudes in the early 1990s (Webb 1995), however, NEPI does not see any possibility for a multilingual policy and expects that the preference for English as the main and, for higher education, the only medium of instruction, would lead to a different policy, namely one of transitional bilingualism from the various L1s to English.

The third line of argumentation, finally, stands for an integrative approach which recognises all the languages as being equally functional and which identifies multilingualism as a national resource to be used to the better of the nation and its inhabitants. In order to pay credit to this linguistic plurality, these self-declared ' "hard-nosed" multiculturalists' (Heugh 1995a: p. 344) – such as the National Language Project (NLP) and the Project for the Study of Alternative Education (PRAESA) – propose bottom-up, flexible policies on the basis of the existing language situation. These policies should provide people with access to a language of wider communication of their choice, which would presently be English. At the same time, the roles of the other languages need to be acknowledged, and their status, where necessary, to be improved upon. This option translates into a language-in-education policy which acknowledges the rights of all the 11 official languages, the importance of additive multilingualism, and the retention of the L1 as language of learning. Then education should lead to competence in at least two, preferably three languages, including a language of wider communication. This should then ideally also be the requirements for further education or the job market (Heugh 1995a; Heugh, Siegrühn & Plüddemann 1995).

WORK IN PROGRESS

Of the three lines of argumentation discussed above, the first one was effectively eliminated from further discussion by the Interim Constitution of South Africa (Act 200 of 1993) and the Constitution of South Africa 1996. A purely assimilative language-in-education policy could not be correlated with the declaration of 11 official languages and further promotion of multilingualism: 'Recognising the historically diminished use and status of the indigenous languages . . . , the state must take practical and positive measures to elevate the[ir] status and advance the[ir] use' (Constitution of South Africa 1996: section 6.2). With regard to education, the Constitution furthermore specifies that '[e]veryone has the right to receive education in the official language or languages of their choice in public educational institutions where that education is reasonably practicable' (Constitution of South Africa 1996: section 29.2). This means that the future language-in-education policy can adhere to either the second – the recognition of societal multilingualism and that of English as language of intranational communication – or the third line – the equal treatment of all 11 languages.

These two lines of argumentation, in their diversified realisations by various governmental and non-governmental bodies, have been taken up by the Department of Education in its quest for a new language-in-education policy. According to the overall principle of grassroots' democracy and ongoing consultation with all concerned, the Department of Education (1995) has not simply issued a new language policy in education, but has asked for further input and reactions to a discussion document preceding the final report. While input to this debate has come from all sides, one of the most important bodies is the Language Plan Task Group (LANGTAG) instigated by the Department of Arts, Culture, Science and Technology with the brief to investigate various aspects of a national language plan, including language-in-education policy. LANGTAG's general plea for functional multilingualism is reflected in the goals of language-in-education policy they have formulated in their final report (LANGTAG 1996), namely 'to promote . . . additive multilingual[ism] . . . in South African . . . educational institutions' and by that 'to promote respect for linguistic diversity in the context of a nation-building strategy' (LANGTAG 1996: ch. 4).

Since, at the time of writing, the consultative process has not been completed and South Africa's future language policy in education (Policy Report 500) not been issued yet, the following outline of the main points relies on the discussion document *Towards a Language Policy in Education*, in its first and second drafts (November 1995, May 1996). From the present discussions, which concentrate on details and questions of implementation, these fundamental points can be seen as generally acceptable in accordance with the Constitution of South Africa and are thus very likely to also be included in the final Policy Report 550.

- Additive bilingualism should be fostered throughout schooling. Wherever this is not yet possible, the necessary social and linguistic provisions will need to be created.
- Multilingualism should be fostered by having at least 2 official languages either as mediums of instruction or as subjects from the 7th school year onwards till the school leaving/university entrance exam. Extra credits should be given for additional languages.

An unanswered question is the grouping of the 11 languages. Pre-1994 they were divided into three groups: the then official languages (English and Afrikaans), the Sotho languages (Sepedi, Sesotho, Setswana) and the Nguni languages (isiXhosa, isiZulu, isiNdebele and siSwati). While both official languages were obligatory for all pupils, restrictions were placed on the Sotho and Nguni groups, of which only one language each could be chosen for the school-leaving examination. Presently the debate is not concluded whether there should be any grouping at all and, if so, what constellation it should be.

- Up to now disenfranchised languages, i.e. all official languages apart from English and Afrikaans, should be specifically promoted through the relocation of financial and human resources.
- All the language requirements should finally be pursued in all educational institutions on all levels, as well as on the employment market.
- Language-in-education policies must be interconnected with other policies, e.g. curriculum development including assessment and promotion, with the provision of material and human resource, and with democratic governance at all levels.
- Language-in-education policies must be cyclical (constant democratic consultation with grassroots and other bodies) and flexible in order to permit adaptations of the requirements at school level.

PROBLEMS AND DIFFICULTIES

The problems facing South African students, teachers, and others involved in education alike are manifold. The present language policies combine principles that seem to be contradictory to some extent (cf. Department of Education 1995). For example, the principle of promotion of previously disadvantaged languages could be in conflict with the non-diminution of existing language rights explicitly included in the Interim Constitution (section 3.2). Similarly, the principle of affirmative linguistic action could limit the individuals' right to their own language choice. At the same time these principles, especially the one of individual choice, must be reconciled with existing pragmatic constraints, such as the limited material and human resources presently available.

Multilingualism has, for a long time, been regarded as a problem in education rather than as a national resource. Ideally, this opinion has to be reversed. Awareness campaigns should bring South Africans to realise the practical advantages of being bi- or multilingual in languages other than English or Afrikaans. Such an awareness is directly linked to the eventual social status and roles of the various languages. If English should retain its de facto privileged position in the South African economic, political and social life, then it is utopian to believe that the other languages, presently functionally restricted to private domains, would ever become equally functional and prestigious. At present, the use of an African language as medium of instruction after basic schooling is, due to the apartheid history, highly unpopular in South Africa. Affirmative action to increase the use and status of African languages in education will be necessary to remove this stigma. Therefore, the functions and uses of these languages must expand to improve the general attitudes displayed towards them. Such changes in popular perceptions are imperative for the African languages to become attractive as school subjects and as languages of instruction in education.

In practice, the choice of languages immediately available as school subjects and mediums of instruction will be relatively limited. Whether the proposed policies of additive and functional multilingualism, and socio-linguistic and -cultural integration are effectively implemented, will depend on the ingenuity, flexibility and good will of administrators, teachers, parents and students alike.

FUTURE DIRECTIONS

The afore-mentioned internal tensions and inconsistencies of the present language-in-education policy will most probably be addressed in policy amendments, once structures for implementation and evaluation come into place. So, for instance, the principle of flexibility and stakeholders' integration might lead to school-based policies which contradict the basic tenet of functional multilingualism. Here, either specific teacher education and community involvement programmes will have to be provided, or stricter formulations for the national policy will have to be found. Similarly, the tension between the right of individual choice and the right to development of hitherto disadvantaged languages will have to be resolved either by a laissez-faire approach – which fosters tolerance and lets development take its own course – or by governmental intervention with regulations concerning the hierarchical and contextually-linked status of these two rights.

Present indications therefore point to a primary concern for practicable measures to balance out three factors, namely (i) the present functional superiority of English and Afrikaans, (ii) the overwhelming, country-wide preference for English, especially in the more formal domains, and (iii) the need to enhance the status and roles of the African languages. As the latter has to overcome financial hurdles on the one and widespread antipathy on the other hand, it will take considerable effort to attain this goal set by the present policy. One practical problem is the number of languages involved and the resulting split of finances and attitudinal support. One suggestion that might be taken up to alleviate this point concerns the long-term plan of reducing the number of standard languages by harmonising each of the two main African language groups – Nguni and Sotho. At present there is not a substantial thrust towards such a standardisation of linguistically related languages. If this idea – first voiced in the 1940s and taken up again in the late 1980s (Alexander 1989) – is to be realised, concerted efforts will have to be made, firstly, to generate popular support for it and, secondly, to find practical ways of its implementation (Brown 1992; Msimang 1992).

To conclude, the central aim to the impending language-in-education policy, i.e. additive multilingualism, can only be pursued constructively if a way is found to strike a balance between the competing interests and the diversified language situations presently found in South Africa. In order to facilitate this difficult task, an independent, consultative body of linguistic experts, the Pan South African Language Board (PANSALB) has been constituted by law (Pan South African Language Board Act, no. 59 of 1995). While PANSALB will have to play a crucial role in putting the principles and beliefs underlying the future language policy into practice, it depends on everyone involved to ensure that future South African generations will be practising additive multilinguals and will understand their linguistic diversity as a national resource.

University of Vienna, Austria

REFERENCES

Alexander, N.: 1989, *Language Policy and National Unity in South Africa/Azania*, Buchu Books, Cape Town.

Alexander, N.: 1995, 'Multilingualism for empowerment', in K. Heugh, A. Siegrühn & P. Plüddemann (eds.), *Multilingual Education for South Africa*, Heinemann, Johannesburg, 37–41.

African National Congress (ANC): 1992, *Ready to Govern. ANC Policy Guidelines for a Democratic South Africa Adopted at the National Conference 28–31 May 1992*, ANC, Johannesburg.

African National Congress (ANC): 1994. *A Policy Framework for Education and Training*, ANC, Johannesburg.

Brown, D.: 1992, 'Language and social history in South Africa. A task still to be undertaken', in R.K. Herbert (ed.), *Language and Society in Africa. The Theory and Practice of Sociolinguistics*, Witwatersrand University Press, Cape Town, 71–92.

Constitution of the Republic of South Africa (Act 200 of 1993, as amended by acts 2, 3, 13, 14, 24 & 29 of 1994), February 1995.

Constitution of the Republic of South Africa 1996, as adopted by the Constitutional Assembly on 8 May 1996 and as ammended on 11 October 1996.

Davenport, T.R.H.: 1991, *South Africa. A Modern History* (4th edition), Macmillan, London.

De Klerk, V. (ed.): 1996, *Focus on South Africa* (Vol. 15 in series: Varieties of English Around the World), John Benjamin's, Amsterdam/Philadelphia.

Department of Education: 1995, *Towards a Language Policy in Education. Discussion Document* (November 1995), Pretoria.

Department of Education: 1996, *Language-in-Education Policy Document* (Draft of May 1996), Pretoria.

Gough, D.: 1991, 'Medium of instruction in South Africa: An historical overview', working paper to NEPI (National Education Policy Investigation).

Hartshorne, K.B.: 1987, 'Language policy in African education in South Africa, 1910–85, with particular reference to the issue of medium of instruction', in D.N. Young (ed.), *Bridging the Gap Between Theory and Practice in English Second Language Teaching. Essays in Honour of L. W. Lanham*, Maskew Miller Longman, Cape Town, 62–81.

Hartshorne, K.B.: 1995, 'Language policy in African education: A background to the future', in R. Mesthrie (ed.), *Language and Social History. Studies in South African Sociolinguistics*, David Philip, Cape Town & Johannesburg, 1995, 306–18.

Heugh, K.: 1995a, 'Disabling and enabling: Implications of language policy trends in South Africa', in R. Mesthrie (ed.), *Language and Social History. Studies in South African Sociolinguistics,* David Philip, Cape Town & Johannesburg, 329–48.

Heugh, K.: 1995b, 'From unequal education to the real thing', in K. Heugh, A. Siegrühn & P. Plüddemann (eds.), *Multilingual Education for South Africa,* Heinemann, Johannesburg, 42–52.

Heugh, K., Siegrühn A. & Plüddemann P.(eds.): 1995, *Multilingual Education for South Africa*, Heinemann, Johannesburg.

Language Plan Task Group (LANGTAG) of the Minister of Arts, Culture, Science and Technology: 1996, *Towards a National Language Plan for South Africa. Summary of the Final Report of the Language Plan Task Group*, Department of Arts, Culture, Science and Technology, Pretoria.

Luckett, K.: 1993, ' "National additive bilingualism": towards the formulation of a language plan for South African schools', *Southern African Journal of Applied Language Studies* 2(1), 38–60.

Malherbe, E.G.: 1977, *Education in South Africa Volume II*. 1923–1975, Juta, Cape Town.

Msimang, C.T.: 1992, *African Languages and Language Planning in South Africa (the Nhlapo-Alexander Notion of Harmonisation Revisited)*, BARD Publishers, Pretoria.

NEPI (National Education Policy Investigation): 1992, Language, National Education
    Co-ordinating Committee & Oxford University Press, Cape Town.
'Pan South African Language Board Act', 1995, Government Gazette, Act no. 59.
Reagan, T.G.: 1995, 'Language planning and language policy in South Africa: A perspec-
    tive on the future', in R. Mesthrie (ed.), *Language and Social History. Studies in South
    African Sociolinguistics*, David Philip, Cape Town & Johannesburg, 319–28.
Schuring, G.K.: 1992, 'Bilingual and trilingual language policies for South Africa', in K.
    Prinsloo, Y. Peeters, J. Tuir & C. van Rensburg (eds.), *Language, Law and Equality.
    Proceedings of the Third International Conference of the International Academy of
    Language Law (IALL) Held in South Africa, April 1992*, University of South Africa,
    Pretoria: 239–46.
Steyn, J.C.: 1989, 'Vroeg-twintigste-eeuse argument vir een ampstaal in Suid-Afrika',
    South African Journal of Linguistics 7(2), 74–83.
Webb, V.N.: 1993/94, 'Language policy and planning in South Africa', *Annual Review of
    Applied Linguistics* 14, 254–73.
Webb, V.N. (ed.): 1995, *Language in South Africa. An Input into Language Planning for
    a Post-Apartheid South Africa*, The LiCCA Research and Development Programme,
    University of Pretoria.

LACHMAN M. KHUBCHANDANI

LANGUAGE POLICY AND EDUCATION IN THE INDIAN SUBCONTINENT

The ideology of language in school is interwoven with the ideology of education in society. Education planners in the contemporary South Asian context have, by and large, committed themselves to *education for all* without seriously questioning the elitist framework of education inherited from the colonial set up (prevailing till 1947).

In India, with a multilingual population and a federal polity, one finds a wide variation in different states as far as the medium, content, duration and nomenclature of educational stages are concerned. The decadal census enumerates two hundred and odd languages, spoken by over 930 million, spread in 26 states and 5 Union territories (Verma 1987). Over eighty languages are used as media of instruction in different stages. Fourteen of them are counted as principal media language, comprising two pan Indian languages – Hindi and English ; two languages without a specific region – Urdu and Sindhi ; and ten languages concentrated in different regions – Assamese, Bengali, Gujarati, Kannada, Malayalam, Marathi, Oriya, Punjabi, Tamil and Teliou. In addition, four more languages – Kashmiri, Konkani, Manipuri and Nepali – are being promoted as a medium for secondary education by different states. Distinct scripts, based on Brahmi, Perso-Arabic and Roman systems of writing, are in vogue for these language(s) (for details. ct. Khubchandani 1983).

The Constitution of India provides full freedom to the states to choose a language or languages in a region as official language(s) (Article 345). It also allows linguistic minority groups to receive education in their mother tongue and to set up institutions of their choice for this purpose (Articles 30).

Neighbouring countries in the region – Bangladesh, Pakistan, Srilanka and Nepal – are also characterized by varied milieu where apart from locally dominant languages pan-regional languages such as Hindustani and English play a significant role in overall education structure. Bangladesh consists of a relatively homogeneous Bengali population. Pakistan is composed of two-third population speaking Punjabi: other prominent languages being Sindhi (16 per cent). Pushtu (8) Urdu (5) Baluchi (3 per cent) (Kazi 1987). Srilanka is going through the trauma of adjustments between two Sinhalese and Tamil-speaking populations (also see reviews by Agnihotri in Volume 2; by Khubchandani in Volume 5; and by Farah in Volume 8).

R. Wodak and D. Corson (eds), Encyclopedia of Language and Education,
Volume 1: Language Policy and Political Issues in Education, 179–187.
© *1997 Kluwer Academic Publishers. Printed in the Netherlands.*

EARLY HISTORY

Before the consolidation of British rule on the Indian subcontinent at the turn of the nineteenth century, there were two competing systems of education: the *pāthashālā* (school) and *gurukul* (residential school) system of Brahmins ; and the *maktab* (school) and *madraseh* (college) system of the Muslims. Education in the traditional set up was regarded as an extension of primary socialization imbibed through the immediate environments of family, caste, creed, and heritage. Two patterns, shaped by vocational relevance, were prominently recognized: *Ordinary* Tradition for providing practical education to administrators and merchants to cope with the day-to-day needs of society through locally dominant languages: and *Advanced* tradition for providing education to the elites (sons of priests, the ruling class and high officials) by reading of scriptures and historical texts, through the classical languages – Sanskrit or Arabic-Persian.

The Great Debate about language policies between colonial administrators and the native elite during one hundred and fifty years of the British rule has left a deep imprint on the role of language for plural societies in the region. The rival British education system known as *schools* soon eclipsed the traditional *pathashala* and *maktab* education system in most parts of British India. The British administration could not resolve the three basic issues of education: the content, the spread and the medium (Dakin 1968). Macaulay's hard line, recommending a policy of imparting Western knowledge through a Western tongue (English) and then only to a minority (ct. the famous Minute of 1835), echoed in education programmes of the British throughout their stay in the subcontinent (Sharp 1920). During a later phase, the 1854 Wood Despatch suggested the use of a vernacular medium "to teach the far larger class who are ignorant of, or imperfectly acquainted with, English" (Richey 1922; Naik 1963). But the introduction of vernacular education was extremely slow, and Macaulay's commandment of *first* developing Indian vernaculars to qualify them for use in education and administration prevailed to a great extent: thus, effectively postponing their introduction in formal domains (Khubchandani 1981).

During the long struggle for Indian Independence, the selective education structure was vehemently criticized by the national leaders – Gokhale, Gandhi, Tagore and other intellectuals – who saw the need for universal elementary education and also put forward pleas for the use of mother tongue in administration (Saiyidain, Naik and Abid Hussian 1962). Mahatma Gandhi in 1938 proposed a scheme for Basic Education which was practically the antithesis of the rulers elitist moorings concerning the questions of content, spread, and medium (Zakir Hussain 1950). It attempted to resolve the conflict between quality and quantity in education by laying stress on integrating education with experience, and language acquisition with communicability as advocated in Gandhijli's approach to Hindustani.

In actual terms, three patterns of education emerged during the British rule:

1. The English medium, in urban centres for the education of the elite, right from the primary stage;
2. the two-tier medium, vernacular medium for primary education and English medium for the advanced stage, in towns;
3. the vernacular medium, in rural areas for primary education.

The politicization of the language issue in India during the struggle for independence dominated the medium controversy, pushing into the background the ideological issues concerning the content of education. The demand for vernacularization by the native elite was associated with the cultural and national resurgence, and eventually with the growth of democracy promoting equality of opportunity through education (Tagore 1906; Gandhi 1916).

CONCEPT OF MOTHER TONGUE

Many modern education experts, uncritically accepting Western theories of education of the early twentieth century, regard it as axiomatic that the best medium for teaching a child is his/her mother tongue (UNESCO Report 1953). These claims did not take into account the plural character of Indian society at large, which reveals apparent ambiguities in defining the concept of mother tongue itself. In linguistic and educational accounts, the terms mother tongue and native speech are often used indistinguishably. The term *native speech* can be distinguished as "the first speech acquired in infancy, through which the child gets socialized: it claims some bearing on intutive competence, and potentially it can be individually identifiable". The term *mother tongue* is mainly "categorized by one's allegiance to a particular tradition, and it is societally identifiable" (Khubchandani 1983).

During the initial years after gaining independence different expert bodies on education such as 1948 Central Advisory Board of Education, 1949 University Education Commission, and 1956 Official Language Commission put a greater weight on the *broad* interpretation of mother tongue i.e. regarding all minority languages not having a written tradition as 'dialects' of the dominant language in the region. This interpretation amounted to an implicit denial of equal rights to linguistic minorities on the ground of practicability similar to the French view of treating minority languages (such as Provencal, Breton and Basque) as dialects of the dominant French. A study conducted in the seventies by the National Council for Education Research and Training (NCERT) viewed that minority language being less cultivated will create unequal opportunities for higher education and employment for minority communities (Goel and Saini 1972).

But ultimately the linguistic minorities succeeded in getting the authorities to accept the *narrow* interpretation of mother tongue, which is closer to the definition of native speech: "the home language of child, the language spoken from the cradle" (*1951 Census of India* 1954).

MULTILINGUAL REPERTOIRE

In mulitligual societies of the Indian subcontinent, one notices an inevitable measure of fluidity in the verbal repertoire of many speech groups who command native-like control over more than one language. The demands of active bilingualism in a plural society expose an individual to 'doing' language activity by accomplishing diverse tasks through a variety of speech styles, registers, dialects, and even language. Mother tongue *identity* and its *image* in this context do not necessarily claim congruity with *actual usage*, and these are again not rigidly identified with specific language *territories*, as is the experience of most European countries either in the past or in the present.

One notices a super-laid homogeneity in communication patterns on the 'cline of urbanization in the entire Hindi-Urdu-Puniabi region divided between India and Pakistan. Language boundaries in this region have got stabilized not so much on account of the barriers of intellingibility between two speech varieties, as on the considerations of identity and value systems among the speakers of those varieties. The highbrow registers of Hindi and Urdu are sharply marked by the polarization in the patterns of borrowing (Sanskritic or Perso-Arabic), whereas at the lowbrow level, distinction between the two is not regarded as so significant. In a communication paradigm the split between Hindi, Urdu and Puniabi traditions is more ideological than lingusitic (Khubchandani 1983). In this context, the issues concerning the facility of expression in mother tongue get highlighted in somewhat simplistic terms i.e. juxtaposing mother tongue against the colonial language English.

A child's earliest first hand experiences in native speech do not necessarily show semblance with the formal school version of his/her mother tongue. The heterogeneity of communication patterns in many regions of the subcontinent, the unequal cultivation of different languages for use as medium of instruction, the demands of elegant versions of mother tongue for formal purposes, the non-availability of personnel with adequate command over the *textbook* language, and the switching over to another medium in the multi-tier media system without adequate preparation are some of the difficulties faced by the learners who are initiated into education through the mother tongue medium. These ground realities have led to the re-examination of the supremacy of the mother tongue medium stretched over to the *entire* education career.

Today many education programmes are geared to facilitate the scope of communication with the prevailing socialization values in a community. Against the background of a multiple-choice medium policy continued after the independence, many newly-cultivated languages (mostly of tribal populations and other minorities) are initiated as *preparatory* medium at the primary stage. Many states have introduced a bilingual education policy where a developing language in a region is used as a *partial* medium together with English, Hindi or the regional language as the major medium. At the tertiary stage, English continues to dominated the scene as a developed medium, and Hindi and regional languages as *emerging* medium (Khubchandani 1978; Sridhar 1988).

Types of media are very much diversified in character. Though many states prefer to promote the exclusive use of regional languages as the medium of instruction, in practice many students experience a shift in language medium at one or another stage, depending upon context, domain and channel such as: students listen to one language and write answers in another: formal teaching in the classroom is conducted in one language but informal explanations are provided in another. In a multi-tier media system, elementary education is initiated through mother tongue, but when a student move upward in the education ladder he shifts to a more cultivated medium.

In multilingual societies the *ideal* claim and the *real* function of a language might be at variance. One notices a wide gap between the language policies professed and actual practice in a classroom. It is not unusual to find in many institutions anomalous patterns of communication where the teacher and the taught interact in one language, classes are conducted in another, textbooks are written in a third, and answers are given in a fourth language/style. This milieu promotes a good deal of code-switching and hybridization of two or more contact languages.

LANGUAGE CULTIVATION

Such multilingual repertoires have played a significant role in cultivating many Indian languages for their increasing use in higher education. Different educational subjects require a different type of preparation for a shift in the medium. Demonstration – oriented subjects of hard core sciences and technology stress the autonomous, well-formulated and unambiguous use of language, utilizing language structures at the rudimentary level accompanied by non-linguistic systems (such as mathematical formulae). In abstract subjects dealing with human phenomena (most of the arts, creative writing, religion and social sciences) language needs mature expression but the content tends to be less vigorously formulated, the likelihood of ambiguity is greater, and interpretations are relatively less precise than in hard core scientific subjects. There is another category identified as meta subjects where the object of interpretation is language itself, such as law, logic, philosophy, semiotics, and linguistics. These subjects develop a kind of meta-language by exploiting subtleties of the language structure for sophisticated and well-formulated communication. The puritanic insistence on developing highbrow *tatsamized* styles based on artificial coinage from non-native classical stocks (Sanskrit, Perso-Arabic, classical Tamil, Medieval lelugu) in preference to adopting borrowed expressions from live situations, has been a great deterrent to introducing Indian languages for this purpose (Loan words from Sanskrit retained in a language without any phonological adaptation are termed *tatsama*, unassimilated, words, in contrast to those adapted to the phonological system of the borrowing language, which are called *ladbhaya*, assimilated, words).

LANGUAGE STUDY

In a nation such as India no single language caters to all the needs of an ordinary citizen. Amid sharp controversies concerning the role of different languages in education, a broad consensus was arrived in the Three Language Formula around the sixties which provided a basis of policy for a minimum requirement of languages in school education. In 1966 the Education Commission recommended a liberalized version of the Formula; it expected a student to acquire sufficient control over three languages by the time he/she completes the lower secondary stage (class x): mother tongue and two non-native modern languages, broadly, Hindi as an official medium, and a link language for the majority of people for inter-state communication, and English as an associate official medium and a link language for higher education and for intellectual and international communication.

The Formula has been differently interpreted by different states. The choice of determining the second or third place for Hindi or English was left to the individual states. Hindi states, by and large, provide classical Sanskrit as the third language in place of a modern Indian language; whereas, a few non-Hindi states (W. Bengal and Orissa) favour Sanskrit at the cost of Hindi as the third language. The safeguards of mother tongue education for linguistic minorities, at least up to the primary stage, were spelled out in the Formula. For several linguistic minorities, it has become virtually a four-language formula, as many states insist on the compulsory teaching of the respective regional language. At certain places language programmes are allotted an out-of-proportion share in the total teaching load in order to suit the climate of language privilege.

LITERACY DRIVES

At this juncture the aspirations of restless masses and of educators are at crossroads, and many diverse claims are being made for bringing radical transformation in the education structure as such. One of the serious handicaps in implementing language education policies by different education agencies at the central and state levels is the continuance of the inherited dichotomies of Ordinary and Advanced tradition, discussed above, and the urban-biased system of education as shaped during the colonial rule.

Many of the present goals of language development in the subcontinent seem to be out of step with the reality in the region. The highbrow values of speech do not actually meet the demands of adequacy and effect in everyday life communication among rural and working-class children. Such requirements of elegance in education (such as stress on urban idiom and sophistication) have created a wide gap between the language(s) of home and that of school, leading to a large number of school dropouts in the country.

In the contemporary world, the uncritical pursuits of modernization promulgate our current perceptions of literacy as the universal truth. During the eighties the Indian government launched a nation-wide Literacy Mission to achieve the target of universal literacy by Year 1995. According to the 1991 Census, the literacy rates in the country have increased to 52.1 per cent during the decade 1981–91, crossing the 50 percent mark (compared to the 1981 literacy rate 44 per cent). At the same time, the total number of illiterates in the country has increased from 302 million in 1981 to 324 million in 1991 (Nanda 1991).

Problems of discontinuity for the rural and working-class entering the predominantly middle-class world of literacy question the goals of universal literacy in removing inequalities in the social structure. Many visionaries rather regard literacy in the modern ethos serving as a discriminating device of identifying advantaged versus disadvantaged classes in a society.

In the Oriental tradition both oral and literate traditions have played a vital role. The Indian heritage rejects the supremacy of one culture over the other. There is now a growing understanding of the assets of oral tradition among illiterate communities transmitted from generation to generation through folklore festivals and rituals, in the backdrop of this it is necessary to focus upon the *continuum* between oral tradition and written culture, and to consider strategies of incorporating the characteristics of *mass* culture into the literate culture (Bright 1988).

Formal education is, initiated by literacy and streamlined through certain time-bound stages in a credential-based system; whereas non-formal education is enmeshed in the cultural milieu of the society, as a part of life-long education through literacy or *without it*. Traditional societies such as India, while relying heavily upon the implicit mechanisms of oral tradition for the transmission of knowledge, assign literate societies (or individuals) certain essential liaison/intermediary functions; literacy in these societies, no doubt, forms an important asset and accomplishment of an individual, but *not a necessary* condition of his/her survival and dignity.

In this endeavour diverse approaches of transmitting literacy skills on a universal basis have emerged on the Indian scene; (1) Conventional educators profess strict adherence to the *standard* language prevailing in the region. (2) Liberal educators recommend a bi-dialectal approach of gradual phasing in time from home dialect to the standard speech; (3) Some educators plead for a *dichotomous* approach by accomodating diversity of dialects/speech varieties at the spoken level, but at the same time insisting on the uniformity of standard language at the written level; (4) Those supporting a grassroots approach endorse a *pluralistic* model of literacy by which variation in speech is regarded as an asset to communication; thus cultivating *positive* values for the diversity in response to the demands of situation, identity and communication task. In this scheme, literacy in the standard variety is, no doubt, promoted for economic-oriented situations and communicative tasks; at the same time, learners are educated to diffuse the pejorative attributes to non-standard varieties which prevail in the society.

The grassroots approach emphasizes making education more meaning-ful useful and productive to work-experience. Sensitivity to speech varia-tion and a grasp over the communication ethos prevailing in the society is, no doubt, enhanced by 'doing' verbal events in natural settings. An elab-oration of Gandhiji's thinking concerning Basic Education could provide a sound basis for launching the schemes concerning education for all, as discussed earlier.

Various constraints in the spread of education are attributed to the multi-plicity of languages, whereas the real issues to cope with are the confronta-tion between tradition and modernity concerning the role of language in education, and the dogmatic rigidity in claiming privileges and parity of different languages in the thrust for autonomy. It is necessary to adopt a pragmatic approach to linguistic usage in education and take into account the mechanisms of standardization of languages in plural societies. When dealing with plural societies, we shall do well to realize the risks involved in *uniform* solutions.

Centre for Communication Studies, Pune, India

Bright, W.: 1988, 'Written and spoken language in South Asia', in C. Duncan-Rose & T. Vennamann (eds.), *On Language: Rhetorica, Phonologica, Syntactica*, Rutledge, London.
Dakin, J.: 1968, 'Language and education in India', in J. Dakin, B. Tiffien & H.G. Widdowson (eds.), *The Language in Education: The Problem in Common Wealth Africa and the Indo-Pakistan Subcontinent*, Oxford University Press, London, 1–61.
Gandhi, M.K.: 1916, 'The present system of education', in *The Problem of Education* (Collected works 1962). Navajivan Press, Ahmedabad.
Goel, B.S. & Saini, S.K.: 1972, *Mother Tongue and Equality of Opportunity in Education*. National Council for Education Research and Training (NCERT), New Delhi.

Government of India: 1948, *Report of the Committee on the Medium of Instruction at the University Level,* Pamphlet 57, Ministry of Education, New Delhi.

Government of India: 1949, *Report of the University Education Commission,* Ministry of Education, New Delhi.

Government of India: 1950, *The Constitution of India,* Ministry of Law, New Delhi.

Government of India: 1954, *Census of India – 1951, Language Tables,* Registrar General of India, New Delhi.

Government of India: 1956, *Report of the Official Language Commission,* Ministry of Home Affair, New Delhi.

Government of India: 1966, *Report of the Education Commission,* Ministry of Education, New Delhi.

Kazi, A.A.: 1987, *Ethnicity and Education in Nation-Building: The Case of Pakistan,* University Press of America, New York.

Khubchandani, L.M.: 1978, 'Multilingual education in India', in B. Spolsky & R. Cooper (eds.), *Case Studies in Bilingual Education* Vol. 11, Newbury House, Rowley Mass; also in the Series; *Studies in Linguistics* Vol. 8, 1981, Centre for Communication Studies, Pune.

Khubchandani, L.M.: 1981, *Language, Education,* Social Justice, Series: In Search of Tomorrow Vol. II, Centre for Communication Studies, Pune.

Khubchandani, L.M.: 1983, *Plural Languages, Plural Cultures: Communication, Identity and Sociopolitical Change in Contemporary India,* An East-West Center Book, University of Hawaii Press, Honolulu.

Naik, J.P.: 1963, *Selections from Educational Records of the Government of India, Vol. 2, Development of University Education 1860–1887,* National Archives of India, New Delhi.

Nanda, A.R.: 1991, *Census of India – 1991, Provisional Population Totals*, series 1: India, Paper 1 of 1991, Registrar General India, New Delhi.

Richey, J.A.: 1922, *Selections from Educational records of the Government of India: 1840–59,* Part II, Bureau of Education, London.

Saiyidain, K.G., Naik, J.P. & Abid, H.S.: 1962, *Compulsory Education in India. Studies on Compulsory Education*, Vol. 11, UNESCO, Paris.

Sharp, H.: 1920, *Selections from Educational records, 1781–1839,* Part 1, Bureau of Education, London.

Sridhar, K.: 1988, 'Language policy for education in multilingual India: Issues and implementation', Conference of South Asian Linguistics Association, Hyderabad.

Tagore, R.: 1906, 'The problem of education', in *Towards Universal Man* (Collected works 1961), Asia Publishing House, Bombay.

UNESCO: 1953, *the Use of Vernacular Language in Education,* Series: Monographs on Fundamental Education, Paris.

Verma, V.S.: 1987, *Census of India 1981*, Series 1 – India. *Household Population by Language,* Government of India Press, Shimla.

Zakir, H.: 1950, *Convention on the Cultural Unity of India,* T.A. Parekh Endowment, Bombay.

NOEL WATTS

LANGUAGE POLICY AND EDUCATION IN NEW ZEALAND AND THE SOUTH PACIFIC

The language situation in an area as extensive as the South Pacific region is, not surprisingly, characterised by its complexity and diversity.

A wide range of languages is employed for different purposes, from indigenous languages which may or may not have written forms and a number of pidgins and creoles each of which may act as a *lingua franca* for groups of people with varied language backgrounds to languages of wider communication such as English or French that are the linguistic artefacts of colonialist expansion in the region in the nineteenth century.

As linguistic situations have changed during the past century and a half, so too have governments responded in different ways with a variety of policy measures to meet perceived needs in relation to language provision. The review below attempts to summarise major trends in language policy formulation and implementation in the countries in the region (also see reviews by Watts in Volume 4; and by Durie and by Lotherington in Volume 5).

EARLY DEVELOPMENTS

The entry of colonial powers into the Pacific in the early nineteenth century imported a range of European languages – Dutch, English, French, German, Portuguese, Spanish – with profound effects on the status of local languages.

In New Zealand at the time of the signing of the Treaty of Waitangi in 1840 between Maori chiefs and the British Crown the dominant language of most people dwelling in New Zealand was Maori. However, this situation rapidly changed as the numbers of Anglo-Celtic emigrants increased and eventually greatly surpassed that of the indigenous population. Although the early mission schools did provide instruction for young Maori in the Maori language, after the 1850s as the colonial government assumed control over education emphasis was placed on learning in English. The 1867 Native Schools Act, for instance, discouraged teaching in Maori. By the end of the century English was firmly established as the medium of instruction and use of Maori by Maori school children either inside or outside the classroom was discouraged. This devaluing of Maori was a feature of the assimilationist policies followed by successive governments up to the mid-twentieth century (Benton N. 1989).

R. Wodak and D. Corson (eds), Encyclopedia of Language and Education,
Volume 1: Language Policy and Political Issues in Education, 189–197.
© *1997 Kluwer Academic Publishers. Printed in the Netherlands.*

Colonial languages also brought major changes to the status accorded to indigenous languages in other countries in the South Pacific during the course of the nineteenth century. As colonial administrations extended their powers educational policies were directed towards promoting English as the language of instruction (or French in New Caledonia, French Polynesia and the New Hebrides).

There were differences, however, in the area of initial schooling where some Pacific Island countries gave a restricted role to the vernacular in literacy development at the elementary level with a transition to the English medium for higher levels, for example in Fiji (Tavola 1991), while other countries rigorously excluded use of indigenous languages from the beginning of schooling as in the case of New Caledonia (Schooling 1990) and American Samoa (Baldauf 1990).

MAJOR CONTRIBUTIONS

It was not until the 1940s and 1950s that the foundations were set for reestablishment of the place of Maori in the New Zealand education system. Increased support was given from the 1960s on to the teaching of Maori as a subject in the secondary schools with the aim of promoting cross-cultural understanding on the part of non-Maori as well as developing the language skills of students of Maori descent and deepening their knowledge of their own cultural heritage. In the primary schools encouragement was also given to including Maori components in the common curriculum. This strengthening of the position of Maori in schools coincided with increased concern in New Zealand about linguistic factors affecting the educational performance of Maori children in English-medium schooling (Benton R.A. 1966). Arguments were advanced that school performance could be enhanced if Maori-speaking entrants were allowed to begin their schooling in Maori. Strong calls for Maori-English bilingual policies in education also came from prominent Maori leaders who were concerned at the apparent sharp decline in the use of Maori language in the community.

Graphic evidence of this decline was found in the data obtained in a major sociolinguistic survey of language use in Maori households between 1973 and 1978 which found that fluent speakers comprised a minority within the Maori population and that these speakers were mainly in older age groups in rural areas (Benton R.A. 1978).

The period since the late 1970s has been characterised by a number of moves to revitalise Maori, the most significant of which involve the establishment of bilingual and immersion programs. In 1976 a bilingual school opened in Ruatoki, one of the few remaining Maori-speaking areas, and this pilot scheme was later extended to other areas. However, disenchantment with the mainstream educational provision persuaded Maori groups to consider other alternatives for their children with the aim of ensuring that Maori children from mainly English-speaking backgrounds could also have opportunities to immerse themselves in a language and cultural environment that closely resembled traditional Maori family life. As a result the first *kohanga reo* centres were set up in 1982 by the Maori people themselves to provide pre-school education entirely in the Maori language. The rapid development of these "language nests" has led to a demand for Maori medium programmes to be continued at the primary and secondary levels. This has occurred in the form of Maori schools called *kura kaupapa Maori* (Spolsky 1989). Support for *kohanga reo* centres and *kura kaupapa Maori* is now part of Government policy.

The 1970s and 1980s also witnessed belated attempts in New Zealand to cater for speakers of languages other than English or Maori to meet the needs of larger numbers of new arrivals from countries where English is not spoken as a first language (Kaplan 1980). Support was provided for pre-school Pacific Islands language centres and the inclusion of community languages such as Tongan and Samoan in a number of primary and secondary schools. However, as Hawley (1987) and Peddie (1992) observed, language maintenance provisions were piecemeal and inadequate to halt the rapid intergenerational loss in community language use which has been observed in sociolinguistic studies of different ethnic groups (Holmes 1991).

There was also pressure from educators and the business community to halt the decline in enrolments in international languages (Working Party on Second Language Learning 1976) resulting in efforts being made from the 1980s to increase the relevance of the foreign language curriculum through new syllabuses and widen the range of languages offered by including languages related to New Zealand's developing trade interests in countries in East Asia (Chinese, Japanese, Korean) and South America (Spanish).

Throughout the Pacific Islands rapid expansion also occurred in the post-war period in primary and secondary education. Concerted attempts were made in a number of countries where English had been adopted as the language of instruction to improve the language competence of students and English syllabuses were revised and updated (Whitehead 1986).

In addition, increasing interest was shown in bilingual education. After many Pacific Island countries achieved independence from colonial powers in the late 1960s and early 1970s developing national awareness was evident in proposals to give local languages a more legitimate place in education. The 1974 Bilingual Education Conference in Pago Pago, for instance, emphasised the advantages of vernacular education, particularly in the initial stages before transition to a second language as the medium of instruction. However, it was recognised that while vernacular education might be more easily implemented in countries with one dominant language variety, such as Kiribati, Tonga and Western Samoa, there were considerable problems in following this approach in socially complex multilingual countries such as Papua New Guinea and Vanuatu (Benton R.A. 1981). The report of a regional workshop on vernacular languages held at Port Vila in 1988 (Liddicoat 1990) documented progress towards moving towards bilingual education policies in the South Pacific with countries such as Fiji, Niue, Western Samoa, Tonga and Tuvalu strengthening the place of local vernaculars at the primary level. It was noted that while Vanuatu continued with English-only or French-only policies because of problems in reconciling two colonial languages, a widespread pidgin (Bislama) and almost one hundred vernaculars, an even more linguistically heterogeneous country, Papua New Guinea, was experimenting with vernacular pre-schools.

WORK IN PROGRESS

At the present time a variety of policy directions are being explored in many of the countries in the region both at national and local levels.

The 1987 Curriculum Review made a recommendation that a national policy on languages be developed in New Zealand embracing Maori, English, Pacific Island languages and foreign languages, including first as well as second language learning. This was followed in 1992 by a detailed discussion document, *Aoteareo: Speaking for Ourselves*, commissioned by the Ministry of Education to examine language issues (Waite 1992).

A priority area identified in the *Aoteareo* document concerned the inclusion of Maori, which had been declared an official language in 1987, in the common curriculum of primary schools. Other key points in the discussion of language needs included the commencement of the study of a LOTEM (a language other than English or Maori) at age 10–11, the extension of ESL and language maintenance programs and increased provision of language services such as translation and interpreting. A further important suggestion was the establishment of a Languages Research Institute to act as a focus for research into second language issues.

However, despite widespread consultation there has been no official endorsement of a substantive national languages policy along the lines of the proposals suggested in *Aoteareo*. Neither has the option of a symbolic national languages policy been taken up. Kaplan (1993) has argued that, at the least, there should be a symbolic policy in which the New Zealand Government signals its serious intent in regard to language education even if it does not wish to commit itself financially to specific courses of action.

Although language issues have been mentioned in subsequent official documents such as *Education for the 21st Century* (Ministry of Education 1993) which suggested a target of 50% of students studying a LOTEM for at least two years at secondary school by the year 2001 and *Nga Haeata Matauranga* (Ministry of Education 1995) which set out a ten-point for Maori education, in many ways present attention in second language policy formulation in New Zealand appears to be shifting from the national level to the local level. Following the Picot Report (Department of Education 1988) radical reforms of educational administration have been made which involve devolution in policy decision-making down to the schools themselves. As a result schools have assumed responsibility for formulating and implementing their own language policies within broad national guidelines. The steps taken by some New Zealand schools in developing policies that reflect the language needs of the surrounding communities are described by Corson (1990). Case studies of different approaches to establishing school-based language policies may also be found in McPherson and Corson (1989).

Progress is also being made to develop and implement new language policies in a number of other South Pacific countries. Two main examples will be given: the Papua New Guinea situation which illustrates a major shift from previous policies and the situation in Tonga which represents refinements to policies rather than a major change of direction.

In Papua New Guinea, a new language policy has been instituted that differs markedly from the English-only policy previously advocated for formal education. English-medium instruction had been viewed as the most practical solution to the problems of providing access to education in a country with over 800 vernacular languages even though it was recognised that English was the second or third language for many children. However, throughout the 1970s and 1980s there were calls for English-only policies to be reconsidered (Kale 1990). The *Education Sector Review* document (Papua New Guinea Department of Education 1991) emphasises that initial learning should occur in the local vernacular. The restructured education system builds on the success of the vernacular pre-school movement (*Tok Ples Pri Skul*) which had developed in several provinces in the 1980s and provides for a three-year elementary school program in which the vernacular acts as the medium of instruction followed by bridging to English in Grade 3 (Siegel 1996).

Tonga can be seen as unique in Polynesia in that it was not subject to colonial rule in the nineteenth century. This has had the advantage of minimising outside influence on language in education policies (Benton R.A. 1981). The result has been to give more prominent place to the vernacular in education than many other South Pacific countries though the importance of English is also recognised. In order to achieve increased competence in both languages programs are being developed which involve a bilingual approach to the teaching of Tongan and English beginning in Class 1 with instruction 90% in Tongan and 10% in English, progressing to 50% in Tongan and 50% in English by Class 6. This approach is based on the view that skills developed in Tongan will assist learners to acquire English more effectively (Taufe'ulungaki 1994).

PROBLEMS AND DIFFICULTIES

As can be seen from the preceding sections, although significant policy initiatives have been made in recent years many decisions on language-related policy matters remain outstanding. In New Zealand, for instance, there is concern at the lack of overall planning in second language education in the absence of a carefully-defined national languages policy. As a result, the separate initiatives taken in areas such as Maori language education and English language provision for migrant children may seem to be lacking an explicit philosophy and a clear sense of direction. The devolution of decision-making to schools which has occurred since the Picot Report can be viewed as a positive move in that it has empowered local communities to seek ways of meeting their particular language-related needs. However, this may also be seen as contributing to fragmentation of effort in addressing important language issues which are of national importance.

The same criticisms of a lack of a guiding philosophy also applies to many of the other countries in the South Pacific region. According to Luke and Baldauf (1990) there is a general need for language policies that are clearly thought out and based on a full understanding of the complexity of language development and use.

As regional meetings such as the 1988 Workshop on Vernacular Education (Liddicoat 1990) have reported, there is a serious lack of information on language matters: numbers of speakers of different languages, community attitudes to language learning, language learner needs. A further cause of concern is that language policies do not always take into consideration important psycho-social factors such as personal and group identity, social justice and access to power sharing (Corson 1993). As Romaine (1992) points out, countries in the South Pacific which continue to pursue English-only (or French-only) policies tend to maintain unequal power distribution by favouring elites.

Apart from the question of developing second language education policies in tune with national and local needs there is the obvious problem of the availability of resources necessary to the achievement of the desired policy outcomes. Throughout the South Pacific region there is a serious shortage of experienced teachers who are fluent in the second language they are teaching as well as versed in modern language teaching methodologies. Similarly, there is a lack of suitable materials. This resource situation is likely to remain a major stumbling block to language policy formulation and implementation unless considerably increased support is provided from outside agencies.

FUTURE DIRECTIONS

Throughout the region there is a need for further research into the principles upon which language policies are based and the ways in which these policies are implemented. Consideration should be given to conducting comparative studies of language policy development in different countries along the lines of the work conducted by Peddie (1993) who contrasted the different approaches adopted in New Zealand and in Victoria, Australia. These studies would be useful to highlight points of similarity as well as differences which relate to the specific linguistic, social, cultural and political factors in individual countries which influence language policy.

In addition to broad surveys of language policies across countries, further research will be required to provide precise information essential for informed language policy decisions. Comprehensive sociolinguistic surveys are required to provide up-to-date data on language use and distribution. As well as large-scale studies, detailed ethnographic research should be carried out to provide qualitative data relating to language issues in specific speech communities, particularly the interconnections between language and cultural identity.

In addition to studies of the ways in which languages are used for ordinary communication in informal domains such as the home there is a need for more concentrated research into language requirements in specialised contexts, for example studies of foreign language use in trade and tourism as outlined by Levett and Adams (1987), Watts (1994).

Finally, development of language policies in the South Pacific region should not be viewed solely as an educational concern. Although schools and other educational institutions certainly play an important role in providing new opportunities for language learning they cannot by themselves create a favourable climate of opinion in society at large that will encourage greatly increased numbers of students to take up these opportunities. The New Zealand situation is a case in point. Despite the widening of the range of language options in schools, only a minority of students include study of another language in their programs. This may reflect, as pointed out by Kaplan (1993), a certain negativity in the population as a whole towards languages other than English, or even a degree of hostility that could stem from "vestigial racism".

The challenge in second language policy formulation in the South Pacific region, then, is to link language in education policies with a wider range of policies involving amongst others, language in government administration, language in the media and language in international affairs to form a comprehensive plan for increasing public awareness of second language issues and promoting positive attitudes towards second language learning.

Massey University
New Zealand

REFERENCES

Baldauf, R.B.: 1990, 'Education and language planning in the Samoas', in R.B. Baldauf & A. Luke (eds.), *Language Planning and Education in Australasia and the South Pacific*, Multilingual Matters, Clevedon, Avon, 259–76.
Benton, N.: 1989, 'Education, language decline and language revitalisation: The case of Maori in New Zealand', *Language and Education* 3, 65–82.
Benton, R.A.: 1966, *Research into the Language Difficulties of Maori Children* 1963–64, Maori Education Foundation, Wellington.
Benton, R.A.: 1978, *The Sociolinguistic Survey of Language Use in Maori Households*, New Zealand Council for Educational Research, Wellington.
Benton, R.A.: 1981, *The Flight of the Amokura: Oceanic Languages and Formal Education in the South Pacific*, New Zealand Council for Educational Research, Wellington.
Corson, D.: 1990, *Language Policy across the Curriculum*, Multilingual Matters, Clevedon, Avon.
Corson, D.: 1993, *Language, Minority Education and Gender: Linking Social Justice and Power*, Multilingual Matters, Clevedon, Avon.
Department of Education: 1988. *Administering for Excellence: Effective Administration in Education: Report of the Taskforce to Review Education Administration*, Department of Education, Wellington.
Hawley, C.: 1987, 'Towards a language policy', in W. Hirsh (ed.), *Living Languages: Bilingualism and Community Languages in New Zealand*, Heinemann, Auckland, 45–53.
Holmes, J.: 1991, 'Threads in the tapestry of languages: An introduction', in J. Holmes & R. Harlow (eds.), *Threads in the New Zealand Tapestry of Languages*, Linguistic Society of New Zealand, Auckland, 1–6.
Kaplan, R.B.: 1980, *The Language Needs of Migrant Workers*, New Zealand Council for Educational Research, Wellington.
Kaplan, R.B.: 1993, 'New Zealand languages policy: Making the patient more comfortable', *Working Papers in Language Education* 1, 3–14.
Kale, J.: 1990 'Language planning in Papua New Guinea', in R.B. Baldauf & A. Luke (eds.), *Language Planning and Education in Australasia and the South Pacific*, Multilingual Matters, Clevedon, Avon, 182–96.
Levett, A. & Adams, A.: 1987, *Catching up with our Future: The Demand for Japan Skills in New Zealand*, New Zealand Japan Foundation, Wellington.
Liddicoat, A. (ed.): 1990, *Vernacular Languages in South Pacific Education: Report on a Workshop held at the Pacific Languages Unit of the University of the South Pacific, Port Vila, Vanuatu, October 1988*, National Languages Institute of Australia, Melbourne.
Luke, A. & Baldauf, R.B.: 1990, 'Language planning and education: A critical rereading', in R.B. Baldauf & A. Luke (eds.), *Language Planning and Education in Australasia and the South Pacific*, Multilingual Matters, Clevedon, Avon, 349–52.
McPherson, J. & Corson, D.: 1989, *Language Policy across the Curriculum: Eight Case Studies of School Based Policy Development*, Department of Education, Massey University, Palmerston North.
Ministry of Education: 1993, *Education for the 21st Century*, Ministry of Education, Wellington.
Ministry of Education: 1995, *Nga Haeata Matauranga: Annual Report on Maori Education 1994/5 and Strategic Direction for Maori Education*, Ministry of Education, Wellington.
Papua New Guinea Department of Education: 1991, *Education Sector Review, Vol. 2: Deliberations and Findings*, Papua New Guinea Department of Education, Port Moresby.
Peddie, R.A.: 1992, 'Language and languages policy in New Zealand: Defining the issues', *English in Aotearoa* 18, 40–50.
Peddie, R.A.: 1993, *From Policy to Practice: The Implementation of Languages Policies*

in Victoria, Australia and New Zealand, Centre for Continuing Education, University of Auckland, Auckland.

Romaine, S.: 1992, *Language, Education and Development: Urban and Rural Tok Pisin in Papua New Guinea*, Clarendon Press, Oxford.

Schooling, S.: 1990, *Language Maintenance in Melanesia: Sociolinguistics and Social Networks in New Caledonia*, Summer Institute of Linguistics, Arlington, Texas.

Siegel, J.: 1996, *Vernacular Education in the South Pacific* (International Development Issues No. 45), Australian Agency for International Development, Canberra.

Spolsky, B.: 1989, 'Maori bilingual education and language revitalisation', *Journal of Multilingual and Multicultural Development* 10, 89–106.

Taufe'ulungaki, A.M.: 1994, 'Language community attitudes and their implications for the maintenance and promotion of the Tongan language', *Directions* 16, 84–108.

Tavola, H.: 1991, *Secondary Education in Fiji: A Key to the Future*, Institute of Pacific Studies, University of the South Pacific, Suva.

Waite, J.: 1992, *Aoteareo: Speaking for Ourselves. Part A: The Overview, Part B: The Issues*, Learning Media, Ministry of Education, Wellington.

Watts, N.: 1994, 'The use of foreign languages in tourism: Research needs', *Australian Review of Applied Linguistics* 17, 73–84.

Whitehead, C.: 1986, *Education in Fiji since Independence: A Study of Government Policy*, New Zealand Council for Educational Research, Wellington.

Working Party on Second Language Learning: 1976, *Second Language Learning in New Zealand*, Department of Education, Wellington.

Section 4

Practical and Empirical Issues

ROBERT PHILLIPSON

THE POLITICS OF ENGLISH LANGUAGE TEACHING

The expansion of English worldwide has been predicted ever since British occupation of North America. Throughout the British empire English was the language of power. Postcolonial states have largely perpetuated the role of English in government and education, and are heavily influenced by Anglo-American academic structures, know-how and books. English Language Teaching (ELT), a general term for the teaching of English as a second/foreign language (TESOL), has expanded exponentially since the 1950s so as to promote and service English worldwide and to meet a demand domestically in Britain and the neo-Europes (USA, Australia, New Zealand, . . .). It has been prominent in foreign 'aid'. In Europe, moves towards greater economic and political integration have consolidated the position of English as the first foreign language. Although English is currently the triumphal 'world' language, and is therefore a major political factor, the primary concerns of ELT professionalism are linguistic and pedagogical. The educational, social and political ramifications of ELT are however increasingly of concern to scholars in 'North' and 'South' countries.

EARLY DEVELOPMENTS

The professionalism that evolved in ELT drew on a range of sources. One was adult foreign language learning in continental Europe and Japan, under the influence of pioneer phoneticians and linguists at the University of London, who were in turn influenced by the European movement to reform foreign language learning (Howatt 1984). A second was the immigrant linguistic melting-pot in the USA and the growth of anthropological and structural linguistics. A third was colonial education. This largely imitated what happened in the metropolis, and seldom addressed the cultural, linguistic or educational needs of colonized peoples, except as loyal servants of empire (Mühlhäusler 1996; Pennycook 1994; Phillipson 1992). 'Eng. Lit.', English Literature, was developed as a school subject in nineteenth-century British India even before its implementation in Britain (Viswanathan 1989). A possible fourth influence was other European powers, particularly France, actively promoting their languages.

During the Cold War, English was spread as a conscious means to extend American influence. Substantial funding was made available for educational and cultural work worldwide, and by 1964 at least 40 US

R. Wodak and D. Corson (eds), Encyclopedia of Language and Education,
Volume 1: Language Policy and Political Issues in Education, 201–209.
© *1997 Kluwer Academic Publishers. Printed in the Netherlands.*

governmental agencies were involved (Coombs 1964). English teaching was a major concern of the US Information Agency. Ford, Rockefeller and other foundations provided grants to develop resources in ELT, and played a decisive role in establishing TESOL as an academic discipline (Berman 1982). Ford funded the establishment of the Center for Applied Linguistics in Washington in 1959 and had projects in 38 countries by the mid-1960s (Fox 1979).

The British government's concern, as can be seen in planning documents of the 1950s, was to ensure that the post-colonial era did not harm British investments and influence (Phillipson 1992: chapter 6). The career opportunities for ELT worldwide and an academic infrastructure in Britain were therefore progressively expanded: applied linguistics was set up in Edinburgh in 1957 explicitly to serve the cause of ELT, and a dozen or more universities have been added each decade since. There is also a huge private language school market in Britain (catering for over half a million people following courses each year), and large numbers of ELT people, often with minimal qualifications, are recruited for short teaching contracts abroad.

MAJOR CONTRIBUTIONS

The professional traditions governing ELT classroom activities, curriculum development, testing and the relevant teacher training have developed largely in separation from mainstream education, including foreign language learning in the 'English-speaking countries' and the teaching of English as a foreign language as it is successfully practised in continental Europe (the Netherlands, Scandinavia, etc). The strengths of the ELT profession have been in developing practical communicative skills and functional language learning, such as English for business or for academic study purposes, following a monolingual approach (Howatt 1984).

There is considerable sophistication in ELT in relation to the description of English (communicative, pragmatic and discourse dimensions) and of processes facilitating its learning (second language acquisition, 'SLA'), due to the strong influence of linguistics on this branch of the teaching profession. However, issues of the power or politics of English and ELT are seldom overtly present in such state-of-the-art volumes as Quirk and Widdowson's (1985) *English in the World: Teaching and Learning the Language and Literatures*, or its successor a decade later *Principles and Practice in Applied Linguistics: Studies in Honour of H.G. Widdowson* (Cook & Seidlhofer 1995). Such concerns belong to the covert agenda of ELT.

ELT has not been without its critics. These have included outsiders to the profession: political leaders such as Gandhiji and Rabindranath Tagore who were worried about cultural alienation and pedagogical ineffectiveness; intellectuals such as Philippines academics protesting about American agenda-setting when English is the medium of higher education; and creative writers such as Ngũgĩ wa Thing'o, who see English as a key instrument of cultural imperialism and subservience to foreign interests in Kenya (see Ngũgĩ 1993).

There has also been a strong reformist tradition within the ELT profession. Questioning the established order is creeping into such key professional fora as *English Language Teaching Journal* and *TESOL Quarterly*, both of which are aimed at ELT practitioners. *English Today* and *World Englishes* cover global variation in English and standards, and have given prominence to scholars who have queried Anglo-American dominance in linguistics and pedagogy. A key figure is Braj Kachru (1986), whose work has focussed on the way English has 'indigenized' in many parts of the world and taken on new social roles and cultural and linguistic forms, and the need to create learning conditions that respect this multilingual diversity (see the review by Pakir in Volume 4).

WORK IN PROGRESS

The political dimensions of ELT are increasingly being addressed by scholars in North and South. Phillipson's *Linguistic Imperialism* (1992) sees English linguistic imperialism, and the ELT profession in particular, as a key interlocking constituent of North-South domination, and identifies the evolution of key tenets in the ELT profession in its formative years:
- English is best taught monolingually,
- the ideal teacher of English is a native speaker,
- the earlier English is introduced, the better the results,
- the more English is taught, the better the results,
- if other languages are used much, standards of English will drop.

Adhering to these tenets has had major consequences, structural and ideological, for the entire ELT operation, and been of major significance both in the education of immigrants and in post-colonial education systems where English has functioned as the medium of education. This occurred despite the tenets being in conflict with the scientific evidence on the role of L1 in L2 learning, even though an understanding of these issues underpinned a seminal UNESCO report (1953) on the use of the vernacular languages in education. The tenets are rooted in a monolingual world view and are therefore highly functional in making the "world" dependent on native speaker norms, expertise, textbooks and methodologies, even though these are unlikely to be culturally, linguistically or pedagogically appropriate. They have contributed to language policies which have perpetuated the neglect of African and Asian languages, and to the underpinning of linguistic imperialism as one element of global dominance of the South by the North and the maintenance of elite privileges in the South. They conform to the classic pattern of hegemonic structures and ideologies in being complex and largely covert, so that their nature and function and the injustice they entail are often unnoticed and uncontested, not least within the ELT profession itself. The tenets could be more appropriately labelled as the monolingual, native speaker, early start, maximum exposure, and subtractive fallacies.

Pennycook's *The Cultural Politics of English as an International Language* (1994) adduces very similar evidence from a number of Asian countries. His analysis focusses less on the structural dominance of English at the expense of other languages and more on how the 'worldliness' of English (the language never being 'neutral') is internalized in discourse, and on how the cultural politics of English and ELT in postcolonial settings is worked through. He also aims to show that a critical pedagogy approach can lead to a validation of 'insurgent' knowledge and address the inequalities that English mediates and creates.

Tollefson has documented how the ELT offered to future immigrants to the USA in Asian refugee camps condemns them to menial tasks and subservience (see Forum 1990). Canadian research has shown how the refusal of refugees of Mayan background from Guatemala to learn English is rooted in deep distrust of both the pedagogy involved (senseless oral drill exercises) and the function of the dominant language in socializing them into an inferior societal status (Giltrow & Colhoun 1992). Many political issues, such as links between ELT and gender, the workplace, higher education admissions, and above all, educational policy are being addressed, for instance in Canada (Burnaby & Cumming 1992). The USA-based organization TESOL has a 'socio-political concerns' committee which has played an important role in assisting the association and its members to address such issues as language rights, the employment of non-native teachers, and advocacy skill-building (see the bi-monthly *TESOL Matters*). There is an expanding scholarly literature on the politics of ELT (see the thematic number of *TESOL Quarterly* 30/3 1996; Tollefson 1995).

Attempts by scholars in the 'North' to situate ELT in a broader socio-political perspective, and make its covert agenda more visible, are occurring in parallel with analyses by 'South' scholars of global dependence relations, of the failure of education and 'development' policies in many post-colonial states, and of the ambivalence of language policies in these. Two anthologies from India explore the identity of 'English' as a higher education subject, and its divorce from pressing social and educational issues (Joshi 1994; Rajan 1992a). The British Council has played a crucial mediating role between Britain and such states, one that has been insightfully analysed by a 'recipient' of such western patronage, who pinpoints its significant agenda-setting role: 'The connection between higher education and the western academy undeniably exists – it is not only historical and paradigmatic but is also a *continuing* relation of dependence and support in matters of scholarship and expertise, material aid, the training of personnel, the framing of syllabi, and pedagogical methods' (Rajan 1992b: p. 141).

There are radical critiques from those who cannot see English truly reflecting Indian cultural traditions (e.g. Dasgupta 1993 and see the reviews by Agnihotri in Volume 2), and those who see current educational language policy as pernicious, and plead for the culture-specific forms of local users of the language to be de-hegemonized and validated, e.g. in Sri Lanka (Parakrama 1995), or see local ELT as a site of resistance and emancipation (Canagarajah 1995). Likewise, scholars from Nigeria and the Caribbean have advocated the use of a pidgin language instead of standard (= British) English in education, so as to make learning more culturally appropriate and successful. In Tanzania the inappropriacy of much western educational 'aid' has been well documented (Brock-Utne 1993) and its impact on language policy (Rubagumya 1990). The ideological content of textbooks in the two Koreas has been analysed (Baik 1995).

'English' in the contemporary world is immensely varied (for a survey see Fishman, Conrad & Rubal-Lopez 1996). Its role is widely contested, but there are few signs in postcolonial education systems of any significant break from ELT in its Anglo-American variant. The North-South relationship that underpins ELT involves not merely products (books, scholarships, academic links, etc), but also ongoing hegemonic processes which are constantly being redefined and legitimated, and can be contested. This was true a century ago: 'Until curriculum is studied less as a receptacle of texts than as an activity, that is to say as a vehicle of acquiring and exercising power, descriptions of curricular content in terms of their expression of universal values on the one hand or pluralistic, secular identities on the other are insufficient signifiers of their historical realities. The nineteenth-century Anglicist curriculum of British India is not reducible simply to an expression of cultural power; rather, it served to confer power as well as to fortify British rule against real or imagined threats from a potentially rebellious subject population' (Viswanathan 1989: p. 167).

This analysis holds with equal validity in the late twentieth-century world: English is the language in which a great deal of 'international' activity (trade, politics, media, education, ...) takes place. Worldwide, competence in English is seen as opening doors. This means that ELT in its global and local manifestations is intricately linked to multiple uses of the language and access to power. It is therefore vital to know what forces and values it embodies, what the purposes and effects of its professional ideologies are, what economic and cultural factors propel it forward, and ultimately whose interests it serves.

PROBLEMS AND DIFFICULTIES

English is taught as a second or foreign language so widely that there is a risk of any generalizations not applying globally. Ango-American-driven ELT has had relatively little influence on English learning in western European countries, except through the influence of textbooks and reference works and informal professional links. Most teachers of English are locals with appropriate training, often with high levels of language proficiency.

In post-communist European countries, ELT has expanded vigorously since 1990, encouraged by the US government (via the Peace Corps and other support programmes) and the British government. The British Council has established an 'ELT Projects in Europe' (ELTECS) service to support British involvement in ELT through stationing staff in eastern and central Europe, conferences, publications, and networking. There is a 'cultural diplomacy' thrust to such work, to do with influence and agenda-setting. There is also a commercial interest because of the vast potential market. For the US and the UK, ELT has significant economic dimensions. Through books, courses and degrees, examinations, and related services, ELT in the mid-1990s is reportedly worth £6 billion *per annum* to the British Exchequer (McCallen 1989). This market is now also of considerable importance to Australia and other English-using countries (for instance Malta as a venue for English-language courses).

While English as a foreign language in continental Europe has tended to function relatively independently in each country, there is widespread awareness that standards of competence achieved in school English teaching could be improved. Strengthening the teaching of foreign languages has been a major concern of the Council of Europe for two decades, and has been recommended as European Union policy since 1995. Measures to ensure that all schoolchildren learn two foreign languages are unlikely to dislodge English from its preferential position, nor is the drive for 'early foreign language learning' that politicians seem to favour. This presumed panacea is as suspect as is an increased use of native speakers as foreign language teachers, unless the more fundamental issue of teacher qualifications is addressed and more attention paid to alternative ways of achieving successful bilingualism in schools (see, e.g. Skutnabb-Kangas 1995). The naivety of faith in native speakers has been elegantly dissected by a Hungarian, Medgyes (1999), partly in response to the way ELT was marketed in central Europe (see the review by Medgyes in Volume 4).

One of the intriguing aspects of a profession that has been booming for forty years is that its members often have peripheral status and uncertain job prospects. This is true even though it has been estimated (by the British Council) that one billion people worldwide will be learning English by the turn of the century. It is the case in the USA, where TESOL has a membership of many thousands, and where professional associations are attempting, like comparable bodies in Britain, to strengthen professional standards and their certification. The uncertainty is undoubtedly connected to unresolved debates in the USA about bilingual education and to the strength of the 'English Only' movement (see the reivew by Ricento), and in the UK to the strong pressure on immigrants to drop their languages and switch to English (see the review by Nassoul). Perhaps the marginal status of ELT is linked to the fact that power in the 'English-speaking' countries rests with monolingual speakers, leaders who are responsible for education systems that, unlike those of most countries in the world, do not succeed in providing schoolchildren with success in learning more than one language. Perhaps at root the belief is that the need for ELT will disappear because ultimately everyone will be 'English-speaking'. An alternative, and more plausible, scenario is that English will strengthen its position worldwide as the first foreign language, in which case the need for ELT can only increase.

FUTURE DIRECTIONS

There are many countries in the world in which it is difficult to predict whether the role played by English will expand or contract. A case in point is South Africa, which has accorded official status to 11 languages, and aims to 'reduce English to equality', in Neville Alexander's memorable phrase, in order to ensure the linguistic rights of the many who do not speak this dominant language – but where the pressures towards an expanded use of English are enormous (see the review by Smit). In many states in Africa and Asia vast populations are ruled in a language that they do not understand. It is arguable that ELT is contributing to unjust political and social systems through its support for English as an elite language that ensures social stratification internally and key commercial and political links externally.

ELT is not the only educational export from Britain and the US to South countries. It is striking that in much of the educational 'aid' from North states, for which the World Bank currently sets the tone, language policy receives very little attention (e.g. in King's 1991 survey), implying continued support for English as the medium of education at secondary and tertiary levels. Such policies reflect the colonialist belief that it is only European languages that can serve the purposes of 'development'. Not only is such a belief, and the educational policies it entails, an infringement of the fundamental human rights of the speakers of non-dominant languages (Skutnabb-Kangas & Phillipson 1994, 1997). It also fails to correctly diagnose why development policies hitherto have failed, and why expenditure on basic education in many South countries is currently substantially lower than earlier, as a direct result of interest payments on loans. Language policy, including ELT, is only one among several factors in this equation, but it is definitely of importance. The politics of ELT in postcolonial contexts therefore needs careful scrutiny globally and locally.

University of Roskilde
Denmark

REFERENCES

Berman, E.H.: 1982, 'The foundations role in American foreign policy: the case of Africa, post 1945', in R.F. Arnove, (ed.), *Philanthropy and Cultural Imperialism*, Indiana University Press, Bloomington, 203–232.

Baik, M.J.: 1995, *Language, Ideology and Power in English Textbooks of two Koreas*, Thaehaksa, Seoul (Ph.D. dissertation, University of Illinois at Urbana-Champaign).

Brock-Utne, B.: 1993, *Education in Africa. Education for self-reliance or recolonization*, University of Oslo, Institute for Educational Research, Oslo.

Burnaby, B. & Cumming, A. (eds.): 1992, *Socio-political aspects of ESL*, Ontario Institute for Studies in Education, Toronto.

Canagarajah, A.S.: 1995, 'Review of Robert Phillipson: Linguistic imperialism', *Language in Society* 24/4, 590–594.

Cook, G. & Seidlhofer, B. (eds.): 1995, *Principle and Practice in Applied Linguistics. Studies in Honour of H.G.Widdowson*, Oxford University Press, Oxford.

Coombs, P.H.: 1964, *The Fourth Dimension of Foreign Policy: Educational and Cultural Affairs*, Harper & Row, New York.

Dasgupta. Probal: 1993, *The Otherness of English: India's Auntie Tongue Syndrome*, Sage, London & Delhi.

Fishman, J.A., A.W.Conrad & A. Rubal-Lopez (eds.): 1996, *Post-Imperial English: Satus Change in Former British and American Colonies, 1940–1990*, Mouton de Gruyter, Berlin & New York.

Forum: 1990, Comments on James W.Tollefson's 'Alien Winds: The Reeducation of America's Indochinese Refugees' and Elsa Auerbach's Review, *TESOL Quarterly* 24/3, 529–568.

Fox, M. (ed.): 1979, *Language and Development: A Retrospective Survey of Ford Foundation Language Projects, 1952–1974, vol 1: Report, vol 2: Case Studies*, Ford Foundation, New York.

Giltrow, J. & Colhoun, E.R.: 1992 'The culture of power: ESL traditions, Mayan resistance', in Burnaby & Cumming (eds.), *please provide book's name*, 50–66.

Howatt, A.P.R.: 1984, *A History of English Language Teaching*, Oxford University Press, Oxford.

Joshi, S. (ed.): 1994, *Rethinking English. Essays in Literature, Language, History*, Oxford University Press, Delhi.

Kachru, B.B.: 1986, *The Alchemy of English. The Spread, Functions and Models of Non-native Englishes*, Pergamon, Oxford.

King, K.: 1991, *Aid and education in the developing world. The role of the donor agencies in educational analysis*, Longman, Harlow.

McCallen, B.: 1989, *English: A World Commodity. The International Market for Training in English as a Foreign Language*, Special Report 1166, Economist Intelligence Unit, London.

Medgyes, P.: 1995, *The Non-native Teacher*, Macmillan, Basingstoke.

Mühlhäusler, P.: 1996, *Linguistic Ecology. Language Change and Linguistic Imperialism in the Pacific Region*, Routledge, London.

Ngũgĩ wa Thiong': 1993, *Moving the Centre. The Struggle for Cultural Freedoms*, James Currey, London and Heinemann, Portsmouth, NH.

Parakrama, A.: 1995, *De-hegemonizing language standards. Learning from (Post) Colonial Englishes about 'English'*, Macmillan, Basingstoke.
Pennycook, A.: 1994, *The Cultural Politics of English as an International Language*, Longman, Harlow.
Phillipson, R.: 1992, *Linguistic Imperialism*, Oxford University Press, Oxford.
Quirk, R. & Widdowson, H.G. (eds.): 1985, *English in the World: Teaching and Learning the Language and Literatures*, Cambridge University Press, Cambridge.
Rajan, R.S. (ed.): 1992a, *The Lie of the Land. English Literary Studies in India*, Oxford University Press, Delhi.
Rajan, R.S.: 1992b, 'Brokering English studies: the British council in India', in Rajan (ed.), *please provide book name*, 130–155.
Rubagumya, C.M. (ed.): 1990, *Language in education in Africa: a Tanzanian perspective*, Multilingual Matters, Clevedon.
Skutnabb-Kangas, T. (ed.): 1995, *Multilingualism for All*, Swets & Zeitlinger, Lisse.
Skutnabb-Kangas, T. & Phillipson, R. (eds.): 1994, *Linguistic human rights: overcoming linguistic discrimination*, Mouton de Gruyter, Berlin & New York.
Skutnabb-Kangas, T. & Phillipson, R.: 1997, 'Linguistic human rights and development', in Hamelink, C.J. (ed.), *Ethical Dilemmas in Development Co-operation. Should there be a Code of Conduct for Development Workers?* Kok, Kampen.
Tollefson, James W. (ed.): 1995, *Power and Inequality in Language Education*, Cambridge University Press, Cambridge.
UNESCO: 1953, *The Use of the Vernacular Languages in Education*, UNESCO, Paris.
Viswanathan, G.: 1989, *Masks of Conquest: Literary Study and British Rule in India*, Columbia University Press, New York and Faber & Faber, London.

T. VAN LEEUWEN

MEDIA IN EDUCATION

The media entered education in three ways: (1) as *teaching aids*, to enliven school subjects and make them appear more relevant to the outside world or to students' extra-curricular experience (especially in the case of students considered to be under-achieving); (2) as an *object of study* in itself, usually to encourage a critical and analytical attitude towards media products with which students might already be familiar as consumers; and (3) as a *practical activity*, through the production of photographs, 8 mm films, videos and so on.

Often media education amounted to an education *against* the media. Everywhere educators felt that the media could threaten the seriousness of education, foster misconceptions about the world and create all kinds of harmful effects. In recent years attitudes have become more positive, at least in Europe. The gap between education and the media industry is closing. This development was heralded by changes in media theory, which moved from theories of passive, manipulated viewers to theories of active, discerning audiences; which began to problematize the distinction between reality and fiction in the media; and which started to legitimate pleasure and entertainment, rather than regarding it as bait to hook gullible viewers with.

Media practice has generally been relatively marginal in education and regarded as creative self-expression rather than as a form of literacy and a potentially vital skill. This may change as the distinction between 'professional' and 'amateur' is much attenuated in the era of the computer.

EARLY DEVELOPMENTS

Fears for the corruption of youth by the media go back at least as far as Plato, who, in his *Republic*, considered most of the literature of his day unsuitable for the purposes of education, because it misrepresented reality and would 'breed in our young men an undue tolerance of wickedness' (Part 3, Book 3: p. 392).

In the 19th century Matthew Arnold (1887: p. 638) condemned the 'new journalism', calling it 'feather-brained' and claiming that 'to get at the state of things as they truly are it seems to feel no concern whatsoever'. In the next century similar criticisms would be levelled against film, against popular songs (e.g. by Theodor Adorno in Germany), against

R. Wodak and D. Corson (eds), Encyclopedia of Language and Education,
Volume 1: Language Policy and Political Issues in Education, 211–218.
© *1997 Kluwer Academic Publishers. Printed in the Netherlands.*

comic strips (e.g. in Frederic Wertham's *Seduction of the Innocent,* in the US) and against many other kinds of media product. Everywhere the media were seen as threatening high cultural values and high art forms, as manipulating gullible mass audiences, and as adversely affecting children's behaviour, cognitive abilities and emotional development – in short, as subverting everything education is to uphold and foster. This tradition is still evident whenever the debate about television and violence flares up, or when politicians proclaim that they want 'William Shakespeare in the classroom, not Ronald McDonald' as did John Patten in 1992. It also exists in developing countries, where (Anglo-American) media are often seen as an arm of cultural imperialism (cf. Tunstall 1977; Dissanayake et al. 1983; Bazalgette et al. 1992).

Education countered by keeping the media out. But from the 1960s onwards, after the full impact of television had become evident, it was increasingly thought necessary to explicitly teach critical attitudes towards media products. 'Discrimination' was the keyword, discrimination between 'good' and 'bad' films, 'good' and 'bad' popular songs, and so on. However, media education rarely entered the school curriculum. In most countries it took place (and still takes place) outside school, in youth clubs, adult education, and so on. Church organizations have played a particularly significant role, in France, Italy, Germany and the Netherlands as well as in many developing countries. Only Norway, Sweden and Finland have made media education a compulsory school subject. In several other countries it was introduced as an elective, for instance in Britain, where it has been an increasingly popular 'A-level' subject since 1989 and is also written into the curriculum of other, traditional school subjects. In the United States concern about the effects of media violence led to the introduction of media studies in the late 1970s, but American-style 'back to basics' curtailed it during the recession of the early 1980s. In general, media education has often been called for or endorsed by Governments, but rarely made an integral and significant part of public education – see UNESCO (1977), Morsy (1984) and Bazalgette et al. (1992) for further information about media studies across the world.

Meanwhile the media had long been used as a teaching aid. As early as 1903 newspapers were introduced in geography lessons in Britain, to provide a 'window on the world'. Other media followed: slides, educational films, educational radio broadcasts, and so on. Such media were welcomed provided they were produced specifically for educational purposes and not marred by the 'sensationalist' and 'stereotyped' approach of the mass media (cf. Ploszajska 1996). Eventually this changed. As already mentioned, critical studies of mass media products also became part of traditional school subjects such as language, science, geography and history. Geography lessons, for instance, began to investigate 'popular and non-rationalized images of, for example, climate, social systems, terrain, social attitudes, etc.' (Lusted 1991: p. 176).

MAJOR CONTRIBUTIONS

Essentially education and the media are rivals. Both provide information about the world. Both seek to influence the minds and hearts of the population. But they do so for different masters, with different interests at heart, and different purposes in mind. In developing countries, for instance, education might be enlisted to teach new methods of agriculture in an attempt to try and make people stay on the land, while the mass media disseminate attractive images of urban life. By introducing media studies, educationalists have sought to counter the influence of the media, and to affect patterns of media consumption and ways of talking about the media.

In many countries this initially centered on film. 'Good' films were films which could be interpreted as dealing with socially significant themes in approved ways, films with religious themes (e.g. Ingmar Bergman), or adaptations of good literature (e.g. Shakespeare films). The language of a 1959 Dutch course booklet, published by the (Christian) Filmcentrum, is typical: 'Already there are some films which reach the level of a work of art. This should be welcomed. The fact that it has been possible to reach this level in a mere sixty years is proof that here too the human spirit triumphs'.

Following the serious attention given to Hollywood films by European intellectuals such as the critics of the French film magazine *Cahiers du Cinema,* it became possible to discern also between 'good' and 'bad' Westerns, or gangster movies, or other Hollywood genre films. Such films would be seen, not as the product of a manipulative 'culture industry', but as the work of 'authors' with individual styles and sets of themes. Nichols, ed. (1976: P. 224–305) contains a series of now classic film theory papers along these lines. The same approach was applied to other forms of popular art, especially jazz. In other words, what before would have been discussed only as a *medium* ('film' or 'radio' in general) or as a *genre* ('the western' or 'jazz' in general), could now be discussed in terms of individual *works*, and given the kind of critical attention which previously would only have been accorded to novels, paintings, symphonies, and so on, or to their creators. The *Popular Arts*, by Stuart Hall and Paddy Whannel, written in 1964, is a good example of this approach to media education.

In the late 1970s and early 1980s, television series also began to be considered. The 'quality' issue continued to play a role (and explicitly returned, e.g. in Feuer et al. 1984), but gradually diminished in importance. It now became possible to introduce any media product into education, regardless of quality, in part by shifting emphasis from teaching the difference between 'good' and 'bad' media products to teaching the difference between 'good' and 'bad' ways of talking about media products, through ethnographic study of the way different audiences talk about the same media product, (e.g. Morley 1980).

Besides the 'popular arts', factual media products such as television news and current affairs (Glasgow Media Group 1976; Hartley 1982) and documentary (Nichols 1981) became an important focus of media studies, especially from the mid 1970s onwards, and usually in a neo-Marxist vein. The aim was to show that these factual media products were not transparent windows on the world or 'slices of life' but 'constructed realities' with an ideological dimension. This was brought out in studies of the media products themselves as well as in studies of their production, with telling titles like *Putting 'reality' together: BBC News* (Schlesinger 1978).

Another neo-Marxist strand of media theory which strongly influenced media studies for a time was a critique of mainstream Hollywood story-telling techniques, inspired especially by the ideas of Bertolt Brecht, Louis Althusser and Jacques Lacan. The 'classic Hollywood narrative' and the 'pleasure of looking' were subjected to a critique which left only a minority of 'radical' films and television programmes as 'good' media products, which construed viewers (and especially female viewers) as wholly and passively at the mercy of structures which ultimately oppressed them, and which saw their pleasures as something to be destroyed: 'It is said that analyzing pleasure, or beauty, destroys it. That is the intention of this article' (Mulvey 1975). Rosen (1986) is a collection of key papers in this tradition.

Finally there was an important emphasis on language, especially in France and Italy. Instead of viewing photographs and films as the ultimate empirical medium, uniquely equipped to reveal reality-as-it-is, a point of view defended by earlier film scholars such as Siegfried Kracauer and Andre Bazin, photographs and films were now seen as constructs, articulated through a visual language which could be analyzed with structuralist methods inspired by Ferdinand de Saussure and Louis Hjelmslev (cf. Barthes 1967, 1977). Although the protagonists of this school moved on to different approaches, the influence of their early work remains profound. Curiously, little attention was given to the use of language and speech in the media, despite the linguistic inspiration. This includes its rather devastating impact on minority languages, especially but not exclusively aboriginal languages and cultures (see the review of Indigenous Language Policies by Corson in this volume). Such work on language and speech in the media as did appear (e.g. Fowler et al 1979; Kevelson 1977) remained on the margins of media studies. It was the visual, not the linguistic medium (that is, not the medium the critics themselves used) whose truth was deconstructed and critiqued. Most recently this has changed somewhat (cf. e.g. Scannell 1991; Fairclough 1995), but for the most part because sociolinguists are gradually becoming less narrow in their concerns of what linguistics should be about, rather than from within media studies.

As most media education was 'education against the media', it was these *critical* approaches which provided the crucial formative influence on media education. Another strand of media studies, (American) mass communication research, was hardly taken up, and classified as social science rather than part of the humanities.

WORK IN PROGRESS

Recent developments have brought a change in the relation between (European) media studies and (American) mass communication theory – it should be noted that the latter is not only practised in the USA, nor the former only in Europe, and that in particular Asian mass communication scholars have developed alternative approaches, more suited to Asian cultural values (cf. Dissanayake et al. 1983). Until recently (American) mass communication theory was a theoretically relatively fragmented collection of methodically rigorous, quantitative studies of media effects, agenda setting and so on, while (European) media studies were qualitative, and based on broad theoretical conceptions of society and the place of the media in it, often on a neo-Marxist basis. As a result of the postmodern turn, (European) media studies have now fragmented into a collection of subjectivist text explications and micro ethnographic studies of a heterogeneity of audience groups. The earlier emphasis on critique has made place for a pluralist and populist approach which sees media products as open to a wide variety of readings, so that they can be read 'subversively' or 'resistantly' even if they are the products of global media empires. Scholars from the mass communication tradition, on the other hand, have moved towards broader concerns, such as the formation of social identities and issues of globalization, localization, and media and social change generally (e.g. Katz & Szecsko 1989 and esp. the *European Journal of Communication*).

The pluralist and populist approach, meanwhile, has had most influence in education: 'A celebratory approach to the subject, one which emphasizes the positive and pleasurable aspects, is long overdue', said the influential British media educator Len Masterman (1985: p. 238). Many media educators no longer seek to change their students' already established preferences and pleasures in favour of other preferences and pleasures, or, more generally, to 'educate against the media'. Even advertising can now go scotfree, especially since it has embraced postmodern values like *pastiche* and self-reflexivity. Instead, they encourage students to give expression to their own identities and lifestyles, to acknowledge their pleasures in the media products which form part of these identities and lifestyles, and generally to diminish the gap between the world inside and the world outside the school. Frequently they are asked to do project work which makes them researchers of their own cultural identity, and this means that they must both embrace that identity and analytically distance themselves from it (cf Buckingham and Sefton-Green, 1994). All this can result in a turning away from larger political issues, a focus on 'cultural' rather than 'media' studies, and an emphasis on the local rather than the global.

Following the rapid development of the 1970s and early 80s, the field as a whole now seems relatively quiescent. The work of the preceding period is being gathered in numerous anthologies, but, apart from the tendencies signalled above, there have been few new developments, either in media theory or in media education. Work on the new digital media is going on (cf. e.g. Hayward ed. 1991), often in a celebratory vein, but much of it is self-published or, indeed, electronically published, heralding changes in the very notion of what constitutes academic work and research, changes which may well contribute to a new set of attitudes towards the aims and objectives of practical media work in education, and of media studies generally (see the review by McGonigal in Volume 3).

PROBLEMS, DIFFICULTIES AND FUTURE DIRECTIONS

The tradition of 'educating against the media' which still underlies a good deal of media education has already been undermined to a considerable extent. Education has made place for the media's traditional emphasis on combining information and entertainment by legitimating viewing pleasures and ways of 'reading' media products and talking about them which it formerly sought to critique and replace. At the same time the media industry has stepped up production of 'edutainment' products suitable for home as well as school use. This diminishes the difference between the world outside school and the world inside school as well as the traditional opposition between education as a site of logic and reason and the media as a site of pleasure and imaginary identification, with attempts to grasp pleasure intellectually as a kind of last-ditch defense. On the positive side, this creates for media education a potential new role of confirming educational subjects in local and specific cultural identities and lifestyles, and so providing a microcosmic model of the multicultural and heterogeneous world in which they will have to live, and a useful complement to the increasing 'vocational' tendencies in education.

It should not be forgotten, meanwhile, that the older, critical model may continue to be highly relevant in developing countries, whose endeavours to articulate their own cultural values against those of the West have found powerful support in the West's own internal critics and critical discourses.

The new media also challenge traditional media studies in that they foster dynamic, action-oriented and constructive, rather than reflective, conceptually oriented and critical approaches, and in that they diminish the traditional opposition between the (professional) producer and the (mass) audience. This is likely to encourage an expanded and more autonomous space for practical (production) work and a continuation of the trend towards ethnography: what computer users do with computer programmes is a good deal more amenable to observation than what television viewers think of television programmes, and interviewing people is a more interactive mode of research than text analysis. On the other hand, there is in all this a danger of forgetting that computer programmes, like texts, are ultimately 'authored', rather than simply part of the environment. Studying what choices they offer to all their heterogeneous users, across the globe – and what choices they do not offer – remains as important as studying what choices are actually made by specific users in specific contexts, and suitable methods for this have hardly begun to be developed.

Future media studies are thus likely to reflect the simultaneous trends towards globalization and localization which can also be observed in other spheres of life. Public education in the developed countries is likely to concentrate on the local, fostering small-scale, local media production, micro 'ethnographies' and a sense of heterogeneity and pluriformity, a postmodern cultural relativism. It is to be hoped that insight in the equally important globalizing tendencies, and the structures of power behind it, will not be accessible only to the few.

London College of Printing, England

REFERENCES

Adorno, T.: 1978, 'The fetish-character of music and the regression of listening' in A.Arato & E. Gebhardt (eds.), *The Essential Frankfurt School Reader*, Blackwell, Oxford.
Arnold, M.: 1887, 'Up to Easter', *The Nineteenth Century*, May 1887.
Barthes, R.: 1967, *Elements of Semiology*, Cape, London.
Barthes, R.: 1977, *Image-Music-Text*, fontana, London.
Bazalgette, C., Berort, E. & Savino, J. (eds.): 1992, *New Directions – Media Education Worldwide*, BFI and CLEMI, London and Paris.
Buckingham, D. & Sefton-Green, J.: 1994, *Cultural Studies Goes To School – Reading and Teaching Popular Media*, Taylor and Francis, London.
Curran, J., Morley, D. & and Walkerdine, V. (eds.): 1996, *Cultural Studies and Communications*, Arnold, London.
Dissanayake, W, Rahman, A. & Said, M. (eds.): 1983, *Communication Research and Cultural Values*, AMIC, Singapore.
Fairclough, N.: 1995, *Media Discourse*, Arnold, London.
Feuer, J., Kerr, P., & Bahimagi, T.: 1984, *MTM: Quality Television*, BFI, London.
Fowler, R., Hodge, R., Kress, G. & Trew, T.: 1979, *Language and Control*, Routledge, London.
Glasgow Media Group: 1976, *Bad News*, Routledge, London.

Hall, S.: 1980, *Culture, Media, Language*, Hutchinson, London.

Hall, S. & Whannel, P.: 1964, *The Popular Arts*, Hutchinson, London.

Hartley, J.: 1982, *Understanding News*, Methuen, London.

Hayward, P. (ed.): 1991, *Culture, Technology and Creativity in the Late Twentieth Century*, John Libbey, London.

Katz, E. & Szecsko, T. (eds.): 1989, *Mass Media and Social Change*, Sage, London.

Kevelson, R.: 1977, *The Inverted Pyramid*, Indiana University Press, Bloomington.

Lusted, M.: 1991, *The Media Studies Book*, Routlege, London.

Masterman, L.: 1985, *Teaching the Media*, Comedia, London.

Morley, D.: 1980, *The 'Nationwide' Audience*, BFI, London.

Morsy, Z. (ed.): 1984, *Media Education*, UNESCO, New York.

Mulvey, L.: 1975, 'Visual pleasure and narrative cinema', *Screen* 16(3).

Nichols, B. (ed.): 1976, *Movies and Methods, vol I*, UCLA Press, Berkeley, Los Angeles.

Nichols, B. (ed.): 1981, *Ideology and the Image*, Indiana University Press, Bloomington.

Ploszajska, T.: 1996, *Geographical Education, Empire and Citizenship*, PhD Thesis, Univ. of London, pp. 1870–1944.

Rosen, P. (ed.): 1986, *Narration, Apparatus, Ideology: A Film Theory Reader*, Columbia Univ Press, New York.

Scannell, P. (ed.): 1991, *Broadcast Talk*, Sage, London.

Schlesinger, P.: 1978, *Putting 'reality' together: BBC News'*, Constable, London.

Tunstall, J.: 1977, *The Media Are American*, Constable, London.

UNESCO: 1977, 'Media studies in education', UNESCO Reports and Papers on Mass Communication No. 80.

Wertham, F.: 1954, *Seduction of the Innocent*, Rinehart & Co., New York.

HERBERT CHRIST

LANGUAGE POLICY IN TEACHER EDUCATION

Ever since educating *every* child became *a public responsibility*, language policy in teacher education became the order of the day. From this point on, several decisions needed to be made. The first issue concerned the language which children were to be taught to read and write as well as receive instruction. The second point requiring clarification was whether children should study another language (or languages) in school besides the *language of instruction*. And the third question to be decided upon was what children should learn about language and languages in general: about the value, cultivation, importance, prestige, etc. of one's own and of other languages.

Teachers at public schools must therefore be implicitly or explicitly prepared for their role as mediators of language(s) in the sense described above. In the following, an overview and discussion will be presented on (a) the role the language of instruction plays in teacher education, (b) how teachers are prepared for work in schools that are in fact multilingual schools, and (c) how foreign language teachers are prepared for their work in today's schools (also see the reviews by Widdowson in Volume 4, and by Brumfit and by Corson in Volume 6).

EARLY DEVELOPMENTS

If the role of language policy in teacher education is to be examined from a historical perspective, one must go back a long way in time. When national states were established, decisions pertaining to language and language policy were, of course, quite influential in most cases. Let us review the much quoted and well documented case of the role of French in the formation of modern France. It was, at the latest, François 1st (1515–1547) who made certain decisions of language policy in the interest of national unity. The French Revolution further promoted the French language and fought against what was called *patois* in order to establish the nation's – and the republic's – unity and to familiarize all citizens with the blessings of republican law. The Third Republic, in which compulsory education was introduced (in 1880/1881), made the elementary school teacher the most important agent of not only republican education ("*les hussards de la République*"), but also an agent of enforcing the French language among the general population; and in this latter task the teacher was greatly supported by the military (as the second place of the nation's education). (Bruneau 1958)

R. Wodak and D. Corson (eds), Encyclopedia of Language and Education,
Volume 1: Language Policy and Political Issues in Education, 219–227.
© *1997 Kluwer Academic Publishers. Printed in the Netherlands.*

Naturally, this ideology of language policy (of which the French case is only one example) was bound to have its effect on teacher education. Future teachers were judged primarily by their abilities in written and oral expression in the national language, and it was made clear to them that their most important duty was to ensure careful and correct usage of the same. Instruction in the classical languages was to support that of the national language. As competition for modern languages, classical languages were considered neutral and thus did not appear to be questionable when the position of the national language needed to be secured.

MAJOR PROBLEMS TODAY

Since the end of World War II, the role and function of language policy in teacher education have become more diverse than before. First, in light of global migration, the question of the *language of instruction* can no longer be answered with the same impartiality as before. Globally viewed, schools with a monolingual population are the exception. School children of language minorities are not as in earlier times (in different political and social contexts) ready to integrate and prepared to settle down. In this respect the language of instruction has become a new problem. On the one hand, the child's or the adult learner's right to self-determination of language is to be respected and the resulting demand for instruction in the native language or one of the languages of origin. On the other hand, the claim of the majority of the resident population should be regarded as well. They want to be able to communicate with all residents in this territory in the language of this majority and thus want knowledge of this language enforced. How the language of instruction should be applied, how its usage by learners of different linguistic background may be prepared, are didactic problems with relevance to language policy that all schools and all teachers are confronted with today. Therefore they must be considered in teacher education. Should the reaction be *bilingual instruction*? (See Porter 1990 on this discussion in the United States). Or should consistent instruction in the majority language be the solution? Or should a third alternative be chosen, namely offering special courses in which parallel instruction in the national language as well as in the language of origin is given?

A second problem is closely connected with this: the problem of individual *bilingualism*. How should teachers react to *bilingual* or *multilingual* students who are today no longer a rare exception in the school population? How can their knowledge, abilities, and skills be used, how can they be helped in their situation of Other-ness, how can their language skills be developed and consolidated as a valuable individual asset as well as for the use of the (own) community and all of society? Individual bilingualism can hardly be overlooked in today's teacher education. The topic has been discussed controversially for decades. Now that the debates have cooled down, it is possible to describe this phenomenon *sine ira et studio* (cf. Hagège 1960) and deal with *bilingual education* in teacher education (cf. Kielhöfer/Jonekeit 1993/1994).

A third problem is – at least in most of the so-called developed countries – the attitude of the resident population towards languages and their own language behavior, which may be termed in accordance with I. Gogolin (1994) the *"monolingual habitus"*. They live with the impression that their own language is the normal case which speakers of other languages must adjust to. Changing this habitus is one of the tasks of foreign language instruction.

This aspect has received much attention worldwide since the end of World War II. It is even now a field of growth inside and outside the schools. Three reasons can explain this: (1) Aside from the previously mentioned global migration, international co-operation in all fields as well as international conflicts have created an objectively ascertainable demand for foreign language skills, which has drawn the attention of many researchers (cf. for example the overview by Oud-de Glas 1981). (2) This objective demand has – in correspondence with the growing mobility of the settled population (business trips, educational trips and study abroad, tourism) created a *demand for foreign languages* and a *need to learn foreign languages* which have led to an increased demand for language courses. (cf. also from the extensive literature the theoretical contribution by Richterich/Chancerel 1977 and as a comprehensive national empirical study see Claessen et al. 1978). (3) Schools, universities, and institutions for adult education have adjusted to this increased demand as well as the growing number of learners who have followed the call to learning for a life time. Aside from the quantitative expansion of schools and universities, one must consider, for example, a qualitative change in form of a massive expansion of early foreign language learning, the development of subject oriented language classes, a conceptualisation for intensive phases in learning languages. As to the learners, many youths and adults are willing to learn several languages at the same time, go abroad for an intensive study of one language, and resume language studies at a later point in life.

Nevertheless, many observers are not satisfied with these results. The number of persons who insist on remaining monolingual is still too large especially in industrial countries (see the above mentioned monolingual habitus) and refuse to react to society's challenge of multilingualism. The situation in developing countries certainly varies from country to country and within each country, but all in all appears in a more favorable light.

Closely related to this problem of language behavior is the problem of the awareness of language policy in language communities – from the individual as well as from the collective point of view. This refers to a population's distributed and shared knowledge about language and languages, about its value and its evaluation, and finally about language policy. Evidently, awareness of language policy not only refers to language and language behavior in a narrow sense, but also influences attitudes and behavior towards speakers of one's own and of other languages. At one time a Breton or Basque was discriminated against in France as a *patois*-speaker, and Indians were called savages because they did not – to use the Spanish term – speak *cristiano,* just as the linguistic competence of speakers of African languages was measured only by their command of the colonizers' languages. These are examples of an (objectively wrong) awareness of language policy which without doubt influenced political and interpersonal interaction. What is needed here is educational work in language policy (e.g. in schools, universities, public opinion in the media) in order to change the public debate and public opinion.

THEORETICAL STUDIES ON LANGUAGE POLICY IN TEACHER EDUCATION

Teacher education can be divided into three typical phases: the theoretical instruction at colleges and universities (often combined with in-school practical studies), practical instruction based on theory (e.g. offered at special teacher training institutions or at universities), and finally, continuing education throughout the teacher's professional life. The practical implementation of this three step program varies from state to state. In some places, the phases are interwoven to the extent that training only begins on the job.

Theoretical and internationally comparative studies on teacher education have been initiated and supported by numerous international and supranational organizations, namely by the Council of Europe, the OECD, and UNESCO. A good overview of the activities of these organizations is compiled in a study published in English, French, and German by Bernaert, van Dijk, and Sander (1993/1994), namely in chapter 9. *The Association of Teacher Education in Europe (ATEE),* an association of European institutions for teacher education with its headquarters in Brussels, is responsible for this publication.

These studies will be presented in the following four parts: (1) the language of instruction, or the monolingual habitus, (2) the preparation for learning *in foreign languages*, or bilingual instruction, (3) the internationalization of schools by networking, or student and teacher exchange, and (4) the development of language and language policy awareness of future teachers, or language policy as a subject in teacher education.

The language of instruction is generally linked with *instruction of language and literature* (e.g. Spanish language and literature in Spain or Mexico, English language and literature in Great Britain or the United States) but not with *its usage in other subjects* (e.g. in history or mathematics or art (see May's review)). This is unquestionably a flaw in teacher education but also marks a deficit in research. *One* way of compensating for this deficit is teacher research. It asks what the relation is between teachers' understanding of the language of instruction and their usage, and how they deal with this problem. Using the example of Gogolin (1994), some suggestions will be presented on how to go about this. Gogolin collected data in teacher interviews and class observations on the following questions: what is the actual, the subjectively assumed or declared linguistic behavior of teachers in class? What are their opinions concerning bilingualism? How do they see schools in factually multilingual societies?

These data, which imply subjective theories, present a basis not only for discussions with the interviewed teachers, but can also be used in teacher education and advanced training to create awareness and initiate a change in behavior.

Compared internationally, learning at school *in* foreign languages has been put into practice in a variety of ways. In America (Canada and US) methods under the name of *(total) immersion* have been tried, which strongly contrast with European approaches of *bilingual education*. Both approaches are to be understood within the respective social circumstances. In teacher education they are only occasionally considered, even though they are quite successful in practical teaching situations and are supported by educational institutions.

Behind both differing approaches we may recognize positions of language policy, e.g. in the Canadian case of immersion the will to preserve and to strengthen the confederation's bilingualism and in the European approaches promoting individual multilingualism.

Research on teaching and studying in foreign languages has greatly increased in the last few years. Points of particular interest included first taking inventory (cf. for example Endt 1992), second, the typology and its political background (cf. Baetens-Beardmore 1993), third, the methods used, fourth, the development of curriculum, and fifth, the development of materials.

Literature on methods for bilingual teaching and learning is very extensive even without a general theory for this method so far. Older approaches are not useful because they – inspite of the title "Method in Bilingual Education" (Dodson 1967) – focus on a traditional type of foreign language classroom (concentrating on the language and not on the subject matter). The difficulty in finding a comprehensive methodological concept is so great because of the diversity of the subjects involved (what subjects are discussed in bilingual classes?) as well as of the target languages taught (English or French or German or Spanish) – not to mention the learners' native languages, the social context and the resulting social relevance of bilingual education (see reviews in Volume 5).

The internationalization of school has reached a new qualitative level in the nineties. Besides the classic forms of an international orientation – student exchange, teacher exchange, class correspondences – electronic networking has been developed in the last few years. The classic means of exchange are still being continued, and are partly supported by modern communication media, but they have also led to new forms of cooperation between schools in which the purely person oriented exchange has been replaced by a project oriented one with new forms of communal learning. Such new forms of student exchange are given an increasing amount of attention by researchers, politicians, and the general public and are thus supported by supranational organizations, e.g. the *Deutsch-Französisches Jugendwerk (DFJW)/Office franco-allemand pour la jeunesse (OFAJ)*, the European Union and its respective programs, or private organizations e.g. the *Robert-Bosch-Stiftung* in Stuttgart with its *Frankreichpreis/Prix Allemagne* for students at vocational schools. All forms of project oriented exchange are finding enormous support through the use of the new media such as e-mail, fax, as well as video communication. Language classes of the classic type as well as learning in foreign languages are thus offered new opportunities. Research on these new forms of teaching and learning is being taken up in these years at the same time as test classes are being conducted. From the fields of German-American and German-French cooperation one example each may be quoted: Kabok (1996), who reports on cooperations between German and French schools in the form of "*centres d'information et de documentation*", and Legutke (1996), who observes joint projects of German and American schools via e-mail.

Hardly any research has been conducted thus far on language and language policy as a subject in teacher education. This can be explained by the above mentioned statements: the language of instruction is almost never questioned and not recognized as a factor in language policy (see the reviews on non-standard varieties by Corson in this volume and in Volume 6). Schools were generally regarded as national agents. Not until the last two or three decades have they been recognized as an instrument for international contacts and as a place of intercultural learning and intercultural interaction.

The fact that schools act as the most important mediators of national languages *and* foreign languages and thus massively intervene in the ecology of languages – their radii of communication, their circle of speakers – is seldom reflected upon. Up until a few decades ago, foreign language classes were exclusively considered to be a place to educate the individual character. Their political, economic, and ecological dimensions were overlooked.

While UNESCO has done much to advance instruction in native languages all over the world, the European Council has succeeded in drawing wide public attention since the sixties towards the political and social importance of learning foreign languages. Under these auspices, it is obvious that language must be discussed in teacher education as a social force and language policy as part of educational and cultural policy, but also as part of the entire domestic and foreign policy if teachers are to be prepared for schools in the next century (Van Deth 1979; Claessen 1980; Christ 1991).

FUTURE DIRECTIONS

A new development that is bound to change schools and will also affect the future of teacher education is the growing internationalization of teachers. Countries that will be affected most by these foreseeable developments cannot be determined yet. But one thing is certain: With the freedom of movement act that came into effect in 1992 in the European Union, the national monopoly of teacher education has been broken. Citizens of the EU may apply for positions on the basis of their national diplomas in any state of the EU and must not be discriminated against. A growing number of union citizens is making use of this. Outside the EU, middle and eastern European states have hired a considerable number of Westeuropean teachers. And the United States, too, has attracted more teachers from overseas than in previous decades.

If it is assumed that this internationalization of teachers (which especially but not exclusively concerns foreign language teachers) will be a long-term process more likely to increase than decrease, it will also become a problem for teacher education. Topics that will have to be dealt with in teacher education will include preparing teachers for a profession in another country and in an unfamiliar educational system, taking consideration of the attitudes of native teachers, students and their parents, opportunities and limitations of co-operation, synergy effects and frictional losses in a new multinational and multicultural context. Here, too, language policy will play a role. Aside from formulating new questions concerning language policy, those concerning didactics will have to be rewritten as well, if the above mentioned difficulties are to be addressed adequately.

Justus-Liebig University, Germany

REFERENCES

Australia's Language: 1991, *Australia's Language and Literacy Policy (ALLP)*, Australian Government Publishing Service, Canberra.
Baetens-Beardsmore, H. (ed.): 1993, *European Models of Bilingual Education*, Clevedon/Philadelphia/Adelaide.
Baetens-Beardsmore, H. (ed.): 1994, 'Les cadres institutionnels de l'éducation bilingue: quelques modèles', *Etudes de Linguistique Appliquée 96 "Aspects de l'enseignement bilingue"*, Paris, 45–65.

Bernaert, Y., van Dijk, H. & Sander, Th.: 1994, *Die Europäische Dimension der Lehrerbildung*, ATEE The Association of Teacher Education in Europe, Brüssel/Onabrück (also available in English and French).

Bone, T.R. & Macchall, J. (eds.): 1990, *Teacher Education in Europe. The Challenge ahead*, Jordanshill College, Glasgow.

Bruneau, C.: 1958, *Petite histoire de la langue française*, 2 tomes, Colin, Paris.

Cheshire, J. (ed.): 1989, *Dialect and Education. Some European Perspectives*, Multilingual Matters, Clevedon.

Christ, H.: 1991, *Fremdsprachenunterricht für das Jahr 2000. Sprachenpolitische Betrachtungen zum Lehren und Lernen fremder Sprachen*, Narr, Tübingen.

Claessen, J.F.M.: 1980, *Moderne vreemde talen uit balans: Een onderzoek naar behoeften aan moderne vreemde talen en relatie tot het vreemdetalenonderwijs*, Instituut voor Toegepaste Sociologie, Nijmegen.

Claessen, J.F.M., van Galen, A.M. & Oud-de Glas, M.M.B.: 1978, *De Behoeften aan Moderne Vreemde Talen. Een onderzoek onder leerlingen, oudleerlingen en scholen*, Instituut vor Toegepaste Linguistiek, Nijmegen.

Crawford, J.: 1989, *Bilingual Education. History, policy, theory and practice*, Crane, Trenton, N.J.

Delnoy, R., Herrlitz, W., Kroon, S. & Sturm, J. (eds.): 1988, *Portraits in Mother tongue Education. Teacher diaries as a starting point for comparative research into standard language teaching in Europe*, IMEN/SLO, Enschede.

van Deth, J.: 1979, *L'Enseignement scolaire des langues vivantes dans les pays membres de la communauté européenne. Bilan, réflexions et propositions. Bruxelles*.

Dodson, C.: 1967, *Language Teaching and the bilingual Method*, London.

Endt, E.: 1992, *Immersion und bilingualer Unterricht. Eine Bibliographie. EKIB*, Eichstätt/Kiel (Informationshefte zum Lernen in der Fremdsprache 3).

Extra, G., van Hout, R. & Vallen, T. (eds.): 1987, *Etnische minderheden. Taalverwerving, Taalonderwijs, Taalbeleid*, Foris, Dordrecht.

Fruhauf, G., Coyle, D. & Christ, I. (eds.): 1996, *Teaching Content in a Foreign Language. Practice and Perspectives in European Bilingual Education*, Stichting Europees Platform voor het Nederlandse Onderwijs, Alkmaar.

Gogolin, I.: 1994, *Der monolinguale Habitus der multilingualen Schule*, Waxmann, Münster/New York.

Gogolin, I., Krüger-Potratz, M., Kroon, S./Neumann, U. & Vallen, T. (eds.): 1991, *Kultur- und Sprachenvielfalt in Europa*. Waxmann, Münster.

Hagège, C.: 1996, *L'enfant aux deux langues*, Odile Jacob, Paris.

van Hout, R. & van Knops, U. (eds.): 1988, *Language Attitudes in the Dutch Language Area*, Foris, Dordrecht.

Kabok, S.: 1996, *Le projet CDI*, in I. Buchloh et al. (eds.), Tübingen, Konvergenzen. Narr, 89–102.

Kielhöfer, B. & Jonekeit, S.: 1993, *Zweisprachige Kindererziehung (8° edition)*, Stauffenburg-Verlag, Tübingen.

Kielhöfer, B. & Jonekeit, S.: 1994, *Education bilingue (2° edition)*, Stauffenburg Verlag, Tübingen.

Kroon, S. & Sturm, J. (eds.): 1986, *Research on Mother Tongue Education in an International Perspective*, IMEN, Antwerpen.

Legutke, M.K.: 1996, 'Begegnungen mit dem Fremden "via e-mail" ', in L. Bredella & H. Christ (eds.), *Begegnungen mit dem Fremden*, Ferber, Gießen, 206–233.

Oud-de Glas, M.: 1983, 'Foreign language needs. A survey of needs', in T. van Els & M. Oud-de Glas (eds.), *Research into Foreign Language Needs*, Augsburger I & I-Schriften 29, Augsburg, 19–34.

Porter, R.P.: 1990, *Forked Tongue; The Politics of Bilingual Education*, New York.

Richterich, R. & Chancerel, J.: 1978, *Identifying the Needs of Adults Learning a Foreign Language,* Council for Cultural Cooperation of the Council of Europe, Strasbourg.
Skutnabb-Kangas, T. & Cummins, J. (eds.): 1988, *Minority Education: From Shame to Struggle,* Multilingual Matters, Clevedon.
Sociolinguistica. International Yearbook of Europen Sociolinguistics 7: 1993, *Multilingual Concepts in the Schools of Europe,* Niemeyer, Tübingen.
Werkverbond voor Onderzoek van Moedertalonderwijs: 1988, *Tussen Apollo en Hermes. Hoofdstukken uit de geschiedenis van moedertaalonderwijs in en buiten Nederlanden,* SLO, Enschede.

STEPHEN A. MAY

SCHOOL LANGUAGE POLICIES

School language policies – or Language Policies Across the Curriculum (LPACs) as they are also known – are viewed by many educationists as a necessary and integral part of the administration and the curriculum practice of modern schools. Since their introduction into educational discourse in the late 1960s, much has been made of their role in highlighting the centrality of language in the learning-teaching relationship (Barnes et al. 1969; Marland 1977; Maybin 1985; Corson 1990; Wells 1991; Crowhurst 1994). Relatedly, advocates have also more recently championed their capacity to address the diverse language needs of students within multi-ethnic schools (Corson 1990, 1993, 1998; May 1994a, 1994b).

Specifically, a school language policy, or LPAC, is a policy document aimed at addressing the particular language needs of a school. It is cross-curricular in its concerns, breaking down traditional subject boundaries, and should normally involve not only staff, but if possible the whole school community, in its development and implementation. The policy, once compiled, identifies areas within school organisation, curriculum, pedagogy and assessment where specific language needs exist. Having identified salient language issues, the policy sets out what the school intends to do about these areas of concern. It should provide staff with direction within a discretionary and flexible framework, and provide a statement of action that includes provision for follow up, monitoring and revision in the light of changing circumstances (Corson 1990).

In this sense, the term 'whole-school policy' (Marland 1977) well describes the educational intentions of a school language policy. Marland has argued that whole-school policies analyse the skills and knowledge required in a particular curriculum field, endeavour to establish how these can best be acquired and developed, and plan contexts and activities to provide the best opportunities for practice and use. As such, school language policies, if successful, should adopt an approach to language which is carried out by teachers 'in the activity context when teaching occurs at the precise point of need, according to the policy, and drawing on the shared knowledge' (Marland 1977: p. 12).

In short then, a school language policy is an action statement outlining the solutions necessary for addressing the diverse language needs of a school. This review will highlight the theoretical evolution of school language policy development within educational research and, more crucially

R. Wodak and D. Corson (eds), Encyclopedia of Language and Education,
Volume 1: Language Policy and Political Issues in Education, 229–240.
© *1997 Kluwer Academic Publishers. Printed in the Netherlands.*

perhaps, the degree to which such policies have been successfully applied in practice.

EARLY DEVELOPMENTS

School language policies emerged from the Language Across the Curriculum (LAC) movement, pioneered in Britain in the late 1960s and early 1970s. The LAC movement had its genesis in 1966 when members of the London Association for the Teaching of English prepared a discussion document entitled 'Towards a Language Policy Across the Curriculum' (Rosen in Barnes et al. 1969; see also, Barnes et al. 1990). These developments, in turn, drew on the seminal work of Vygotsky (1962) and Bruner (1966) on language and learning, and the work of the contemporary curriculum theorists, Britton (1970) and Moffett (1968). In particular, LAC tried to put into practice Moffett's view that rendering experience into words was the real business of schools (Corson 1990). The major tenets of LAC that subsequently emerged were that:

- Language plays a central role in all learning.
- Students must be actively engaged in meaning-making processes. Concomitantly, teachers must facilitate active student-centred learning rather than adopting didactic and transmissionist approaches to teaching.
- Active student learning involves the four principal modes of language – listening, talking, reading and writing.
- Students should be encouraged to use their own language in these various modes as the principal tool for interpreting and mastering curriculum content (for further discussion, see Corson 1990; Crowhurst 1994).

The initial discussion document, and the key principles it enunciated, were to prove a catalyst for change. Schools in Britain, other countries in the British Commonwealth, and in North America, began to develop their own school language policies, drawing on the original document as a model. In 1975 these developments were given further impetus in Britain by the official sanction of LAC in *A Language for Life* (The Bullock Report). In the Report, the Bullock Committee stressed the need for *all* subject teachers to be aware of the importance of language in their classrooms: 'Each school should have an organised policy for language across the curriculum, establishing every teacher's involvement in language and reading development throughout the years of schooling' (DES 1975: p. 514). Elsewhere, the Report recommends that the responsibility for such a policy should be embodied in the organisational structure of the school. A decade later this support for LAC was again reinforced by *Education for All* (The Swann Report) (see the review by Rassool). In discussing solutions to apparent ethnic differences in educational achievement in British schools, the Report observes that: 'Unless there is a school language and learning policy across the curriculum there will be a wastage of effort and often confusion' (DES 1985: p. 417).

In addition to this official support in Britain, further momentum for school language policies was gained in the 1970s/1980s from three parallel developments. First, the prominent advocacy of a more school-based approach to curriculum development – including the development of the action research paradigm – facilitated the expansion of school language policies by promoting the school as the principal site of curriculum change, and teachers as key curriculum innovators (see Stenhouse 1975; Skilbeck 1984; Carr & Kemmis 1986; Elliott 1991; Smyth 1989, 1991). Second, the increasing enthusiasm for collaborative student learning tied in with the emphasis in LAC on active, student-centred language participation (see Slavin 1983, 1989; Johnson & Johnson 1987; Cowie & Ruddock 1988; Bennett & Dunne 1992; Galton & Williamson 1992). Third, the emergence of the 'whole language' movement, particularly in North America (see Goodman 1982; 1989; Shannon 1992), also provided comparable emphases on whole language activities and student-centred learning.

MAJOR CONTRIBUTIONS

During the 1970s/1980s, several key texts were written advocating the specific need for school language policies, especially at the secondary school level. Drawing in many cases on the original outline found in Barnes et al. (1969), these texts outlined the key tenets of school language policies and discussed how best to implement them (see Marland 1977; Martin et al. 1979; Schools Council 1980; Torbe 1980; Knott 1985; Maybin 1985). Marland (1977), for example, sets out the background to the LAC debate, up to and including the Bullock Report (DES 1975), as a basis for his advocacy of 'whole-school' policies. In so doing, he examines the conventional first language questions that confront secondary schools, and how a whole-school language policy might address them.

Knott (1985), in developing this position further, presents a range of useful practical suggestions for implementing school language policies within secondary schools. These include, for example, a draft questionnaire for ascertaining pupil language use, and another for discovering the language attitudes of school staff. Likewise, Maybin (1985) provides practical approaches for working towards a school language policy at the primary (elementary) school level, particularly for schools in a culturally pluralist setting. Practical examples which she suggests include conducting a school language survey, looking at the establishment of a whole-school approach to reading, and working more closely with parents in the community in terms of their language expectations for their children. Staff development activities, and the crucial role of senior management, are also highlighted by Maybin as central to the successful implementation and maintenance of school language policies.

However, it is Corson (1990, 1999) who provides the first comprehensive modern treatment of the theory and practice of school language policies. Drawing on research studies in New Zealand schools in the late 1980s (see McPherson & Corson 1989), Corson provides detailed discussion and example of language policy development at the micro-level of the school – at both the primary and secondary level – with a particular emphasis on the actual process of administration and policy-making in schools. In so doing, Corson also develops previous work on LAC in two new directions. First, he extends the conception of language to include not only the four conventional language modes, but also the additional activities of moving, watching, shaping, and viewing. Second, and more crucially, he extends the original focus of LAC on first language concerns to include second language, bilingual, foreign language and wider social justice issues (see the review by Watts).

In this latter regard, Corson argues that the original concerns of LAC do not address adequately the increasingly multi-ethnic nature of many schools – a point presaged in the Swann Report (DES 1985) and in Maybin (1985). Such issues – including bilingualism, and the related cultural and language needs of ethnic minority children – have subsequently provided a focus for much of the current advocacy of school language policy development. Corson (1993), for example, elaborates on his position in a wide-ranging account that highlights the interconnections between school language policies, social theory, and national language planning. Corson is particularly concerned here to explore differences of language access and use as they relate to gender, ethnic minority groups, and other minority social and cultural groups within schools. As in his earlier work, his aim in promoting school language policies is a specifically emancipatory one. Corson views such policies as having the *potential* to ameliorate the differential power relations in schools, and the wider society, which lead to the privileging of the language uses of dominant groups over those of minority groups. May (1994a, 1994b) develops these themes further in his critical ethnographic account of a multi-ethnic urban elementary school in New Zealand by specifically linking school language policy development with the wider concerns of critical multiculturalism. Marsh and Burke (1992) and Sharpe (1992) provide two smaller-scale examples of language policies at work in multi-ethnic schools. In a special issue of the *Australian Journal of Language and Literacy* devoted to school language policies, they report respectively on language policy development at an elementary school and a Catholic secondary school in Australia, both with multi-ethnic school populations. Crowhurst (1994) provides a useful recent textbook on LAC aimed at pre-service and in-service teachers in Canada which also addresses, albeit briefly, school language policy development in culturally pluralist settings.

PROBLEMS AND DIFFICULTIES

In light of the many claims made about school language policies, there is a noticeable discrepancy between their enthusiastic endorsement in the academic literature and their successful implementation in schools. Many schools are ambivalent about such policies and/or implement them to little effect; the potential and the practice do not always seem to coincide. As Wells observes of the Language Across the Curriculum movement, 'LAC has remained a slogan to rally the converted rather than a policy that is affecting the daily practice of the majority of teachers and administrators across all levels of the education [system] ...' (1991: p. 1). This discrepancy between theory and practice is further illustrated by Corson's observation that school language policies 'are viewed by a growing number of educationists as an integral and necessary part of the administrative and curriculum practices of modern schools, yet relatively few schools anywhere have seriously tackled the problem of introducing them' (1990: p. 1).

A number of key reasons can be ascertained for the desultory implementation of LAC policies within schools. First, while official support for school language policies has been forthcoming at the national level in a number of countries, particularly Britain, financial resources in support of these policies have not. In the Bullock Report (DES 1975), for example, no fewer than 10 of its 17 'principal recommendations' on LAC had significant resource implications (Proctor 1987). At a time of financial stringency, the inevitable result perhaps was that insufficient resources were made available to implement the Report's recommendations while they were still at the centre of educational debate (Wells 1991). Relatedly, other initiatives in Britain in the 1970s/1980s, such as the School Council's funding of subject-based curriculum development projects, directly militated against the success of across-the-curriculum policies (Proctor 1987). In turn, these latter developments were to lead to a return to the more traditional language emphases of the Kingman Report (DES 1988), and to their subsequent reinforcement in the National Curriculum – first introduced in 1988, and revised most recently in 1995 (HMSO 1995). Thus, even in Britain, where LAC received strong endorsement at national policy level, little actual effort was made to support its wide-spread implementation in schools.

Second, where implementation of LAC policies has been attempted in schools – and despite the range of practical suggestions offered in the literature – numerous operational difficulties have ensued. The most common reasons for experiencing difficulties in implementation have centred on three key areas: a lack of acceptance and agreement in schools over the aims and scope of a language policy; an inability to involve all teachers (let alone the wider school community) in the development of the policy, thus ensuring support for the policy; and an inability to change school structures to match the inclusive intentions with which school language policies have been largely associated. I will look at each of these dimensions in turn.

One problem for LAC is simply that many educationists, administrators and teachers have yet to be convinced by its claims. This scepticism is most apparent at the secondary school level where clearly demarcated subject-based teaching remains the norm. There are some examples of successful school language policies at secondary level (see, Corson 1990; Sharpe 1992) but many subject-based teachers continue to resist the aims and influence of LAC. Wells (1991) comments, for example, on the widespread perception among secondary school teachers that LAC is either an act of imperialism on the part of English teachers, or their attempt to avoid responsibility for ensuring their students' continued language development (see also HMI 1982). Conversely, Proctor (1987) observes that some English subject teachers oppose LAC because of its potential to 'dilute' the academic content of their subject.

At the primary, or elementary, level there has been wider acceptance of the aims of LAC. In Britain, for example, the recommendations of the Plowden Report (DES 1967) had prepared the ground somewhat for the cross-curricular themes of LAC. Likewise, in North America, and also in Australia and New Zealand, the work of Smith (1975) and Goodman (1982) in reading, and of Graves (1983) in writing, led to the integration of reading, writing, and oral language under the banner of the 'whole language' movement (Wells 1991); an important adjunct to LAC. Even here, however, the debates about the merits, or otherwise, of 'whole language' – particularly, in relation to a skills-based curriculum – have continued to remain controversial (see, for example, McKenna et al. 1994).

In this regard, the *process* of implementing LAC within the school is crucial to gaining and maintaining teacher support. A school language policy needs to be both carefully thought through and carefully managed if *all* staff are to be convinced of its merits. In particular, the following factors have been identified as essential to the successful implementation of a school language policy: the central involvement of school management; sufficient time and resources to effect real change; and the crucial role of staff development in providing initial and ongoing support. With regard to the role of school management, for example, Corson (1990) argues:

> any 'across the curriculum' issue is by definition outside the range of easy control by individual teachers, who are often con-fined to one class level or subject specialism; by default the task of dealing with 'across the curriculum' issues becomes the responsibility of the school executive. ... Perhaps the design,

oversight, and implementation of these policies, especially a [school language policy], may be the school executive's major curriculum role in future schools. (1990: p. 2; see also, Maybin 1985).

The close involvement of the school executive in supporting and facilitating the changes required by LAC is a feature of many actual studies of successful language policy implementation (Corson 1990; Beaton et al. 1992; Sharpe 1992; May 1994a, 1994b). Also highlighted in these and other studies (Marsh & Burke 1992; Taylor et al. 1992), is the need for sufficient time, and the necessary resources, to effect successful change within the school. May (1994a, 1994b), for example, demonstrates how the school he examined was able to implement a highly effective language policy through gradual and carefully planned change over a number of years, and with the support of an extensive teacher-made curriculum resource programme.

However, as May also argues, and as other studies reinforce, an allied staff development programme is perhaps the pivotal requirement for ensuring the support of teachers for LAC. Without staff development, a school language policy is doomed to fail. Teachers have to have a sufficient basis in theory to understand the educational intentions involved in school language policy development if they are to be able to implement them effectively (May 1994a). As Marland suggests, only a well informed staff 'is able to respond to all issues within the total context of an institution ... and is [thus] able to participate in educational debate' (1977: p. 6). Corson reiterates this point in discussing the difficulties of understanding the concept of LAC:

> One answer to this problem for LAC is for teachers to be given greater access to theory, which is professional knowledge about the processes of language and learning, coupled with better information about what children can be expected to do and what they are doing in progressive settings. (1990: pp. 84–85)

A final obstacle to the successful implementation of LAC within schools, however, relates again to its educational intentions. It is important that teachers understand these fully and that they are all involved in implementing them, but this in itself is not enough. School structures also need to be changed in order to reflect the inclusive and emancipatory concerns of LAC. In effect, school language policies – and the educational tenets of LAC which underlie them – require major pedagogical, curricular, and organisational reform in schools (see Corson 1990, 1993, 1999; May 1994a, 1994b); a process very few schools are actually prepared to undergo. Specifically, developing and implementing a successful school language policy requires the school to be:

- *more democratic*. Organisationally, the formulation and implementation of school language policies should ideally involve both teachers
  and parents in the decision-making process. The language policy
  agreed by such a process should thus reflect the wider language
  expectations of the local community (Maybin 1985; Corson 1990;
  May 1994a). An additional benefit, as Corson suggests, is that
  'schools collaboratively managed [in this way], and with agreed and
  working policies, are more likely to be places of staff and community
  commitment' (1990: p. 59). Pedagogically, establishing collaborative teaching and learning arrangements in the classroom are essential
  if the underlying principles of LAC are to be reflected. This involves
  challenging the didactic and transmissionist approaches to teaching
  that continue to dominate in many classrooms and the summative
  forms of language assessment with which they are often associated
  (Corson 1993; May 1994b; see the review by Waite).
- *critically reflective*. The tenets of LAC require a 'radical rethinking
  of the way in which the triangular relationship between learning,
  teaching and the curriculum is understood, particularly in the context
  of a multicultural/multilingual society' (Wells 1991: p. 2). Put more
  simply, LAC requires major changes in teacher attitudes and in the
  pedagogical choices that they make (Corson 1990). Schools thus need
  to promote *critical* educational reflection as an integral part of school
  language policy development in order to accomplish the degree of
  'radical rethinking' required (May 1994b).
- *whole-school oriented*. School language policies need to be both
  cross-curricular in themselves and to be closely integrated with other
  curriculum policies (Corson 1990; May 1994a, 1994b). This is not
  easy when many schools, particularly at secondary level, remain
  compartmentalised; constrained within rigid subject boundaries. As
  Marland (1977) argues, the key problem many schools have in implementing a school language policy is in first finding a curriculum
  across which to put it.

FUTURE DIRECTIONS

If school language policies are to avoid being just another failed educational innovation, the ambiguities surrounding their aims, and the resulting
problems which schools face in their practical implementation, need to be
addressed and clarified. In this regard, it is necessary to recognise the
difficulties which inhere in any attempt to establish school-based curriculum development (see Stenhouse 1975; Skilbeck 1984). Whole-school
policies, such as a school language policy, involve considerable organisational restructuring at the school level, and much educational thought and
reflection. This process is difficult, time-consuming, and requires the sup-

port and dedication of both staff and the wider school community. Recent developments in national educational policies which emphasise a return to a narrow, skills-based core curriculum model – as in Britain and New Zealand, for example – also militate against such a process (see Bell 1994; Mitchell et al. 1994; HMSO 1995).

However, encouraging counter-tendencies can also be identified. In Canada, for example, the 1980s saw Ontario develop a clearly articulated policy on LAC (Ontario Ministry of Education 1984). This advocacy of school language policies applied to both Anglophone and Francophone schools in the province but has been further clarified recently with regard to the latter (see MET 1993a, 1993b). Relatedly, there have also been recent developments in Canada, Britain, the United States, Australia and New Zealand which have seen an increasing devolution of educational administration to the school level (for school-level language planning developments in the US, see the review by Fattis in Volume 5). While problematic in many respects (see Lingard et al. 1993), these developments, and the degree of autonomy they provide for schools, present perhaps the best opportunity yet for continuing the aims of LAC within schools. Moreover, the pressing language needs of an increasingly multi-ethnic school population – and the broader questions of large-scale cultural pluralism which these raise – suggest that the need for inclusive, cross-curricular and culturally-pluralist school language policies is as urgent as ever.

The key to the future survival of school language policies then may rest in the ability of schools to combine effectively the theoretical and practical dimensions of LAC – something with which many have hitherto struggled. Additionally, schools will need to implement such policies within national educational systems that may be committed to more restricted and restrictive language aims. A possible way forward here – and a means by which both concerns can be addressed – is for LAC to ally itself with the emergent 'critical language awareness' movement (see, Clark et al. 1990, 1991; Corson 1993; Fairclough 1992, 1995). Critical language awareness is specifically concerned with the relationship between language and power, and the differential educational outcomes which result for majority and minority language users. As such, it may, in combination with LAC, offer a useful corrective to present national policy trends in education which ignore such dimensions.

Relatedly, school language policies may also have an invaluable role to play within the broader ambit of critical pedagogy and critical multiculturalism. Until recently, advocacy within these movements has been conducted largely at the level of educational theory (see, for example, Carr & Kemmis 1986; Giroux 1992; McLaren 1986, 1995). Increasingly, however, organisational, pedagogical and curriculum implications for schools are being directly addressed by leading proponents of critical pedagogy and critical multiculturalism (see Nieto 1992; Sleeter & McLaren 1995; New

London Group 1996; May 1994b, 1997). These developments include a recognition of the central role of language policy formation within a culturally pluralist approach to schooling. As such, they offer fresh hope for the successful incorporation of school language policies into the organisation and curriculum practice of today's schools.

University of Bristol
England

REFERENCES

Barnes, D., Britton, J., & Rosen H.: 1969, *Language, the Learner and the School*, Penguin Education, London.
Barnes, D., Britton, J., & Torbe, M.: 1990, *Language, the Learner and the School* (fourth edition), Boynton/Cook, Portsmouth, NH.
Beaton, L., Butler, L., Goebel, A., Mauger, J., Winter, A., & Russell, T.: 1992, 'Whole school language arts', *Australian Journal of Language and Literacy* 15, 55–58.
Bell, A.: 1994, 'New Zealand or Aotearoa? The battle for nationhood in the English curriculum', *Curriculum Studies* 2, 171–188.
Bennett, N. & Dunne, E.: 1992, *Managing Classroom Groups*, Simon & Schuster, London.
Britton, J.: 1970, *Language and Learning*, Penguin, London.
Bruner, J.: 1966, *Towards a Theory of Instruction*, Harvard University Press, New York.
Carr, W., & Kemmis, S.: 1986, *Becoming Critical: Education, Knowledge and Action Research*, Falmer Press, Lewes.
Clark, R., Fairclough, N., Ivanic, R., & Martin-Jones, M.: 1990, 'Critical language awareness, Part I: A critical review of three current approaches to language awareness', *Language and Education* 4, 249–260.
Clark, R., Fairclough, N., Ivanic, R., & Martin-Jones, M.: 1991, 'Critical language awareness, Part II: Towards critical alternatives', *Language and Education* 5, 41–54.
Corson, D.: 1990, *Language Policy Across the Curriculum*, Multilingual Matters, Clevedon.
Corson, D.: 1993, *Language, Minority Education and Gender: Linking Social Justice and Power*, Multilingual Matters, Clevedon.
Corson, D.: 1998, *Language Policy in Schools*, Erlbaum, New York.
Cowie, H. & Ruddock, J.: 1988, *Cooperative Group Work: An Overview*, BP Service, London.
Crowhurst, M.: 1994, *Language and Learning Across the Curriculum*, Allyn & Bacon, Scarborough.
DES (Department of Education and Science): 1967, *Children and their Primary Schools* (The Plowden Report), HMSO, London.
DES (Department of Education and Science): 1975, *A Language for Life* (The Bullock Report), HMSO, London.
DES (Department of Education and Science): 1985, *Education for All: Report of the Committee of Inquiry into the Education of Children from Ethnic Minority Groups* (The Swann Report), HMSO, London.
DES (Department of Education and Science): 1988, *Report of the Committee of Inquiry into the Teaching of the English Language* (The Kingman Report), HMSO, London.
Elliott, J.: 1991, *Action Research for Educational Change*, Open University Press, Milton Keynes.
Fairclough, N. (ed.): 1992, *Critical Language Awareness*, Longman, London.

Fairclough, N.: 1995, *Critical Discourse Analysis: The Critical Study of Language*, Longman, London.

Galton, M. & Williamson, J.: 1992, *Group Work in the Primary Classroom*, Routledge, London.

Giroux, H.: 1992, *Border Crossings*, Routledge, New York.

Goldberg, D.: 1994, *Multiculturalism: A Critical Reader*, Blackwell, Cambridge.

Goodman, K.: 1982, *Language and Literacy: The Selected Writings of Kenneth S. Goodman*, Routledge & Kegan Paul, London.

Goodman, K.: 1989, 'Whole language research: Foundations and development', *Elementary School Journal* 90, 207–221.

Graves, D.: 1983, *Writing: Teachers and Learners at Work*, Heinemann, Exeter, NH.

HMI (Her Majesty's Inspectorate): 1982, *Bullock Revisited: A Discussion Paper*, DES, London.

HMSO: 1995, *English in the National Curriculum*, HMSO, London.

Johnson, D. & Johnson, R.: 1987, *Learning Together and Alone: Cooperative, Competitive, and Individualistic Learning* (second edition), Prentice Hall, Englewood Cliffs, NJ.

Knott, R.: 1985, *The English Department in a Changing World*, Open University Press, Milton Keynes.

Lingard, B., Knight, J., & Porter, P. (eds.): 1993, *Schooling Reform in Hard Times*, Falmer Press, London.

Marland, M.: 1977, *Language Across the Curriculum*, Heinemann, London.

Marsh, V., & Burke, J.: 1992, 'A Whole School Approach to Literacy', *Australian Journal of Language and Literacy* 15, 7–26.

Martin, N., D'Arcy, P., Newton, B, & Parker, R.: 1979, *Writing and Learning Across the Curriculum*, Ward Lock, London.

May, S.: 1994a, *Making Multicultural Education Work*, Multilingual Matters/OISE Press, Clevedon/Toronto.

May, S.: 1994b, 'School-based language policy reform: A New Zealand example', in A. Blackledge (ed.), *Teaching Bilingual Children*, Trentham Press, London, 19–41.

May, S. (ed.): 1998, *Critical Multiculturalism: Rethinking Multicultural and Antiracist Education*, Falmer Press, London.

Maybin, J.: 1985, 'Working towards a school language policy', in *Every child's language: An in-service pack for primary teachers*, The Open University & Multilingual Matters, Clevedon, 95–108.

McKenna, M., Stahl, S., & Reinking, D.: 1994, 'A critical commentary on research, politics, and whole language', *Journal of Reading Behaviour* 26, 211–233.

McLaren, P.: 1995, *Critical Pedagogy and Predatory Culture: Oppositional Politics in a Postmodern Era*, Routledge, New York.

McPherson, J. & Corson, D.: 1989, *Language Policy Across the Curriculum: Eight Studies of School-based Policy Development*, New Zealand Education Department, Wellington.

MET (Ministry of Education and Training).: 1993a, *Pour Les Ecoles Franco-Ontariennes. Volume I: Amenagement linguistique en francais. Paliers elementaire et secondaire*. November, Toronto.

MET (Ministry of Education and Training).: 1993b, *Pour Les Ecoles Franco-Ontariennes. Volume II: Actualisation linguistique en francais. Paliers elementaire et secondaire*. November, Toronto.

Mitchell, R., Brumfit, C., & Hooper, J.: 1994, 'Knowledge about language: policy, rationales and practices', *Research Papers in Education Policy and Practice* 9, 183–205.

Moffett, J.: 1968, *Teaching the Universe of Discourse*, Houghton Mifflin, London.

New London Group.: 1996, 'A pedagogy of multiliteracies: Designing social futures', *Harvard Educational Review* 66, 60–92.

Nieto, S.: 1996, *Affirming diversity: The sociopolitical context of multicultural education*, Longman, New York (2nd edition).
Ontario Ministry of Education.: 1984, *Ontario Schools: Intermediate and Senior Divisions*, Ministry of Education, Toronto.
Proctor, N.: 1987, 'Bullock refreshed: The five languages for life', *Reading* 21, 80–91.
Schools Council Working Paper No. 67: 1980, *Language Across the Curriculum*, Methuen, London.
Shannon, P. (ed.): 1992, *Becoming Political: Readings and Writings in the Politics of Literacy Education*, Heinemann, Portsmouth, NH.
Sharpe, T.: 1992, 'Shifting the focus', *Australian Journal of Language and Literacy* 15, 69–82.
Skilbeck, M.: 1984, *School-based Curriculum Development*, Harper & Row, London.
Slavin, R.: 1983, *Cooperative Learning*, Longman, New York.
Slavin, R.: 1989, *School and Classroom Organization*, Erlbaum, Hillsdale, NJ.
Sleeter, C., & McLaren, P.: 1995, *Multicultural Education, Critical Pedagogy and the Politics of Difference*, SUNY Press, Albany.
Smith, F.: 1975, *Comprehension and Learning: A Conceptual Framework for Teachers*, Holt Reinhart, New York.
Smyth, J.: 1989, *Critical Perspectives on Educational Leadership*, Falmer Press, London.
Smyth, J.: 1991, *Teachers as Collaborative Learners: Challenging Dominant Forms of Supervision*, Open University Press, Milton Keynes.
Stenhouse, L.: 1975, *An Introduction to Curriculum Research and Development*, Heinemann, London.
Taylor, K., Boscato, M., & Beagley, P.: 1992, 'Changing school language teaching: Evolution not revolution', *Australian Journal of Language and Literacy* 15, 43–53.
Torbe, M. (ed.): 1980, *Language Policies in Action: Language Across the Curriculum in Some Secondary Schools*, Ward Lock, London.
Vygotsky, L.: 1962, *Thought and Language*, MIT Press, Cambridge Mass.
Wells, G.: 1991, *Learning and Teaching the Discourses of the Disciplines*, The author, Toronto.

HILARY HANKS

TEACHING LANGUAGE AND POWER

The teaching of language and power as part of language education is a relatively recent phenomenon particularly in primary and secondary schools. Critical Language Awareness (CLA) will be used as a convenient shorthand for classroom applications of work on language, ideology and power although such work is also known by other names such as for example 'critical linguistics', 'critical literacy' and 'critical discourse analysis'. Taken from marxist discourse, this use of the word 'critical' signals a view of language which sees it as central to the workings of ideology, as a key means of mobilizing meaning to sustain or contest relations of domination in society. CLA is a form of language education which views all language as situated social practice and which seeks to enable students to ask and answer the questions – Whose interests are served by the way in which language is used? Who benefits? – so that out of this awareness possibilities for change may grow. It is underpinned by a strong equity and social justice agenda.

The teaching of language and power is designed to enable students to understand that language is not a neutral tool for communication but is everywhere implicated in the ways in which we read and write the world, the ways in which knowledge is produced and legitimated, the ways in which a human subject is constructed as a complex set of identities based on, amongst other things, race, class, gender, education, age, nationality, sexuality.

Research on diversity, difference and othering, often from a feminist, post-colonial or gay and lesbian perspective, has included careful work on language and its power to construct and delimit the ways in which we think the Other and ourselves. Although this work has played a formative role in the development of CLA, it will not be the focus of this review. This review will limit its scope to work in schools and the implications of these new developments for language education (also see reviews by Pennycook, and by van Leeuwen; by Luke and by Auerbach in Volume 2; by Hellerand by Gilbert in Volume 3; by Corson, by Clark & Ivanic, by Wallace and by Wortham in Volume 6; and by Goldstein, by Baugh, by May, and by Norton in Volume 8).

EARLY DEVELOPMENTS

When Hymes argued in 1974 that in addition to acquiring linguistic competence children also had to acquire communicative competence he brought

R. Wodak and D. Corson (eds), Encyclopedia of Language and Education,
Volume 1: Language Policy and Political Issues in Education, 241–251.
© *1997 Kluwer Academic Publishers. Printed in the Netherlands.*

about a fundamental change in language education. He established that language use is a fundamentally social activity and that communicative competence requires an ability to use language appropriately. Such competence includes knowing which language variety and register of a language is most suited to a social occasion; for multilingual children it requires knowing which language to use when, and the complicated social understanding necessary for code-switching. It requires knowledge of one's place in different social contexts and the attendant language rights and obligations. His work made space for the social in language education.

At the same time Labov was doing important work on language varieties. His work demonstrated conclusively that so-called non-standard varieties of English are fully systematic, rule governed languages as capable of abstract logical reasoning as so-called standard varieties (Labov 1972). What sets these varieties apart is their social status, not any inherent linguistic superiority or inferiority. Bernstein's work, although widely misinterpreted at the time (see the review by Corson on pp. 99–109) drew attention to the cultural capital that was necessary for success in schools. Part of that cultural capital included having access to both the linguistic and communicative competences valued uncritically by the school.

The communicative approach was the pedagogic realisation of these theories in second language education. Here the emphasis was placed on effective communication and for the first time fluency and appropriateness were seen to be more important than accuracy, which had dominated earlier structural approaches to language teaching. In the teaching of English as a first language in Britain, the language-in-use approach provided teachers with ways of teaching language in relation to its social functions. Both of these approaches led to a new focus on the communication skills – talking, listening, reading and writing.

The fragmentation of language pedagogy into first, second and foreign language teaching implies distinct students in separate classes which, in a post-modern world, is not the case. Schools have multilingual student populations and students with variable competencies in English. This linguistic and cultural diversity has enabled teachers to enrich the exploration of language by inviting students to compare and contrast their languages thus making space in the 'English' classroom for the languages of multilingual students (see for example *The Languages Book*, Raleigh 1981, produced by the Inner London Education Authority and *Activities for Multilingual Classrooms,* produced by the English Language Teaching Information Centre 1995, in South Africa). At the same time, modern languages teachers in Britain, concerned about the declining numbers of students choosing to learn a foreign language introduced Language Awareness, an approach to language education which focuses on the linguistic and pragmatic properties of language per se. It is an area of applied linguistics defined as the conscious awareness of the nature of language and its role in human life' and it attempts to foster this by drawing data from different alphabets, languages and varieties encouraging students to celebrate language and diversity (See the *Awareness of Language Series* edited by Hawkins 1983). While all these contrastive linguistic approaches are more inclusive, they do little to challenge the status of the dominant languages in the classroom or the society.

It was out of the Lancaster critique of Language Awareness that Critical Language Awareness was born. In the paper that launched CLA, Clarke et al. (1987) show that Language Awareness is underpinned by a view of schooling which does not enable students to question or challenge existing social structures. 'Appropriateness', the concept at the heart of the social in language education, comes under the critical knife because what is appropriate is decided by social norms which, in contexts of power (institutions, prestigious job interviews, the media), are inevitably the naturalised cultural practices of the social elite. And so the move to consider the relationship between language and power was made. Volume 6 includes reviews of Language Awareness and Critical Language Awareness.

MAJOR CONTRIBUTIONS TO THE TEACHING OF LANGUAGE AND POWER IN SCHOOLS

The purpose of this review is to consider the practical issues relating to the teaching of language and power. The major contributions to our understanding of practice are (i) accounts of critical literacy teaching and school-based research and (ii) classroom materials which translate post-structuralist theories about language, ideology and discourse into activities which are accessible to teachers and students.

Critical Language Awareness (Fairclough 1992) was the first edited collection of CLA as practice. Although only five of the chapters refer explicitly to primary and secondary classrooms, the book raises and begins to answer some of the key questions on the teaching of language and power. How are students to be given access to the discourses of power in their educational institutions so that these are not simply reproduced unproblematically? How much language competence do students need before CLA can be taught in second or foreign language classes? What constitutes critical practice in relation to the place of students' own minority languages? What positions on students' access to the standardised variety are compatible with CLA? How does CLA impact on student subjectivities? Is awareness enough? When does CLA become emancipatory?

McKenzie's chapter (pp. 223–237) on school reports is an exemplary account of a CLA project where the step by step account of the practice is clear and the relationship between the practice and the critical ends – the deconstruction and reconstruction of a naturalised discursive practice central to the production of institutionalised student subjectivities – is carefully explained. McKenzie does not claim that this work alters the conditions of production of school reports, he makes no reference to whether teachers' report-writing practices were affected by the process. What he does claim is that the conditions of reception were altered: students were able to produce multiple readings of their own schools reports.

In these first accounts of CLA practice (Fairclough 1992) there is little sense of disruption. Clarke recognises that decisions 'to conform or not to conform' (p. 117) involve real risks and Janks and Ivanic close the collection in the final paragraph with a reminder that 'people endanger themselves when they take on the prevailing power structures' (p. 330). But the accounts themselves are seamless. The staff at McKenzie's school remain apparently unthreatened by the fact that students are asking challenging questions and are deconstructing the reports they have written for them. Janks and Ivanic's post-graduate student manages to transform his relationship with his supervisor without making waves (p. 309) and there is no sense that CLA might impinge on students' and teachers' identity investments and rock the classroom boat.

However, other classroom-based research points to the disruptive potential of a critical pedagogy which disturbs students taken-for-granted discourses and threatens their sense of self. Ellsworth (1989), Janks (1995) and Granville (1996) provide accounts of classroom conflict resulting from the teaching of language and power, particularly in heterogeneous classes. This teaching can only be transformative in situations where the critical processes of denaturalisation and deconstruction allow other voices to enter and be heard so that students come to understand the interested nature of all discourse and all readings, including their own.

In Australia CLA arose from discourses on literacy and came to be known as 'critical literacy', a concept coined by Paulo Freire. The Deakin University course *Language Education,* edited by Christie (1989) uses Halliday's theory of language as a social semiotic as its theoretical foundation. It covers a wide range of school based applications of critical literacy: the ideology of school texts, the politics of reading in schools, language and the social construction of gender, and the role of language in Aboriginal education to name just a few.

Martin's (1989) contribution to this series *Factual Writing: Exploring and challenging social reality* forms part of what came to be know as genre theory. Using Halliday's systemic functional grammar, the genre theorists described the generic and linguistic features of six dominant factual genres – reports, recounts, procedures, explanations, expositions and discussions – in order to be able to teach them to students. Genre theorists argue that marginalised students need access to the dominant genres and the Disadvantaged Schools Project developed both materials and an explicit pedagogy (Bernstein 1990) for providing this access. This strong position on access to dominant literacy is supported by Delpit who works with African American students in the United States (1988).

The genre theorists came into conflict with other critical literacy theorists in Australia (see the review by Freedman & Richardson in Volume 6). Where genre theorists want to enable students to do the dominant genres, critical literacy theorists want students to deconstruct and reconstruct them. Cope and Kalantzis (1993) have argued convincingly that serious attention to genre is not antithetical to the aims of critical literacy provided that genres are not reified and taught as static conventions reduced, in some of the more rigid genre positions, to formulae operating according to fixed rules. What students need is an understanding of the historical and social determinants of these forms and an ability to adapt these forms as the conditions change, and in order to change these conditions.

How this translates into practice is not yet resolved. How *do* teachers work with the contradiction at the heart of educational access? If you provide extensive access to the dominant forms in a society (eg. genres/knowledges/languages/varieties) you contribute to maintaining their dominance. If you deny students access, you perpetuate their marginalisation in a society that continues to recognise mastery of these genres as marks of distinction. CLA has to find a way of working inside the contradiction, of making the contradiction itself available to students. Gee (1990: p. 159) argues that in teaching the discourses of power, schools dislocate students profoundly, often requiring their 'active complicity with values that conflict with [their] home and community-based Discourses' and Bourdieu draws attention to the fact that while the education system fails to provide students from subordinated classes with *knowledge of* and *access to* the legitimate language, it succeeds in teaching them *recognition* [misrecognition] of its legitimacy (1991: p. 62). CLA needs to reverse this.

Australia has also been at the forefront of developing critical literacy materials for use in schools. Chalkface Press has published several workbooks which introduce secondary students to post-structuralist theory for textual deconstruction. These materials include innovative approaches that lead to an understanding of reading positions and how they are produced, regulated and challenged. The workbooks seek to enable students to understand how discourse is implicated in the production of power and inequality. Morgan has also made an important contribution to classroom materials and her *Ned Kelly Reconstructed* (1984) establishes a range of methods for developing students' understanding that all texts are both constructed and interested. Misson's work is also rich with specific examples of critical literacy activities for secondary schools. He raises an important question about the fate of pleasure and desire when we require students to interrogate the popular texts that they enjoy (1994).

Australia has also been at the forefront of introducing critical literacy into primary schools. Here the work of Freebody, Luke and Gilbert has been important for its exploration of literacy practices in primary schools and the way these practices are inscribed on students' bodies to produce docile reading subjects (1991). In South Australia Comber and O'Brien (1993) have introduced the critical reading of everyday texts – cereal boxes, toy catalogues, mothers' day catalogues – into the early years of primary school. Both Luke and Gilbert have drawn attention to the ideologies which inform the books children are given to read in primary schools. Luke studied early readers and Gilbert has concentrated on gender bias. All of this work has affected classroom practice in Australia.

The only other large scale attempt to develop CLA materials for schools is the *Critical Language Awareness Series* edited by Janks (1993) in South Africa. The apartheid context gives a political edge to these workbooks which make it clear that language is both a site and a stake in struggles for a more humane world. The three workbooks in the series by Granville, Newfield and Rule focus on media texts; two others by Janks work with language and position and language and subjectivity; Orlek's workbook addresses the power differentials between different languages and different varieties in a multilingual country. Her work is indebted to *Language and Power*, Afro-Caribbean Language and Literacy Project materials for use in Britain (ILEA 1990).

Watson (1994), also working in South Africa, produced a critical literacy comic with students in a rural school. In addition to providing alternative choices and possibilities for the characters, the comic highlights difficulties that teachers confront when they invite students to generate materials out of their own ideologically constructed commonsense and the responsibilities and dilemmas a teacher faces in moving towards reconstructing students' belief systems.

The contributions to CLA referred to here have been limited to English language education but CLA obviously has applicability across the school curriculum. The discourse-historical method of critical analysis developed by Wodak and her associates has informed their critique of school history textbooks in Austria (1990). Lee (1996) in Australia uses critical discourse analysis for an exploration of the construction of gendered discourses in school Geography and Kalantzis has developed materials on critical social literacies for citizenship education.

FUTURE DIRECTIONS: PROBLEMS AND DIFFICULTIES

Accounts of CLA often include a slippage from 'awareness' or 'critical literacy' to 'emancipation'. This is too easy. Claims for the empowerment of learners need to be further researched. While many students report an ability to interrogate texts, to resist being constructed by othering discourses, to recognise and to refuse interpellation there is very little in the literature that is not anecdotal. Given that human subjects are multiply affiliated identities, we have no clear idea of what discursive emancipation might look like. A student who learns a feminist discourse at school might be severely punished for it in a traditional patriarchal home, particularly where sexist practices in the home are further underpinned by religious beliefs. Mellor and Patterson (1994) in fact argue that critical literacy is simply a new 'reading regime' requiring a new normativity. This needs to be weighed against Simon's (1992) conception of a 'pedagogy of possibility' which ties the critical endeavour to a political project with an ethical social justice agenda. These differing positions have very different outcomes in classrooms. For example Mellor and Patterson would expect students to be able to produce an anti-racist reading of a text whereas Simon would want to go further. He would want students to become transformed human subjects who reject racism. This raises important questions about the teacher's power and responsibilities and the students' rights which lie at the heart of CLA and which are still unresolved.

Different answers are likely to be found in different contexts at different historical moments. For example, it was easy to defend CLA as a transformative political project in South Africa during apartheid. However, in the USA, where liberal humanism is entrenched and the myth of the American Dream is part of the national common sense, language and power is not widely taught in schools. Whole Language which privileges the learning styles of mainstream middle class children predominates. Finally, in the UK, the Language in the National Curriculum materials continue to be embargoed by the State.

The major focus of critical literacy has been on deconstruction and alternative ways of reading the world. Less has been done in schools on re-writing the world. Haas-Dyson's (1995) work with urban African American primary school children is the exception. Using Bakhtin's theory of dialogism to teach students to appropriate other voices she teaches children how to reinvent their world and themselves. Morgan (1993) has also done some work in this area using students autobiograhy and Pennycook (1995) talks of teaching students to 'write back', an idea taken from post-colonial discourse. This is an area that needs further development.

Clearly what is needed in further research is studies based on detailed classroom observation in order to analyse the ways in which students and teachers engage with critical language education. So far what we have are largely descriptive accounts, journal studies, interviews. In addition we need a clearer idea of what is happening in pre-service and in-service teacher education. Granville's (1996) research conducted on a pre-service CLA course for primary teachers is a start. Little of the inservice professional development work in Australia in the area of CLA has been written up.

Some work has been done on the implications of CLA for testing. O'Neill's (1995) research is the most extensive study so far. Working with a range of texts she shows how students in Australia and Canada from diverse social locations and language backgrounds produced different readings of the same texts. She is able to argue that all these readings are possible readings of the texts and that students' answers across a number of questions remain consistent with the reading they have foregrounded. This poses important challenges for the assessment of students, where students from minority groups are less likely to produce the dominant readings and are thereby further disadvantaged by the education system. Stein and Peirce (1995) report similar findings in South Africa where the answers students produced in a test differed from these students' own preferred reading of the text. Post-structuralist theory which posits multiple meanings from different reading positions suggests that right-answer marking memorandums for comprehension and essay tests are no longer sustainable and that alternatives need to be found. O'Neill's work proves that multiple choice testing is also extremely problematic.

Where English is the language of power in the society, it is often students who speak other languages who are most affected by questions of language and power and who are therefore most interested in CLA. More work still has to be done on the teaching of CLA in English as additional language classrooms. ESL teachers often argue that students need to be able to decode the text, make sense of the words, before they can be taught CLA. Clearly CLA does require an understanding of the subtlety and nuances of words but there are texts of different degrees of linguistic complexity and any text that is suitable for the level of learners to read is suitable for critical analysis at that level. The principles of critical literacy do not change. Speakers of African languages in South Africa do not need any sophistication in English to recognise that the pictures of children on cornflakes boxes are usually boys who are usually white, and they are capable of relating this to the verbal text. The Janks *Critical Language Awareness Series* situates itself expressly across the first language/second language divide and is deliberately written in English that is accessible to students who speak African languages. This is not to say that further work is not needed to ensure that CLA materials include activities, texts and issues pertinent to the needs of minority students. CLA also creates the opportunity to include the power-meaning potential when one is teaching linguistic structures. So for example students learning grammar can simultaneously learn about the relationship between modality and power, or about the connection between 'us' and 'them' pronouns and othering discourses, and they can learn to recognise who is a 'doer' and who is a 'done-to' when they are taught transitivity and voice.

Diversity and an ability to recognise that difference is often structured in dominance is central to CLA. Kress (1995: p. 6) argues that diversity in schools could be an important means for making students 'feel at ease with continuous, intense change; comfortable with sharp differences of culture and social values met every day; treat them as normal, as unremarkable and natural; and above all, as an essential productive resource for innovation rather than as a cause for anxiety and anger'. Processes of globalization are going to require such human adaptability. These are the forces that are driving the New London Group's move to theorising *A Pedagogy of Multiliteracies* (1996) which still has to be translated into classroom practice. This coming together of related critical theorists (Cazden, Cope, Fairclough, Gee, Kalantzis, Luke A, Luke C, Kress, Michaels, Nakata) effects a number of important gains. The concept of multiliteracies is extremely generative in harnessing the idea of multiple literacies developed by the New Literacy Studies. This deprivileges the print-based verbal sign and makes way for oracies, visual semiotics, multimodal literacies, non mainstream literacy practices and the new technologies. It also creates a space for thinking links between the range of specialist interests brought by different members of the group: genre theory, discourse theory, language learning in multilingual and indigenous communities, social and citizenship education, cultural diversity in schools, language and learning for 'fast capitalist' workplaces, language and gender. There is an overall attempt to make diversity a productive power.

This influential new direction in the teaching of language and power signals a shift from concerns with asymmetrical power relations and the need for critical literacy to teach students how to recognise and resist such power, to a view which recognises that power is also productive. Foucault (1970: p. 110) in *The Order of Discourse* argues that 'discourse is the power which is to be seized' and this surely is why it is important to teach language and power in schools.

University of the Witwatersrand
South Africa

REFERENCES

Bernstein, B.: 1990, *The Structuring of Pedagogic Discourse Volume IV Class Codes and Control,* Routledge, London.

Bourdieu, P.: 1991, *Language and Symbolic Power*, Polity Press, Cambridge.

Clark, R., Fairclough, N., Ivanic R. & Martin-Jones, M.: 1987, 'Critical language awareness', Centre for Language in Social Life, working paper series, Number 1, Lancaster University.

Christie, F.: 1989, *Language Education Series*, Oxford University Press, Oxford.

Comber, B. & O'Brien, J.: 1993, 'Critical literacy: classroom explorations', *Critical Pedagogy Networker*. Vol. 6, Nos. 1 and 2, June.

Cope, B. & Kalantzis, M. (eds.): 1993, *The Powers of Literacy. A genre approach to teaching writing*, Falmer Press, London.

Delpit, L.: 1988, 'The silenced dialogue: Power and pedagogy in educating other people's children', *Harvard Educational Review* 58, 280–298.

Ellsworth, E.: 1989, 'Why doesn't this feel empowering? Working through repressive myths of critical pedagogy', *Harvard Educational Review* 59(3).

English Language Teaching Information Centre: 1995, Activities for Multilingual Classrooms. ELTIC, Johannesburg.

Fairclough, N. (ed.): 1992, *Critical Language Awareness*, Longman, London.

Foucault, M.: 1970, 'The order of discourse', in M. Shapiro (ed.) (1984), *Language and Politics*, Basil Blackwell, Oxford.

Freebody, P., Luke, A. & Gilbert, P.: 1991, 'Reading positions and practices in the classroom', *Curriculum Inquiry* 21(4), John Wiley, Ontario Institute for Studies in Education.

Gee, J.P.: 1990, *Sociolinguistics and Literacies. Ideology in Discourse*, Falmer Press, London.

Granville, S.: 1996, *Reading beyond the text: exploring the possibilities in Critical Language Awareness for reshaping student teachers' ideas about reading and comprehension,* Unpublished Masters Dissertation, University of the Witwatersrand, Johannesburg.

Haas Dyson, A: 1995, 'The courage to write: child meaning making in a contested world', *Language Arts* (72), 324–333.

Hawkins, E. (ed.): 1983, *Language Awareness Series*, Cambridge University Press, Cambridge.

Hymes, D.: 1974, 'On communicative competence', in C.J. Brumfit & K. Johnson (eds.), *The Communicative Approach to Language Teaching*, Oxford University Press, Oxford.

Inner London Education Authority Afro-Caribbean Language and Literacy Project: 1990, *Language and Power,* Harcourt Brace and Jovanovich, London.

Janks, H. (ed.): 1993, *Critical Language Awareness Series*, Hodder and Stoughton and Wits University Press, Johannesburg.

Janks, H.: 1995, *The Research and Development of Critical Language Awareness Materials for Use in South African Secondary Schools*, Unpublished Doctor of Philosophy Thesis, Lancaster University, Lancaster.

Kress, G.: 1995, 'Making signs and making subjects: the English curriculum and social futures', Professorial Lecture, Institute of Education, London University.

Labov, W.: 1972, 'The logic of non-standard English', in Giglioli (ed.), *Language and Social Context*, Penguin, Harmondsworth.

Lee, A.: 1996, *Gender, Literacy, Curriculum: Rewriting school Geography,* Taylor and Francis, London.

Martin, J.R.: 1989, *Factual Writing: Exploring and Challenging Social Reality*, Oxford University Press, Oxford.

Mellor, B. & Patterson, A.: 1994, 'Producing readings: freedom versus normativity', *English in Australia* 109, 42–56.

Misson, R.: 1994, 'Making it real, making it mine', Conference Proceedings, Australian Association of Teachers of English Conference, Perth.

Morgan, W.: 1994, *Ned Kelly Reconstructed*, Cambridge University Press, Cambridge.

Morgan, W.: 1993, ' Self as text', *Exploring and Connecting Texts,* Education Department of South Australia, Adelaide.

New London Group.: 1996, 'A pedagogy of multiliteracies: Designing social futures', *Harvard Educational Review* 66(1).

O'Neill, M.: 1995, *Variant Readings: A Cross-cultural Study of Reading Comprehension*, Unpublished Doctor of Philosophy Thesis, Murdoch University, Murdoch, Western Australia.

Pennycook, A.: 1995, *The Cultural Politics of English as an International Language*, Longman, London.
Raleigh, M.: 1981, *The Languages Book*, ILEA English Centre, London.
Simon, R.: 1992, *Teaching against the Grain. Texts for a Pedagogy of Possibility*, OISE Press, Toronto.
Stein, P. and Peirce, B.N.: 1995, 'Why the monkeys passage bombed: tests, genres and teaching', *Harvard Educational Review* 65(1), 50–65.
Watson, P.: 1994, *Heart to Heart*, The Storyteller Group, Johannesburg.
Wodak, R. and Kissling, W.: 1990, 'Die meisten KZler zeigten sich fuer jede Hilfeleistung sehr dankbar' Schulbuch und Schulbuchdiskussion als Paradigma politischer Kommunikation in Oesterreich. Austriaca, No 31, 87–105.

SUBJECT INDEX

NAME INDEX

261

TABLE OF CONTENTS

VOLUME 2: LITERACY

TABLE OF CONTENTS

Section 3: Focus on the Social Context of Literacy

Section 4: Focus on Selected Regions

TABLE OF CONTENTS

VOLUME 3: ORAL DISCOURSE AND EDUCATION

TABLE OF CONTENTS

TABLE OF CONTENTS

VOLUME 4: SECOND LANGUAGE EDUCATION

TABLE OF CONTENTS

TABLE OF CONTENTS

VOLUME 5: BILINGUAL EDUCATION

TABLE OF CONTENTS

TABLE OF CONTENTS

VOLUME 6: KNOWLEDGE ABOUT LANGUAGE

TABLE OF CONTENTS

TABLE OF CONTENTS

VOLUME 7: LANGUAGE TESTING AND ASSESSMENT

TABLE OF CONTENTS

TABLE OF CONTENTS

VOLUME 8: RESEARCH METHODS IN LANGUAGE AND EDUCATION

TABLE OF CONTENTS

Encyclopedia of Language and Education

Set ISBN Hb 0-7923-4596-7; Pb 0-7923-4936-9

1. R. Wodak and D. Corson (eds.): *Language Policy and Political Issues in Education.*
   1997   ISBN Hb 0-7923-4713-7
                                             ISBN Pb 0-7923-4928-8

2. V. Edwards and D. Corson (eds.): *Literacy.* 1997   ISBN Hb 0-7923-4595-0
                                             ISBN Pb 0-7923-4929-6

3. B. Davies and D. Corson (eds.): *Oral Discourse and Education.* 1997
                                             ISBN Hb 0-7923-4639-4
                                             ISBN Pb 0-7923-4930-X

4. G.R. Tucker and D. Corson (eds.): *Second Language Education.* 1997
                                             ISBN Hb 0-7923-4640-8
                                             ISBN Pb 0-7923-4931-8

5. J. Cummins and D. Corson (eds.): *Bilingual Education.* 1997
                                             ISBN Hb 0-7923-4806-0
                                             ISBN Pb 0-7923-4932-6

6. L. van Lier and D. Corson (eds.): *Knowledge about Language.* 1997
                                             ISBN Hb 0-7923-4641-6
                                             ISBN Pb 0-7923-4933-4

7. C. Clapham and D. Corson (eds.): *Language Testing and Assessment.* 1997
                                             ISBN Hb 0-7923-4702-1
                                             ISBN Pb 0-7923-4934-2

8. N.H. Hornberger and D. Corson (eds.): *Research Methods in Language and Education.* 1997   ISBN Hb 0-7923-4642-4
                                             ISBN Pb 0-7923-4935-0

KLUWER ACADEMIC PUBLISHERS – DORDRECHT / BOSTON / LONDON